Only for Peace

Selected Speeches
and Writings

Only for Peace

by

A. A. GROMYKO

PERGAMON PRESS

OXFORD · NEW YORK · TORONTO · SYDNEY · PARIS · FRANKFURT

U.K.	Pergamon Press Ltd., Headington Hill Hall, Oxford OX3 0BW, England
U.S.A.	Pergamon Press Inc., Maxwell House, Fairview Park, Elmsford, New York 10523, U.S.A.
CANADA	Pergamon of Canada, Suite 104, 150 Consumers Road, Willowdale, Ontario M2J 1P9, Canada
AUSTRALIA	Pergamon Press (Aust.) Pty. Ltd., P.O. Box 544, Potts Point, N.S.W. 2011, Australia
FRANCE	Pergamon Press SARL, 24 rue des Ecoles, 75240 Paris, Cedex 05, France
FEDERAL REPUBLIC OF GERMANY	Pergamon Press GmbH, 6242 Kronberg-Taunus, Pferdstrasse 1, Federal Republic of Germany

Selection, arrangement, illustrations and translation copyright © 1979, VAAP

First Edition 1979

British Library Cataloguing in Publication Data
Gromyko, Andrei Andreevich
Only for peace: selected speeches and writings.
1. Russia—Foreign relations—1953–1975—
Addresses, essays, lectures
2. Russia—Foreign relations—1975
Addresses, essays, lectures
I. Title
327.47   DK274.3   78–41262
ISBN 0-08-023582-4

Printed in Great Britain at Aberdeen University Press

CONTENTS

CONTENTS

CONTENTS

ILLUSTRATIONS

ILLUSTRATIONS

AUTOBIOGRAPHICAL INTRODUCTION

In my view it is no easy task to write an introduction, especially for a book that is to be published in a foreign country. Tradition demands at least some autobiographical data. But this is, of course, not the main thing. The main purpose of any book about the milestones in the diplomatic work and views of any political personality is to bring into focus the basic international problems confronting mankind and affecting the destinies of the world, to show the difficulties involved in surmounting various barriers to the consolidation of international security, and to expose the broad possibilities that do in fact exist for transcending these barriers.

In other words, when the story is about a political personality, it must necessarily touch upon the main political events with which he has been associated. In my case they are international developments in which I have been and still am a participant. I feel that this is mirrored best in my articles and speeches over a period of more than thirty years, beginning with the Second World War, when the Soviet people crushed Nazism, and ending with the present day, when the CPSU and the Soviet Government are, in fulfilment of the will of the Soviet people, firmly pursuing a policy of *détente* and peace. Some of these speeches and articles, appearing in the last ten years, are preserved in this volume.

I should like to emphasize that in this difficult job I am only one of many Soviet statesmen carrying out the will of the Soviet people, the will of the Leninist Communist Party. It is this in particular which explains the simple fact that Soviet foreign policy is not so strongly susceptible to subjective factors, as is so frequently the case with the policy of some major powers belonging to the other social system. Indeed, dishonesty and sudden shifts in foreign policy are alien to us. Our policy is consistent and peaceful, and safeguards the interests of

1

the Soviet people and of our allies and friends. It is a Leninist foreign policy, a policy of the people. In this lies its strength and the reason for the manifest impotence of those who oppose it, of those who often go so far as to calumniate it.

The 1960s and 1970s brought Soviet foreign policy particularly striking successes. Peace on earth was made more secure, socialism's strength grew immeasurably, and the proponents of cold war suffered telling setbacks. Nonetheless, the efforts to undermine *détente* continue to this day. In many cases they are dressed up with propagandistic fireworks. But these fireworks cannot be an alternative to foreign policy.

All the anti-Soviet propaganda campaigns of the past have sunk into oblivion, and the same fate will overcome all who are today following that inglorious path. It is a labour of Sisyphus to fight peaceful coexistence and *détente*, to endeavour to impose upon other nations one's views and sometimes even way of life, to teach them how to conduct their affairs. The experience of history shows the futility of this approach to international affairs. If we look at it closely, the anti-Sovietism of some foreign politicians and their yesmen, evident at the close of the 1970s, has many points of similarity with the propaganda that emanated from the German Third Reich of the 1930s and 1940s. It is, therefore, heading for the same fate—namely, the scrap-heap of history. Some readers may perhaps find my words much too harsh, but, frankly, I can find no others for those who are trying to destroy the structure of peace and plunge nations into the abyss of a thermonuclear war.

Led by the CPSU, the Soviet people clearly see this danger. But we also know our influence and potentialities. That explains why the Soviet leadership is conducting its international affairs so calmly and confidently, counterposing political myopia with competence, composure, and purpose in defence of *détente* in the world. An especially hard worker for peace is the leader of the Soviet Communists and head of the Soviet state, Leonid Brezhnev. He often repeats, quite justifiably, the wise dictum that one cannot take peace for granted, as something that goes without saying, but that one must constantly fight for it. This is borne out by my own experience of international politics, an experience that covers a period of nearly forty years.

Briefly, about myself. I was born in 1909 into the family of a semi-peasant, semi-worker. This population category existed in pre-revolutionary Russia. It consisted of people who had neither sufficient land to feed themselves and their families, nor steady employment in industry. In short, ours was a poor man's household. There were days when there was not even enough bread in the family. On top of that, my father's 'allotment' of land was infertile. When I was still a juvenile, from the age of 14, I joined him in looking for work on the side—in industry or in cutting timber.

The region of Gomel, where I was born, is situated in the south-western part of the East European plain, approximately halfway between Moscow and Kiev. It has always been richly forested, but there is also no lack of swamps alternating with stretches of sand. The winters are usually relatively mild, and the summers are quite warm. The people there are always kind and responsive, but not to those who come with sword in hand. During the Great Patriotic War, when the USSR was attacked by the fascists, all of Soviet Byelorussia, the young and the old, fought them with supreme valour. But the Nazis brought great, very great grief and sorrow to that land and its people. One in four perished.

I spent my childhood in the environs of Gomel. The town of Gomel is first mentioned in ancient chronicles of the mid-twelfth century. In the fourteenth century it was part of the Grand Principality of Lithuania; in the sixteenth century it was seized by Poland; in 1772 it was incorporated into Russia. The Gomel of my childhood remains in my mind as a large railway junction with a small amount of industry, the largest enterprise being the big Vesuvius Match Factory. Reduced to ruin during the war, the town has not only been restored but turned into one of the industrial and cultural centres of Byelorussia. In 1970 Gomel was decorated with the Order of the Red Banner of Labour.

In 1931 I married Lydia Dmitrievna Grinevich, daughter of a Byelorussian peasant. We have two children, Anatoly and Emilia. Today Anatoly is a professor and doctor of historical sciences, and heads the African Institute of the USSR Academy of Sciences. My daughter is a candidate of historical sciences, equivalent to an English Ph.D. My wife and I are pleased with our children. Moreover, we have three grandsons, Igor, Andrei, Alexei, and granddaughter Lidia. My two brothers died in the war.

3

In 1930 I joined the All-Union Communist Party (Bolsheviks), as the Communist Party of the Soviet Union was called at that time.

I must admit that as long as I can remember I had an irrepressible passion for study. My parents did all they could to enable me to study regularly. Usually I only had to stop in the summer, when I had to go to work in order to help the family. I finished a rural elementary school, then a seven-year school, a technical college, then an institute and a post-graduate course. The institute where I did my post-graduate work was headed by Professor Borisevich, who gave all of us his closest attention.

An event occurred during this period which unquestionably determined my further career. During my second post-graduate year a group of six, including myself, was transferred from Minsk to Moscow. I completed my post-graduate studies in Moscow with the relevant academic degree in economics. In 1936, soon after I had defended my dissertation, I joined the Institute of Economics of the USSR Academy of Sciences as a senior scientific associate. Academician G. M. Savelyev was director of the institute at the time.

I felt that I had started seriously on a long-term scientific career. I doubled as a lecturer at Moscow's Municipal Construction Engineering Institute. Incidentally, one of my students was Victor Vasilyevich Grishin, who is today a member of the Politburo of the CPSU Central Committee. Sometimes we recall the days when students were often almost the same age as their lecturers, a circumstance that made me, at any rate, feel awkward on occasions.

With the passing of the years the Soviet Union developed and gained strength. The people were building socialism, turning the Russia of the tsars, a downtrodden country on the outskirts of capitalism, into a flourishing state of workers, peasants, and a working intelligentsia. However, already then, at the close of the 1930s, there was an unmistakable smell of gunpowder in the air. All the indications were that the stern test of war was closing in on the Soviet Union. Of course, nobody wanted to believe it, but it was true nonetheless. All of us felt it in our hearts.

At the close of 1938 I was appointed Academic Secretary at the Institute of Economics. I decided to enrol in a flying school without discontinuing my work. In those days this was the dream of many.

But here disappointment awaited me—I had come too late. I was told that 25 was the age limit for enrolment.

I was sorely disappointed; I was so eager to fly. But, I repeat, there were many who wanted to be fliers. In the Soviet Union, as in other countries, there was in those years a veritable cult of aviation, that rapidly advancing area of human endeavour. It was the time when aircraft were being used for the development of the Arctic. There was nothing I could do but resign myself and say: 'Goodbye, flying, evidently you weren't for me.'

I had only just begun to get into the routine of scientific work when unexpectedly I was summoned by Vladimir Komarov, President of the USSR Academy of Sciences, and offered the post of Academic Secretary of the Academy's Far Eastern Division. I did not turn the offer down out of hand, but felt very strongly that this important scientific and organizational job required a scientist with much more experience than I had—in fact, it required an eminent scholar. I believe Komarov agreed with my view and appreciated why I was reluctant to take the job. However, I was not destined to work much longer at the Institute of Economics. True, later, when I was Ambassador in Washington, I began, and then during my tenure as Ambassador in London, I completed and published the book *Export of US Capital* (under the pen-name of G. Andreyev), for which the Academic Council of Moscow State University conferred upon me the academic degree of Doctor of Economic Sciences. Still later, under the same pen-name, I published my second book *US Dollar Expansion*.

In early 1939 I was suddenly notified that I was to present myself to a commission set up by the CPSU Central Committee to select new, trained personnel for foreign policy and diplomatic work. The commission sat in the Foreign Ministry's old building on Kuznetsky Most. When, at the appointed time, I reported to the commission I recognized among its members Vyacheslav Molotov and other leading Party and government officials. I was informed that I was being considered for a foreign policy post, most likely in the diplomatic service. With me on that day were three other candidates.

Today it is, of course, hard to say what exactly motivated the commission when they chose me. I think what decided them was that ever since my early days in the Komsomol I was involved in political education, delivering lectures and reports, and conducting seminars and study groups at offices and factories: in short, I was an activist. Also in my favour was, I believe, the fact that as a post-graduate student I had mastered English, although I was far from being perfect. When I was asked what I had read in English, I named some books, including *Rich Land, Poor Land* by the American economist Stuart Chase. Within a few days I was again summoned to the CPSU Central Committee and informed that I would be transferred to diplomatic work.

Thus, in the spring of 1939 I was appointed head of the American Department of the People's Commissariat for Foreign Affairs. My tenure in that office was short, about six months. I was soon immersed in diplomatic work, meeting officials of the US Embassy. Laurence A. Steinhardt was the US Ambassador at the time, and I must say he left no perceptible trace in Soviet–US relations. In fact, I often wondered why President Roosevelt, with his breadth of views, including those on Soviet–US relations, had chosen the man. Life, however, corrects decisions of this kind. Steinhardt did not stay long in Moscow, apparently to the satisfaction of both sides.

One day I received a summons from Stalin. Until then I had only seen him at a distance, in Red Square, where he took the salute at parades or waved back to anniversary processions. Of course, within minutes of receiving the summons I was in the waiting room of Stalin's office in the Kremlin. I introduced myself to his assistant and secretary Poskrebyshev. He reported my arrival. I soon found myself in Stalin's office. He was sitting not at his desk but at the head of the long table usually used at meetings of the Politburo. With him was Molotov, who was People's Commissar for Foreign Affairs at the time and with whom I had often discussed questions concerning relations with the USA.

I was courteously greeted by Stalin and Molotov. Stalin spoke first. He said that they proposed to post me to the Soviet Embassy in the USA as the number 2, as counsellor. Frankly, this took me somewhat by surprise, although I had already come to the belief that, like soldiers, diplomats had to be prepared for unexpected transfers.

Sparing of words, as was his custom, Stalin named the areas of priority in Soviet–US relations. He noted that the USSR could maintain good relations with a major power like the USA, especially in view of the mounting fascist menace in Europe. German fascism, he said, was marching towards war, and this was obvious to any observant person. Molotov put in a few remarks in support of what Stalin was saying. From what was said I realized that I was not being sent to the USA for a month or a year, particularly as the Soviet Ambassador in the USA, Umansky, who evidently did not impress Stalin or Molotov very much, had been recalled to Moscow. Although Umansky returned to the USA it was felt that his work there was coming to an end. Indeed, he did not stay long. He was replaced by Maxim Litvinov, who likewise held the post of Ambassador for a short time. After Nazi Germany had attacked the USSR it was believed that Roosevelt would perhaps like to see as Soviet Ambassador to the USA a diplomat who had won a name for himself in the League of Nations and was associated with the League. But developments made it plain that Stalin, and Molotov for that matter, regarded this as a purely temporary step.

Thus the author of this book soon replaced Litvinov as Ambassador in the USA.

Incidentally, Stalin asked me how well I knew English. I replied that I was struggling with it and seemed to be gradually mastering it, although the process was very difficult, especially when there was little or no opportunity to speak the language. Here Stalin gave a piece of advice that was both puzzling and enlivening. It helped me to shed some of my constraint. Stalin said: 'I don't see why you shouldn't go to American churches and cathedrals and listen to the sermons from time to time. They usually speak good English. And their diction is excellent. You know, when Russian revolutionaries lived abroad they used this method to improve their knowledge of a foreign language.' I remember, I was confused at first that Stalin, an atheist, should suddenly recommend that I, also an atheist, should go to foreign churches. I almost blurted out: 'Did you, Comrade Stalin, use this method?' But I resisted the temptation to put that question, for I knew that Stalin spoke no foreign language, and my question would obviously have not been quite proper. I held my tongue, so to speak. Although I am sure Stalin would have made a jest of it, as I often saw him do in later years in similar circumstances.

This was perhaps the only instance of a Soviet Ambassador not carrying out Stalin's instructions. I can just imagine the impression my visits to American churches would have made on hustling reporters. Unquestionably, they would have been puzzled, nonplussed, lost in conjecture over the reason why the atheist Soviet Ambassador was regularly visiting American churches and cathedrals and whether there was some threat to the USA in this.

In the autumn of 1939 my family and I were aboard the Italian luxury liner *Rex* en route to the USA. We had had to change trains several times on the way from Moscow to Genoa.

We had a curious experience in the Atlantic on 7 November when the ship's master invited Ambassador Umansky and me to his cabin out of considerations of etiquette. Treating us in private to excellent Italian wine, he proposed the toast: 'To the Great October Revolution in Russia, to Lenin.' We seconded him enthusiastically, of course. It must be remembered that fascism ruled Italy in those years. Umansky and I later recalled that toast, saying that had the Duce learned of it our captain would most certainly have been in trouble. But there obviously were decent Italians among the captains of the Italian merchant marine, who held fascism and the fascist order in contempt.

A few days after encountering our first-ever real storm in the Atlantic we arrived in Washington, where I soon made the necessary contacts with officials of the US government, mainly of the State Department, and later with President Franklin D. Roosevelt. I saw him for the first time at the opening of the National Art Gallery in Washington towards the end of 1939.

The first period of my stay in the USA bore the imprint of the military clash between the USSR and Finland. The nation's press was mostly hostile to the USSR. In those days very few Americans gave much thought to fascism's intention in the south and north of Europe. Subsequently an ever-growing number of them began to see the actual objectives of the fascist military plans. The mood changed, of course, when Nazi Germany attacked the Soviet Union and the USA's own existence was in peril.

However, the complexity of international processes made itself felt. Even the tragedy of Pearl Harbor, inflicted by the perfidy of Germany's accomplice, militarist Japan, failed to open the eyes of all Americans to the designs of German fascism. Moreover, even after the Nazis attacked the Soviet Union, there were American politicians who wanted to see the USSR and Germany bleed each other and thereby, in their view, increase the chances of the USA having the last say in the war. It was during the first days of the war that Harry S. Truman, who was later to be the US President, declared that the Germans and Russians should be allowed to bleed each other as much as possible. It is not surprising that on this man's orders atomic bombs were needlessly dropped on the Japanese.

A new phase commenced. The Soviet people rose to a man to fight for their independence and freedom. The Soviet Union and its allies, one of whom was the USA, began a life-and-death struggle against mankind's most sinister enemy—Nazi Germany and its accomplices.

Together with Britain, the USA became our ally. In some European countries a Resistance movement sprang up that was to play a major part in the great anti-fascist struggle.

In a short introduction it is not possible to write in detail of wartime events. I must, however, note that from 1943 onwards I was a direct participant in the political events that developed on the crest of the wave of the heroic military struggle waged by the Soviet Union and its allies against fascism.

I took part in the Crimea (Yalta) Conference in early 1945, and some of the intermediate Allied conferences, for instance, in Atlantic City.

The Potsdam Conference was held in May 1945. It passed historic decisions on the denazification, demilitarization, and reintroduction of democracy in Germany. At both the Yalta and Potsdam Conferences, I was a member of the Soviet delegation in my capacity as Soviet Ambassador to the USA.

Towards the end of the war, after Molotov's departure, I led the Soviet delegation at the San Francisco Conference that drew up the UN Charter, and prior to that I led the Soviet delegation at Dumbarton Oaks.

Much water has flowed under the bridge since then. The world has changed perceptibly for the better. But this change has not, of course, taken place by itself. It is a result of the persevering efforts of the anti-fascist and progressive forces to end the terrible world war and then the cold war. There passed before my eyes, to speak only of American Presidents, Franklin Roosevelt, Harry Truman, Dwight Eisenhower,

John Kennedy, Lyndon Johnson, Richard Nixon, and Gerald Ford, and now the incumbent President is James Earl Carter. I am no longer surprised when American political personalities ask me what one or another President thought about this or that international issue. You see, they have never met them.

My meetings with the great American Franklin Roosevelt have left me with a cherished memory. He was a wise statesman and had a wide range of interests. I remember when I handed him my credentials he said with his usual directness: 'Give me your speech, and here's mine; both will be in the newspapers tomorrow. We'll spend our time more profitably exploring the possibilities for a summer meeting between the three powers: the USA, the USSR, and Great Britain.'

The correspondence between Stalin and Roosevelt passed through the office of the Soviet Ambassador in Washington. These documents have now been published and become the property of the world.

As had been agreed, General Watson, the President's military aide, usually came to the Soviet Embassy in Washington, on 16th Street, whenever letters were received from Stalin to Roosevelt or from Roosevelt to Stalin. Everything was done in a rush. There were no matters of inconsequence in those days. I particularly remember my discussion with Roosevelt on some matters that were considered later at Yalta.

In 1945, soon after Yalta, the world learned of President Roosevelt's untimely death. In Yalta, when Roosevelt caught a cold and fell ill, the conference was postponed for one day, and Stalin, Molotov, and I called on the American President. He was resting in the former bed-chamber of the Tsaritsa in the Livadia Palace. On our way back, as the three of us descended the stairs, Stalin said: 'Is this man any worse than the rest of us, why has nature been harsh with him?' He obviously had in mind not the cold but the President's disabling malady—polio accompanied by the paralysis of both his legs. Frankly, Stalin liked Roosevelt.

Soon Truman came to power in the USA. As a statesman he was only a pale reflection, like the moon, of his predecessor. Grave tensions began to creep into Soviet–US relations.

In the post-war situation the main thing was to enforce the Potsdam Agreements. Although the agreements themselves were profound and far-reaching, the true face of the new American foreign policy was soon seen when the time came to translate them into reality. By working towards the formation of the Bipartite Zone, the Tripartite Zone, and then a separate West German state, Washington, London, and Paris demonstrated that they had jettisoned the idea of creating a single, genuinely democratic, demilitarized Germany. Subsequent Soviet proposals on this issue were invariably turned down.

I had many meetings also with British statesmen, including Winston Churchill, Clement Atlee, Ernest Bevin, Harold Macmillan, Anthony Eden, Hugh Gaitskell, Selwyn Lloyd, Philip J. Noel-Baker, R. A. Butler, and Dugald Stewart. Of course later, in 1952, I handed my credentials to Queen Elizabeth II. I had also met her father, King George VI.

I met the King for the first time in St. James's Palace at a dinner for heads of delegations at the First UN General Assembly. Getting up from the table on which were laid massive and, evidently, unique gold plate, all the guests went to a fairly spacious drawing room. On the way I found myself walking beside the King. He suggested a private word in, to my amazement, the centre of the drawing room. The guests stood mostly along the walls.

The King spoke warmly, saying that the relations that had taken shape between the Soviet Union and Great Britain during the anti-Nazi struggle should under no circumstances be weakened. Naturally, I was wholeheartedly in agreement and said so. Our conversation attracted attention but clearly caused no surprise, for the two countries had been allies in the war. I shall not conceal the fact that this conversation impressed me profoundly. Needless to say, upon returning to the Embassy I shared my impressions with the other Soviet delegates.

My second meeting with King George VI and Queen Elizabeth, the present Queen Mother, occurred at a reception for delegations to the UN session. They were very gracious to the Soviet representatives, including the representatives of the Ukraine and Byelorussia. Standing beside the King and Queen as they received the guests were the present Queen Elizabeth II and her sister Margaret. We had a short but extremely friendly conversation.

I would like to say frankly that even then Princess Elizabeth greatly impressed me with the considered nature of her views. I remember several of her remarks, which though brief were interesting and well thought out.

I had a similar impression of the Queen from my conversation with her at the presentation of my Letter of Credence in 1952. This conversation took place before the Coronation. Apart from the quality mentioned above, what struck me at the meeting with the Crown Princess was the fact that she talked in broader concepts on matters concerning the relations between the Soviet Union and Great Britain as well as world politics in general.

I remember vividly the extraordinarily long and disproportionately narrow reception hall at Buckingham Palace. We, the Soviet representatives, looked over the magnificent decoration in the hall and noted that if it were a few metres wider and higher it would perhaps give nothing away to St. George's Hall in Moscow's Kremlin. Its colour scheme is sombreish in the Anglo-Saxon style.

Naturally, I have vivid memories of my meetings with the late Winston Churchill. During the war I usually met the British Prime Minister at important Allied conferences, at which his Soviet negotiating partner was Joseph Stalin. In those days all political matters decided during negotiations came from the common table at which Stalin, Roosevelt, and Churchill sat. I contributed to the talks in my capacity as a member of the USSR delegation and as Soviet Ambassador in Washington.

When, in the discharge of my duties as Ambassador in Great Britain, I met the British Prime Minister after the war he invariably began our conversations with reminiscences of war-time summits, and also of the Potsdam summit held immediately after the end of the war. This summit began while Churchill was still Prime Minister, but witnessed his replacement in that capacity by Clement Attlee, leader of the Labour Party. Correspondingly, Anthony Eden was replaced as Foreign Secretary by Ernest Bevin.

I remember Churchill's confidence as he waited for the outcome of the elections. But life decreed otherwise. I repeat, Churchill later reminisced not about this dramatic episode of his life but about his meetings with the leaders of the other two war-time Allied powers. If I did not put in a word when he got off on the subject he would talk about it endlessly, and it was obvious that he derived pleasure from his reminiscences and that my presence spurred them on.

The same thing happened when I paid my last call on Churchill before leaving for Moscow to take up my duties as First Deputy Minister of Foreign Affairs.

After we had dealt with political matters, Churchill poured some whisky for me, while he himself drank Russian vodka. Then he asked me whether I liked London. I replied that I did, especially now, with the city decorated for the coronation of Queen Elizabeth II. I said that Piccadilly, which was, to all appearances, on the route of the Queen's coronation procession, looked particularly attractive. Churchill smiled with the twinkle in his eye that he reserved for such occasions and said: 'Indeed, Piccadilly and the city itself look beautiful for the forthcoming event. We British feel that it is better to go to a considerable expense once in the lifetime of our monarchs than every four years as the Americans do when they elect their presidents.' Frankly, this bit of typically Churchillian wit impressed me, and I said so, adding that I had personally observed American-style inaugurations during my stay in the USA. The talk ended on a friendly note and Churchill escorted me to the door of 10 Downing Street, where photographers were waiting to photograph my last meeting with him.

The people I have mentioned were of different political calibre, but I would say that what they had in common was the gradual realization that the 'crusade' against the Soviet Union had come to grief and that the cold war was prejudicing the interests of the British themselves. The vast majority of ranking Western statesmen came round to this sober conclusion in the 1960s and the 1970s. However, many irresponsible individuals still cling to cold war positions and now and then emit a shrill hawkish screech. But the future has never belonged and never will belong to them. The people want neither a cold nor a cool war. This is a political axiom and it cannot be refuted by those who like to 'play soldiers' in order to bury *détente*. Soviet people are firmly convinced of this.

The principles of Soviet foreign policy, formulated during the very first days of the Soviet state's existence when Lenin proclaimed the victory of the Great October Socialist Revolution, comprise the basis of this book.

The central idea in this collection of articles, speeches, and statements made in the USSR and abroad is that nations should live in peace and that the differences between them should not be settled by crossing swords and bloodshed. This is further confirmation of the self-evident truth that what Lenin, architect of the Decree on Peace, said at the dawn of Soviet power has become the immutable foundation of the day-to-day work of the Soviet Government.

The statements, articles, and speeches published in this book deal with a wide spectrum of problems—from questions of war and peace and the prevention of another world-wide conflagration to workaday matters concerning economic, political, and cultural relations between nations. Whatever the rostrum used by a representative of the USSR, in this case the Minister of Foreign Affairs, the world hears the Soviet Union passionately calling for peace, *détente*, and neighbourly relations. Moreover, it hears condemnation of those national leaders whose policies and actions deliberately or involuntarily undermine the foundations of peace and come into conflict with the principles and pledges that were worked out and proclaimed during and directly after the Second World War with the aim of upholding peace and preventing further aggression.

Of course, the opinion of some readers of this book may differ in some details from the standpoint of the author—in the final analysis I state the principles underlying the policy of the Union of Soviet Socialist Republics. But I profoundly believe that given an unbiased, honest approach to international affairs no person will fail to agree that there is no reasonable alternative to the course towards peaceful coexistence of countries with different social systems, to the course towards the extension of *détente*, to the course towards ever more diversified and extensive relations between nations.

Naturally, among the problems analysed by the author, considerable attention is given to the problem of disarmament, of ending the arms race, of the ways and means of delivering nations from the burden of armaments, and, as a first step, of actually lightening that burden. Is there any intelligent person in the world who would deny that this is one of the paramount problems of international life, one that must be resolved? The Soviet Union will continue to make every effort to resolve it. This was urged by Lenin, and it is urged today by Leonid Brezhnev, who enjoys enormous prestige in the world and expresses the will of the entire Soviet people.

The author of these lines would be gratified if the reader reflects over this and other international problems. Today, more than ever before, nobody can afford to ignore them.

The will and thoughts of the Soviet people, and their dedicated work to carry out the internal tasks confronting them, are invariably aimed at contributing to the maintenance of lasting peace. The Soviet Union is doing everything in its power to make peace really durable. It is, as it has always been, willing to co-operate with any nation prepared to follow in the same path. The Communist Party of the Soviet Union, its Central Committee and Politburo headed by General Secretary Leonid Brezhnev are firmly determined to keep to that path.

In conclusion, I should like to return once more to what I began with. It has so happened, and I am happy and proud of it, that in effect my entire independent life has been devoted to implementing the Leninist principles of the foreign policy of the world's first socialist state. In this field I have been working in one post or another for nearly forty years.

It would be proper to ask me, and indeed I ask myself, the question: am I satisfied with what I have accomplished?

In my position I could answer emphatically in the affirmative only if the sun of peace were shining unclouded over our planet, and memories of wars, of all types of armaments, of oppression of nations by nations were, to quote Pushkin, 'buried in the remote past'.

Regrettably, this is still not the case. Lasting peace in the world cannot be achieved by the efforts of only one side, however titanic these efforts may be.

Nevertheless, to the above question I can in the main reply in the affirmative because what has been achieved today inspires optimism for the future. The world has indeed become better than it was some decades ago.

One cannot help deriving profound satisfaction from the fact of having made one's modest contribution to accelerating this movement towards peace, towards justice.

People say that to be a pessimist is simple and safe. I have been and remain an optimist. My optimism is based on my faith in human intelligence, which throughout the centuries has illumined the road to a happier, more just and radiant life for all people.

During the recent special UN session on disarmament I had a

15

meeting in Washington with President Carter and other American foreign policy makers. After the meeting, correspondents, as is the custom in the USA, surrounded me on the lawn in front of the White House. The questions were mostly about a second strategic arms limitation agreement. I told them that the vast majority of the issues involved, particularly the substantive problems, had been settled, and that the range of outstanding problems was gradually narrowing. I added, of course, that there were questions on which no final agreement had been reached, that to speed up settlement of these questions we needed further meetings and, above all, positive motivation not only on our part but also on the part of the American side in the negotiations. In our view the efforts of the American side to reach agreement were feeble and did not give the proper rebuff to the opponents of agreement.

When I saw the faint and quite understandable disappointment on the faces of some of the journalists, I said: this agreement must evidently be built as houses are built—brick by brick.

This idea, which I expressed at the time, is still with me today when I think of the world as a whole, and as I end the Introduction to this book for the English-speaking reader.

To build, brick by brick, the edifice of a lasting peace for my people and all other peoples of the earth, and only world peace can be truly lasting—this has been the aim of my whole life, and one to which I intend devoting the years to come.

Part 1: The 1960s

The 50th anniversary of the Soviet diplomatic service. 29 December 1967

In the report delivered at the joint Anniversary sitting of the Central Committee of the CPSU, the Supreme Soviet of the USSR, and the Supreme Soviet of the RSFSR Leonid Brezhnev, General Secretary of the CPSU Central Committee, gave a profound Marxist–Leninist analysis of our country's foreign policy over the past 50 years and characterized the key features of this policy, which springs from the very essence of the socialist social system.

Our foreign policy grew out of the socialist revolution. It has been and remains an instrument of revolutionary transformation in our country.

Our foreign policy is internationalist, for the interests of the Soviet people coincide with those of working people in all countries of the world. It is imbued with the spirit of solidarity with revolutionary, progressive forces throughout the world and is a vigorous factor in the class struggle on the world scene.

One of the main features of Soviet foreign policy is its profound and genuinely democratic spirit, its recognition in practice of the equality of all nations, large and small, its recognition of the equality of races and ethnic groups.

Lastly, a fundamental feature characterizing Soviet foreign policy is that it is a consistent policy of peace, security, and friendship among nations. Socialism has no other aim save concern for the interests of the people, and this presupposes, above all, a struggle against war.

History knows of no more striking and significant fact than what the socialist revolution accomplished in our country under the leadership of the Communist Party of Lenin.

Soviet foreign policy had to help safeguard the gains of the revolution. It was necessary to work out the principles and methods of that policy, and to build up a Soviet diplomatic service that would dependably assist the Party in attaining international aims and successfully cope with the requirements of the situation.

Lenin's work in foreign policy was and remains a most vivid and unfading model of Party commitment and high principles, of the ability to assess social, economic, and political phenomena in all their complexity and contradictory interrelationships and respond opportunely to changes in situation requiring a rapid modification of tactics.

19

Soviet diplomacy is an offspring of the Party. The Party and its Central Committee chart the strategy and tactics of foreign policy and guide the implementation of that policy.

The ruling classes of capitalist society have been disciplining their state machine for ages. They have turned diplomacy into an art of 'using words to conceal reality', to quote Machiavelli, and diplomats into servants of their interests, into an instrument of the exploiting system, the expression of which in foreign policy has been and remains the preaching of militarism, the arms race, and war.

The Bolshevik Party had to train its own proletarian diplomats, to create its own diplomacy that would show the world the superiority and genuine humanity of Soviet foreign policy and of the socialist world-view.

The most important foreign policy documents of the then young Soviet state were written personally by Lenin. He directed negotiations and conducted talks with foreign representatives, and spoke with statesmen, civic leaders, journalists, and writers visiting revolutionary Russia.

The combination of Party and Soviet principles, the day-to-day guidance of foreign policy by the Central Committee and Lenin personally, and the possibility and ability to address the working masses of the capitalist countries and oppressed peoples and express thoughts cherished and appreciated by them were what from the outset gave Soviet diplomacy decisive advantages over imperialist diplomacy.

To this day foreign policy issues are constantly on the agenda of the Party's Central Committee. They are analysed in depth in the documents of Party congresses. Special plenary meetings of the CPSU Central Committee are held to discuss these issues. Our Party's leadership exchanges views on international developments and problems with the leaders of other Communist and Workers' parties and the governments of fraternal socialist countries. The concurrence of basic class interests creates unbounded opportunities for close co-operation between socialist countries on major problems of the day.

The emergence of the great community of socialist states, which exercises a steadily growing influence on the course of social development in the interests of peace, democracy, and socialism, is one of the most outstanding achievements of our epoch. The task of strengthening and consolidating the world socialist system and of further enhancing its role on the international scene holds premier place in the foreign policy and diplomatic work of the CPSU Central Committee and the Soviet Government.

The relations between socialist states are of an entirely new kind. They are based on uniformity of the political, social, and economic system, on the fact that they share the same Marxist–Leninist ideology, and on common aims in the struggle against imperialism and for peace, democracy, and socialism.

In the twenty years since the world socialist system was formed tremendous ground has been covered in promoting and enriching the relations between socialist countries, in evolving new forms of collective economic, political, and military co-operation, and in organizing joint action on the international scene.

Commitments adopted under treaties of friendship, co-operation and mutual assistance are in force between socialist states. These treaties express the vital need of the peoples of socialist countries for fraternal unity and co-operation.

In the system of political and defence co-operation among the countries of the socialist community a special place is held by the Warsaw Treaty. This is well known by the peoples of the socialist countries and it is well known in the other camp as well.

There is really nothing that can compare with the intensity of the foreign policy contacts and links characterizing the relations between socialist countries. The meetings of party and government leaders, sessions of the Warsaw Treaty Political Consultative Committee, which are attended by the general secretaries of the Communist and Workers' parties and by heads of government, the conferences of ministers, the close, business-like relations between ministries and other central institutions, and the steadily broadening contacts between enterprises, institutes, collectives of working people, and public organizations are evidence of the wealth and diversity of the forms of co-operation, and of the solid, inviolable ties between socialist countries.

Much of the foreign policy effort of the socialist countries is directed towards ensuring the system of European security, towards preventing another war in Europe. The whole world has heard the proposals for ways and means of consolidating peace in Europe drawn up by the

21

Warsaw Treaty Political Consultative Committee at its sittings in Warsaw and Bucharest.

The first foreign policy act of the Soviet Government was Lenin's Decree on Peace.

For the first time in world history foreign policy was placed in the service of the working people.

For the first time the world saw an internationalist policy that was not aimed against the peoples of other states and did not pursue mercenary objectives, but was consistent with the interests of other nations as well, and thereby won their sympathy and support.

During the long history of social exploitation people have almost got accustomed to the thought that any more or less protracted period of peace is only a respite between wars. Bourgeois ideologies sought to discipline people to the thought that nothing was more natural than the subjugation and exploitation of many countries by a handful of states that allegedly had the 'mission' of administering the world's affairs.

There are innumerable examples of how even on the eve of wars governments kept the people ignorant of impending catastrophe, sowed illusions, and lied deliberately with the sole purpose of paralysing the will of the masses for peace and freedom, setting one nation against another, and using one nation to oppress another.

The half-century chronicle of Soviet foreign policy and diplomacy contains many stirring pages, for instance, the struggle for the Brest Peace, which, to quote Lenin, 'was significant in being the first time that we were able, on an immense scale and amidst vast difficulties, to take advantage of the contradictions among the imperialists in such a way as to make socialism the ultimate gainer'. (V. I. Lenin, 'Speech Delivered at a Meeting of Activists of the Moscow Organization of the RCP(B)', *Collected Works*, vol. 31, p. 439.)

The Communist Party and the Soviet Government frustrated many a plan of the Western ruling circles, who endeavoured to channel, in the words used before the outbreak of the Second World War, Nazi aggression against our country.

In their reckless attempt to hold a feast during the fascist plague, in their desire to be present at the funeral repast of the first and, as they hoped, last socialist state, these circles betrayed the interests of even their own countries and peoples, pushing them into the abyss, to the edge of which they wanted to propel, above all, the Soviet Union.

The Soviet Union's victory in the Second World War was a triumph of the Soviet social system and of the organizational and political work of the CPSU. It was a victory of Soviet arms and a triumph of the courage, heroism, and selflessness of our great people. Communism was the real force that broke Hitler's backbone, crushed hundreds of his divisions, and forced the fascist aggressors to their knees.

Moreover, it was a triumph of Leninist foreign policy and Leninist diplomacy.

Soviet foreign policy helped to mobilize the anti-Nazi forces during the war, thwarted the diverse back-stage manipulations of our ill-wishers, and contributed towards the creation of favourable pre-conditions for a democratic post-war arrangement, for curbing the forces of aggression, for the triumph of the people's and socialist revolutions in Europe and Asia, and for the national liberation of colonies and dependent countries.

After the war Soviet diplomacy helped the Party and the people to consolidate the results of our great victory.

Almost half a century ago, acting on instructions from Lenin, the Soviet delegation at the Genoa Conference proposed a programme for general disarmament. Since then Soviet foreign policy and diplomacy have been conducting a broad offensive against the positions of the proponents of the arms race.

From a report at a meeting to mark the 50th anniversary of the Soviet diplomatic service, 29 December 1967

The USSR Supreme Soviet. 10 July 1969

Soviet foreign policy is consistently upholding the principle of the peaceful coexistence of states irrespective of their social systems and making every effort to deliver mankind from another world war.

Therefore, as a major world power with wide-ranging international links, the Soviet Union naturally cannot remain passive in the face of developments that affect our security and the security of our friends even if these developments are territorially remote. Responsibility to the Soviet people and our internationalist duty make it obligatory that the high prestige and might of the USSR should effectively serve the cause of preserving and consolidating peace and repulsing the policy of aggravating international tensions and aggression, wherever that policy jeopardizes peace.

Our country's influence on world affairs is growing steadily year after year, even, it may be said, day by day.

The Soviet Union stands shoulder to shoulder with the fraternal socialist countries, whose foreign policy is of the same nature as our foreign policy and pursues the same objectives.

The relations among the countries of the community are a new type of relations emanating from the nature of their social system. These relations spring not only from a common aim in domestic development, from a common ideology, but also from common foreign policy objectives.

In the community a special role is played by the Warsaw Treaty member-countries. The mutual commitments accepted under that Treaty and also under the relevant bilateral state treaties have still further enhanced the influence of the socialist countries in the world, including European affairs.

Military groups were not our idea. Their formation was started by the big Western states, our former war-time allies. The Soviet Union had time and again warned these powers that the world's division into military blocs would not strengthen international security, that, on the contrary, it would undermine that security. In the West the upper hand was gained not by a realistic approach to the situation in the world, but by hostility towards socialism, by a striving for expansion. The Warsaw Treaty Organization was our reply to this policy and these acts of the Western states and, chiefly, to the creation of the aggressive North Atlantic bloc.

Developments have shown that the Warsaw Treaty member-countries acted correctly when they set up their own defensive organ-ization, which is steadily improving its work. An important milestone in strengthening the defensive military mechanism of the Warsaw

Treaty member-countries was the decision passed by the Political Consultative Committee last March in Budapest.

The increased might of the Warsaw Treaty Organization has been placed in the service of peace and security in Europe. But those whom it concerns must know that this Organization will never permit anybody to encroach upon the security of its member-countries, on the gains of socialism in these countries.

The socialist community of states is an historic gain not only for the peoples of the member-states but also for the working people of the whole world. Today no task is more important in the struggle for peace and socialism than to strengthen that community. The CPSU and the Soviet Government will continue doing their utmost to carry out their allied and internationalist duty of further consolidating the socialist community.

On the international scene our country is using the entire weight of its influence to settle major problems, of which there are many, in favour of peace. The Soviet Union tirelessly draws the attention of other countries to the danger of another world war. The task of combating this threat, of achieving international security is plainly evident today.

The Soviet Union has always been and remains opposed to wars of aggression and aggrandisement. Victims of aggression have always had and will always have our support. If only by virtue of this the foreign policy of the Soviet Union comes into conflict in many areas with the foreign policy of some Western powers. Essentially speaking, all present developments in the world bear the deep imprint of this collision of different policy guidelines.

An end to the war in Vietnam and a political settlement of the Vietnam issue would considerably improve the international situation as a whole. This is in the interests of all peoples, of all countries.

The situation in the world as a whole is strongly influenced by the situation in the Middle East. The Soviet Union has given and continues to give much of its attention to that region, which remains a dangerous flashpoint that may have serious consequences for peace. What is the main problem? The fact that Israel has still not evacuated the territory of Arab states—Egypt, Syria, and Jordan—occupied by it.

Following the events of June 1967 chauvinistic heat has evidently turned the heads of some Israeli leaders to the extent that two years have proved insufficient for them to acquire the ability to look at things more realistically. And to be more realistic means to acknowledge that foreign territories seized as a result of aggression cannot be held, that they must be returned to whom they belong.

To set hopes on military superiority, as Israel is doing, is not far-sighted on the part of Israel. The only dependable way to settle the issue is to evacuate Israeli troops from occupied lands and simultaneously recognize the right of all Middle Eastern states, including Israel, to ensure an independent national existence, and to bring lasting peace to the region.

The Soviet Union's stand is that every opportunity should be taken to settle the situation in the Middle East. Procrastination is dangerous and prejudicial to everybody. It is politically prejudicial because of the enormous danger of the situation in that region deteriorating. It is economically prejudicial chiefly because the Suez Canal, which is Egypt's sovereign property and an important international shipping route, is inoperative.

There is another highly important aspect of this problem: if aggression is not to be encouraged, no country that has attacked other states and seized part of their territory by force should be allowed to continue occupying that territory in flagrant contravention of the UN Charter and the relevant Security Council resolutions.

The Soviet Government has taken the important initiative of working out proposals aimed at facilitating a political settlement in the Middle East. These proposals, including the proposals put forward recently, continue to play a vital role in the quest for ways of establishing peace in that region.

We should like to see the US Government, on whose policy Israel relies, adopt a more realistic stance on this question in keeping with long-term interests instead of with various calculations of short-term advantage. All countries, large and small, want the situation in the Middle East to be settled. Moreover, the solution of that problem would benefit the international situation and definitely tip the scales in favour of peace.

European affairs hold a large and important place in Soviet foreign policy. Many vital threads of world politics lead from and to Europe. The destiny of our country has frequently depended on developments in Europe. In other words, the security of the Soviet Union is inseparable from European security.

In pursuing a vigorous, principled policy in European affairs the Soviet Union's point of departure is that the victory in the Second World War, however sweeping it may have been, and it was precisely such, does not by itself ensure the creation of all the conditions precluding further aggression. Comprehension of this underlies the inter-Allied agreements on the post-war arrangement in Europe, and this is borne out by every article and every phrase of those agreements. This continent can deliver itself from the threat of war only if all the European states pursue a policy consonant with the actual situation that has taken shape and exists there as a result of the Second World War and post-war development.

The interests of European security require recognition of the results of the war by all countries, and the building-up on that foundation of the relations between the European countries themselves and also between them and the countries of other regions of the world.

The Second World War fundamentally reshaped the political and social map of Europe. An event of epochal significance was the birth twenty years ago of the first state of German working people, the German Democratic Republic, where the key provisions and principles of Potsdam and other Allied agreements have been implemented in full, provisions whose purport is to uproot German militarism and Nazism once and for all and prevent any revival of the threat of German aggression.

Today every European knows that as a result of the Second World War some countries of the continent live within boundaries that differ from what they were like before the war. These just boundaries, including the Oder–Neisse boundary and the boundary between the two German states, are a major guarantee of security in Europe.

Having taken shape in the flames of the most devastating of wars and being the result of a struggle against aggressors who had set out to destroy entire countries and peoples, the existing boundaries of the European states are immutable.

27

They are immutable because their legality and the obligation for all countries to respect them are based on the Yalta and Potsdam agreements, which are historically significant political acts possessing the strength of international law, and also on other international treaties signed by the states concerned.

They are immutable because for three decades a number of European countries, including the GDR and the FRG, have been arranging their life and their state affairs in their own way within these new boundaries.

Moreover, they are immutable because an entire generation of Europeans, who have grown up under conditions of peace, knows of no other European boundaries than those which exist today and which it justifiably regards as the frontiers of peace.

The inviolability of existing boundaries is the key question for Europe. Peace or war depends on how countries, particularly the big powers, answer that question.

As regards the Soviet Union, our answer is unequivocal: the boundaries of countries—in the East or the West, in the North or the South of the continent—are inviolable, and no force can change this situation.

This is also the stand of our Warsaw Treaty allies, whose words, like ours, are not at variance with deeds.

A clear-cut stand relative to recognition of the immutability of the boundaries existing in Europe is a major indication of the policy of each individual state in European affairs and of how its pronouncements in favour of peace conform to its actual intentions.

Today, as in the early years after the war, the Soviet people closely follow the attempts to regenerate German militarism and Nazism. The struggle against Nazism and militarism, whose extirpation is demanded by the Potsdam Agreement, is one of the principal orientations of our country's foreign policy efforts.

We have noted time and again that the Federal Republic of Germany has no fewer possibilities than other countries for promoting normal relations with the Soviet Union. The difficulties in relations are not created by us. The point is that in return for an improvement in relations the FRG wants neither more nor less than a retreat from the principles of our policy on European affairs, and that is out of the question.

A change in our relations can take place, and this is what we want, if the FRG takes the road of peace. To this end the plans of revenge for the lost war must give way to understanding that the future of the FRG with its large economic and technical potentialities lies in peaceful co-operation with all countries, including the Soviet Union.

Proceeding from these positions, the Soviet Government is prepared to continue exchanging views with the FRG on the renunciation of the use of force, up to the conclusion of the relevant agreement, and also to exchange views on other issues of Soviet–West German relations and maintain the relevant contacts. Needless to say, at the exchange of views the Soviet Union would take into account all the interests of its allies, the fraternal socialist countries.

In the very centre of Europe is a place that demands the close attention of Soviet foreign policy. This is West Berlin. Ever since the war complications have arisen time and again over the city.

West Berlin enjoys a unique international status. It is situated in the heartland of a sovereign state, the German Democratic Republic, and is able to maintain contacts with the external world only by using its means of communication. The social and state system of West Berlin, and its economic and money systems, and other conditions under which its population lives differ from the order and conditions existing in the GDR.

But this is by no means the source of friction. It is generated by FRG encroachments upon West Berlin, by its attempts to use the city for purposes hostile to the GDR, the Soviet Union, and other socialist states.

The policy of the Soviet Union, as of the GDR, relative to West Berlin is clear-cut. We want the population and authorities of West Berlin to operate in conditions that can ensure the city's normal existence as an independent political entity. However, there can be no question of allowing infringements upon our interests, or the legitimate interests of our ally, the GDR, or any violation of West Berlin's special status.

If the other powers, our war-time allies, who bear their part of the responsibility for the situation in West Berlin, approach this question with due account for the interests of European security, they will find the Soviet Union prepared to exchange views on how to prevent complications over West Berlin today and in the future. Of course, we shall take no step prejudicial to the legitimate interests of the GDR or to the special status of West Berlin.

In its efforts to strengthen European security, the Soviet Union proceeds from the belief that the creation of a system of collective security is the most effective way of making Europe more secure.

The Soviet Union's efforts to ensure such security in Europe date from before the war. But in the period preceding the Second World War the governments of the Western powers lulled themselves with the drafts of various pacts and deals, which were an attempt to buy off the aggressors to the detriment of the security of the Soviet Union and other states. They yielded to Hitler and Mussolini, paving their way to aggression with more and more concessions.

It cannot be said that the powers, which together with us fought Nazi Germany during the war, and together with us laid the foundations of the post-war peace, have drawn the correct conclusions in the post-war period. That is far from being the case. They have set collective security aside in favour of closed military–political groups that are in many ways reminiscent of the pre-war military–political combinations. This was brought into bold relief when the aggressive North Atlantic bloc was formed in 1949.

As always, underlying the Soviet Union's approach to problems of European security is the striving to organize relations between European countries on the basis of peaceful, I repeat, peaceful co-operation. This is the aim of our proposals, and for us it does not matter who bears the palm in putting forward various ideas and projects. The Soviet Union is prepared to consider any proposal from other countries if their purpose is to secure an easing of tension in Europe and to strengthen European peace.

The Warsaw Treaty member-countries have adopted the well-known Bucharest Declaration, which contains a wide-ranging programme of measures for ensuring security in Europe. They have proposed concrete steps towards military *détente* in Europe. The signatories to the Bucharest Declaration have proposed that questions of European security should be discussed collectively by all the European nations.

Much has been done to step up the drive for European security by the Karlovy Vary Conference of Communist and Workers' Parties of

Europe. Its programme remains as important today as it was two and a half years ago.

Deputies to the Supreme Soviet of the USSR are, of course, informed of the wide response to the Address of the Warsaw Treaty member-countries to all European states on the convocation of a European conference on security, adopted last March in Budapest. In fact, no European state has raised objections to the proposal for convening that conference.

The Soviet Government expresses satisfaction over the fact that the Government of Finland has taken the initiative in proposing that all the countries concerned should begin preparations for the conference through consultations between the interested governments and that a meeting should be held at a certain stage to discuss questions pertaining to the convocation of the conference. The Soviet Government has responded favourably to this initiative of the Government of Finland and is prepared to facilitate its realization.

The governments of some countries declare that it is important to ensure the success of the European conference by conducting the necessary preparations. This does not conflict with our view. The only thing is that the preparations should not be turned into impassable thickets closing the road to the conference.

The Soviet Union is also a protagonist in the joint efforts by East and West European countries in major energy, transport, and public health projects that have a direct bearing on the welfare of the entire continent. Broad and expanding economic, scientific and technical co-operation, unhindered mutually beneficial trade, and cultural exchanges can and should be an important basis for political co-operation as well.

There are thus many problems that could be considered. All that is wanted is the readiness to examine and resolve them.

The problem of Soviet–Chinese relations is of immense significance from the angle both of our country's interests and of the development of the international situation as a whole.

China is a neighbour of the Soviet Union. We have a common frontier 7,395 kilometres long. The situation in Asia, and by no means only in Asia, depends to a large extent on China's aims and on the orientation of its foreign policy.

A radical reorientation took place in China's policy many years ago. Its leaders steered towards the curtailment and then a virtual suspension of all relations with countries of the socialist community. From a polemic they went over to divisive, subversive actions, to energetic attempts to range modern revolutionary forces against each other. From criticism of peaceful coexistence they went over to direct opposition to the settlement of international disputes, to the provoking of armed conflicts.

China's leaders have done their utmost to shatter the relations that had taken shape between our countries in the early years following the revolution and the formation of People's China. Trade has diminished from nearly 2,000 million rubles in 1959 to 86 million rubles in 1968. Scientific, technical, and cultural exchanges have been cut off entirely. It is the fault of the Chinese side that some treaties on economic co-operation have been annulled and others have been frozen. It is their fault that the work that was done formerly to co-ordinate the attitudes of the two countries to pressing international problems has been halted.

The situation on the frontier, which had been characterized by close contacts between border regions, by broad co-operation in the development of natural wealth and frontier river basins, and by friendly contacts between the population, is now marked by tension, more and more frequent friction, and open conflict.

There is no need to speak in detail of China's hostile, subversive actions against the USSR and other socialist countries or against the international communist movement as a whole. These actions have been assessed only recently by the participants in the International Meeting of Communist and Workers' Parties.

The principled attitude of our country, of our Party and the Government of the USSR to the People's Republic of China has been clearly enunciated in Leonid Brezhnev's speech at that Meeting and in the Soviet Government's statements of 29 March and 13 June of this year. The basis of our policy towards China has been and remains aimed at restoring and in future promoting friendship between the USSR and the PRC with, naturally, an emphatic rebuff to any provocation. The Soviet Union opposes the stream of abuse and insults with a constructive policy that takes the long-term interests of the peoples of both countries into account.

Of course, there is a wide gulf between the Peking leaders' anti-Soviet declarations, which show their hostile intentions against our country and against the Soviet people, and the possibilities for carrying them out. Any attempt to talk with the Soviet Union in the language of threats, much less of arms, has been and will be given a well-deserved rebuff from us. What happened last March on Damansky Island in the Ussuri River should make those concerned weigh the consequences of their actions more soberly.

Despite the attitude they had maintained in the recent past, the Chinese leaders make territorial claims on the Soviet Union. They allege that the Russo–Chinese treaties clearly demarcating the frontiers between the two countries are unequal. But, as the Soviet Government's statements eloquently show, these are false allegations. The treaties of Aigun, Tientsin, and Peking, and the protocols, agreements, and maps demarcating and formalizing the frontiers between China and the USSR are in operation and both sides are committed to respect them.

Along their whole length, including in Central Asia and the Far East, the frontiers of the Soviet Union are inviolable. In the courageous action of every soldier and officer on Damansky Island was seen the will of our people to stand firmly in defence of these frontiers.

The Soviet Union has no territorial claims on any of its neighbours. Its point of departure is that frontiers should not be lines of animosity and hostility. Across frontiers there should be exchanges not of threats, much less of leaden fire, but of economic, cultural, and other values, of everything that strengthens friendship between neighbouring peoples. This is the Soviet Union's attitude to its frontiers with all neighbouring countries; this and only this must be the state of affairs on the frontier with China as well.

The Soviet Government has proposed to the Government of the PRC that measures should be instituted to normalize the situation on the Soviet–Chinese frontier and prevent any incidents, especially such as might cause bloodshed. It proposed resuming the consultations between the authorized representatives of both sides that were conducted in 1964 with the aim of specifying the state frontiers of the PRC and the USSR in individual sectors. This attitude of the Soviet Government is entirely consistent with our policy of settling differences by negotiation.

We should like to believe that the Chinese leaders will come to the only correct conclusion, that incidents have to be excluded, that in the relations between our countries the language of enmity and force is unsuitable.

The Soviet Union has time and again declared that it is prepared to discuss questions of inter-state relations—economic, scientific, and cultural—with the appropriate representatives of the PRC. Acceptance of these and all our other proposals aimed at improving relations between the USSR and the PRC would be consistent with the long-term interests of the Chinese and Soviet peoples. The future will show how the PRC leadership will respond to our readiness to conduct talks on a wide range of questions affecting the relations between the USSR and China without the burden of prior conditions.

One of the most acute problems confronting mankind is that of ending the arms race and achieving disarmament.

The Soviet Government has reported to the Supreme Soviet that it is prepared to begin exchanges of views with the USA on strategic arms. The Government of the USA has declared that it is getting ready to exchange views. The Soviet Government is also prepared to do this. I should like to express the hope that both sides will approach this question with an awareness of its great significance.

Ever since the appearance of nuclear weapons the Soviet Union has stressed that the energy of the atom should be used exclusively for peaceful purposes, for which the relevant international agreement must be signed. It has consistently abided by this stance and continues to urge such a settlement.

All the main questions relating to complete nuclear disarmament, to the abolition of nuclear weapons, in other words, to the prohibition of the use of atomic energy for the production of nuclear arms, can be settled in fact only with the participation of all, I repeat, *of all* the nuclear powers. That is the only way this question can stand. The Soviet Government remains prepared to discuss this colossally important question with representatives of the other nuclear powers.

Directly contiguous to this is the task of preventing the proliferation of nuclear arms. Alongside other countries, the Soviet Union has begun the ratification of the nuclear non-proliferation treaty, which has now been signed by nearly ninety nations. We should like to express the hope that the countries still discussing the question of subscribing to the treaty will come to the only correct conclusion, that it must be signed and ratified.

The Soviet Union has always attached importance to the question of a complete ban on nuclear weapons tests. The 1963 Moscow treaty on the cessation of such tests in the atmosphere, in outer space, and underwater was a major step in that direction. However, underground nuclear tests still remain unprohibited. The Soviet Government is prepared to reach agreement on this question as well.

The Soviet Union has proposed a ban on the use of the bed of seas and oceans for military purposes. There are grounds for expressing satisfaction over the response to this proposal. True, there also have been attempts to reduce the volume of commitments by states. However, the vast majority of countries in the Disarmament Committee want an effective treaty of this kind.

The Soviet Union will continue to act on the assumption that the demilitarization of the bed of seas and oceans is in the interests of all nations.

We have submitted for the consideration of other states, including the member-countries of the Geneva Disarmament Committee, a proposal providing for a ban, more effective than the existing one, on chemical and biological means of warfare. The Soviet Government expresses the hope that this question will be decided by countries with a full sense of responsibility and that the relevant agreement, formalized in international law, is reached in the near future.

Soviet foreign policy aimed at ending the arms race and achieving disarmament has the closest co-operation and support of fraternal socialist countries. Our Warsaw Treaty allies—Poland, Czechoslovakia, the GDR, Bulgaria, Hungary, and Romania—attach paramount significance to the attainment of progress in this field. For their part they are making important proposals on various aspects of disarmament, in particular where it concerns European countries.

The Mongolian People's Republic was recently invited to become a full member of the Geneva Disarmament Committee. Mongolia's attitude to disarmament has always been clear-cut and lucid. It has unfailingly given its backing to every constructive move in the matter of disarmament. Today it is getting still greater possibilities for pursuing this course.

Such is the Soviet Union's line in questions of disarmament and it is determined to continue pursuing it. The line towards curbing and ending the arms race, the line towards disarmament is the only correct one and is dictated by the objective conditions obtaining in the world, of which the present scientific and technological revolution is not the least. The channel into which this revolution turns—towards war or towards peace—is a question of the utmost importance.

In his speech at the International Meeting of Communist and Workers' Parties Leonid Brezhnev set as an important long-term task the creation of systems of collective security in regions where the threat of armed conflict is concentrated. It was emphasized that in addition to Europe, present developments were placing on the agenda the task of creating a system of collective security in Asia as well. Being both a European and an Asian power, the Soviet Union wants all the peoples of Asia to live in peace.

It must be noted that there was a considerable international response to this idea, particularly in Asian countries. True, all sorts of fantasy were woven around it. Hardly had the governments concerned given serious consideration to this idea than certain circles began peddling the assertion that a system of collective security in Asia would be directed against some individual country or group of countries. This sort of fantasy has no leg to stand on. It is purely a matter of collective efforts by all the Asian states to strengthen security in that part of the world in their common interests.

Of course, this entire question requires discussion and consultations between the countries concerned in order to work out mutually acceptable decisions. In the course of such consultations the Soviet Government would be prepared to state its concrete considerations on this exceedingly important problem.

The Soviet Government expresses the hope that its proposal for a system of collective security in Asia is seriously studied by the governments of the countries concerned.

Many forms of contact between countries and many forms of their activity combine on the international scene. One of the most important is the United Nations Organization.

Ever since the war, when the foundations of the UN were being laid, the Soviet Union has attached and continues to attach great significance to this Organization. The UN has done much that is useful and consistent with the interests of peace. Its work has benefited from the adoption of some proposals of the Soviet Union and our friends aimed at relaxing tension, abolishing the colonial system, and halting the policy of expansion.

But when one weighs the work accomplished by the United Nations one comes to the conclusion that one can apply to it an expression that is often used in sport: when people want to praise a side and, at the same time, state a measure of disappointment over the showing of that side they usually say: 'The team could have done better.' This expression is also applicable to the UN; it is still not using all its potentialities in the struggle for peace.

From this the Soviet Union draws the conclusion that the UN member-countries, chiefly the great powers—the permanent members of the Security Council—should not divert the world organization from major, acute problems relating to the maintenance of peace, but that they should do everything possible to enable the UN to deal precisely with these problems, to function strictly in accordance with its Charter, the spirit and letter of which to this day preserve the resolution of the Second World War and have the mission of serving the cause of peace.

There are grounds for declaring from this rostrum of the Supreme Soviet that on the world scene the Soviet Union's position is *stable*.

This is due to the immense day-to-day work of the CPSU Central Committee and its leading core, the Politburo, to the purposeful and effective work of the Soviet Government, the Supreme Soviet of the USSR, its Presidium and standing commissions, and to the vigorous efforts of Soviet public organizations and trade unions. This extensive, manifold work ensures the consistent application and skilful combination in practice of the principles of socialist internationalism and the defence of the Soviet Union's state interests. The foreign policy of our Communist Party and the Soviet Government has the unanimous and undivided support of the entire Soviet people, and in this lies the foundation of its strength and efficacy.

The Soviet people's achievements in economic development, science, technology, and culture, in promoting living standards, furthering socialist democracy, and steadily increasing the Soviet Union's defensive capability are enhancing the scale and depth of the influence exercised by Soviet foreign policy on world developments. Distances cannot weaken the great attractive force of Soviet foreign policy, or the ideas in general that our socialist state is bringing to the world. It is a profoundly peaceful and profoundly humanitarian foreign policy, which serves the interests of the peoples and only these interests.

The Soviet Union champions peace on earth firmly and unswervingly. It has pursued and will continue to pursue a policy of friendship among peoples, the Leninist foreign policy.

From a speech at the 6th session of the 7th Supreme Soviet of the USSR, 10 July 1969

Ratification of the Treaty on the Non-proliferation of Nuclear Weapons. 24 November 1969

The Presidium of the Supreme Soviet of the USSR is today considering the question of ratifying the Treaty on the Non-proliferation of Nuclear Weapons submitted by the Council of Ministers of the USSR. As you all know, on 20 August this year the Foreign Relations Commissions of the Soviet of the Union and the Soviet of Nationalities of the Supreme Soviet of the USSR closely examined the non-proliferation treaty and unanimously recommended its ratification by the Supreme Soviet.

Considerable international significance attaches to the conclusion of the Treaty on the Non-proliferation of Nuclear Weapons. This treaty has established a key norm in international law by which countries must be guided.

The fact that since it was opened for signature on 1 July 1968 the non-proliferation treaty has been signed by nearly 90 nations and ratified by 23 is an indication that this principle has received international recognition.

Broad support for the non-proliferation treaty shows the readiness of the nations of the world to pool their efforts in order to avert the danger of a nuclear war.

It was precisely this aim, preventing a dangerous spread of nuclear weapons, erecting a barrier to the emergence of more nuclear powers, and thereby reducing the danger of a nuclear war, which was set by the CPSU Central Committee and the Soviet Government when they took the initiative in resolving the problem of the non-proliferation of nuclear weapons. Our stance in the talks with the United States and other countries on the treaty was based on our striving to resolve these important issues.

The treaty drawn up as a result of long and difficult negotiations meets this purpose. In accordance with its basic provisions, the signatory states possessing nuclear weapons pledge not to pass this weapon to any country directly or indirectly, or to help in its production or acquisition. In turn, the non-nuclear states pledge not to produce or acquire this weapon. Thus, through the reciprocal commitments of nuclear and non-nuclear states it is possible to quite effectively close loopholes allowing the further spread of nuclear weapons.

As is stated in the treaty, nuclear weapons may not be turned over not only to individual states but also to any groups of states, including military blocs. This is an important provision.

The non-proliferation treaty does not impose on its signatories any commitments that may be regarded as incompatible with their sovereignty or with the principles of equality. It will have no restrictive force on the peaceful uses of nuclear energy. On the contrary, by prohibiting the use of atomic energy for the production of weapons, the treaty opens up prospects for broad co-operation among its signatories in the interests of developing the use of nuclear energy for peaceful purposes. A special article of the treaty is devoted to this question.

In accordance with the relevant wishes of the non-nuclear states, it was agreed by the USSR, the USA, and Britain that in the Security Council they would make co-ordinated statements stressing that the security of the non-nuclear signatories of the Treaty on the Non-proliferation of Nuclear Weapons would be duly safeguarded. These statements have been made. The Council passed a special resolution welcoming the intention of the nuclear powers to extend assistance, in accordance with the UN Charter, to any non-nuclear signatory of the treaty in the event it is the victim of an act of aggression or the object of the threat of nuclear aggression. The Soviet Union declared that it is prepared to fulfil this decision of the Security Council and that it intends to abide firmly by its commitments. Needless to say, this understanding covers all non-nuclear signatories of the treaty without any discrimination whatsoever.

The coming into force of the non-proliferation treaty will help to create a situation in which any country, nuclear or non-nuclear, that has not signed the treaty will find it extremely difficult to act in contravention of the aims of the treaty.

The Soviet Union has always felt and continues to feel that it is of paramount importance that countries possessing a developed nuclear industry and, consequently, having the potential for manufacturing nuclear weapons should be signatories of the non-proliferation treaty.

The conclusion of the Treaty on the Non-proliferation of Nuclear Weapons does not abolish nuclear weapons themselves. However, it places an effective obstacle to the nuclear arms race in breadth, preventing the appearance of new nuclear powers, helping to improve the international situation, and to some extent clearing the way for negotiations on further steps in that direction.

From a speech at a sitting of the Presidium of the Supreme Soviet of the USSR on the question of ratifying the Treaty on the Non-proliferation of Nuclear Weapons, 24 November 1969

Part 2: 1970–74

The 25th session of the UN General Assembly. 21 October 1970

The twenty-fifth session of the General Assembly is of a somewhat unusual character. It is providing an occasion not only for the annual exchange of views between member states of the United Nations on the state of the international situation but also, at the same time, for the observance of a major landmark in the life of the Organization—the twenty-fifth anniversary of its foundation.

The quarter of a century which has elapsed since the founding of the United Nations has been a whole historical era. The starting point of this era was the victory of the peoples of the anti-Hitler coalition over fascist Germany and militarist Japan.

Never before had victory demanded such a high price. The peoples of our country alone had to sacrifice 20 million lives, including those killed at the front and those murdered and tortured by the Nazis; this is more than the whole population of some states. The Soviet people do not forget that the peoples of many countries in Europe, Asia, Africa and America fought beside them against fascism.

The Charter of the United Nations reflected the spirit of those times. The most important provisions of the Charter emerged not just at the negotiating table of the Allied Powers and at conferences, but above all amidst a powerful anti-fascist liberation upsurge. Unlike the pre-war League of Nations, the new world organization was created from the very outset on the basis of universality and the sovereign equality of states irrespective of their social systems. The Charter of the United Nations, of which our country was one of the authors, became the charter of peaceful coexistence, in which the ideas of the 'peaceful cohabitation' of states, advanced by Lenin at the very dawn of the existence of the Soviet state, are translated into the language of international law. It is impossible not to mention the triumph of these ideas at the present time, in this year in which the whole of progressive mankind has celebrated the centenary of the birth of the founder of our state.

Twenty-five years separate us from the day on which the United Nations Charter entered into force.

The task of maintaining international peace has certainly not become simpler. More than once during those years conflicts have broken out, acts of aggression have been committed, and situations threatening universal peace have been created. More than once the United Nations itself has been in a feverish condition. However, if one tries to single out the main feature of the course of world affairs over these years, if one views the complications which have arisen in the world—complications which are against the basic trend in the development of the world situation, but which have nevertheless sometimes reached a point of considerable tension—then one can, we think, conclude with certainty that the task of maintaining and consolidating peace has become more complex but that the conditions for dealing successfully with it have been developing to an even greater extent and more rapidly.

This is a reflection of the immense positive changes which have occurred in the development of human society over the past 25 years—changes which have, in fact, altered the whole social aspect of our planet. The world system of socialism has established itself over one-third of the globe. The socialist community has taken shape and con-solidated itself. It has firmly opposed the aggressive impulses of the forces of imperialism and consistently advocated in international affairs a policy of reducing tension, ruling out the use of force in the settlement of disputes and defending the rights of peoples to independent develop-ment by way of national liberation and social progress—a policy directed against any attempts to intervene in the domestic affairs of peoples or to impose reactionary pro-imperialist regimes from without. This line is organically inherent in socialist foreign policy, which is an expression of the deep-rooted and vital needs of the working classes and the entire people. The policy of consolidating the socialist com-munity and developing relations of friendship, mutual assistance and co-operation of all kinds between the socialist countries is not only in the interests of these countries themselves but also in the wider interests of the security of all peoples.

This is precisely why the foreign policy of the Soviet Union and the countries of the socialist community is having such a profound effect on the activities of the United Nations. No one can deny that the questions raised and proposals made by the socialist countries—questions such as the strengthening of international security, disarma-ment, non-intervention in the domestic affairs of states, the peaceful settlement of conflicts, the elimination of colonialism, the normalization of international economic relations, measures to promote the social progress of peoples and the improvement of United Nations peace-keeping machinery—occupy an important place in the work of the United Nations. These are questions of the highest importance, on which the security of nations to a large extent depends.

The mighty current of the national liberation movement, which has gathered up many of the oppressed peoples of the world and has destroyed colonial empires in its course, has brought into being dozens of young independent states.

The aspiration of the developing countries to escape from the clutches of the economic backwardness which they inherited from colonial times can be realized only in conditions of peace, particularly lasting peace. Since they fully understand this, they are actively advocating the condemnation of aggression and the strengthening of international security. This is the purpose of the decisions taken by the conferences of non-aligned countries, the Organization of African Unity and the meetings of Arab states.

The young independent states are adopting the same positions in the United Nations. The fact that they and the socialist states have a common interest in repelling aggression and strengthening peace serves as a basis for co-operation in the consideration of major international problems.

During the past quarter of a century, the foreign policy lines and doctrines of certain Powers—which, whatever name is given to them, amount merely to attempts to act in international affairs from a position of strength and *diktat*—have been rejected one after another as untenable. Some elements of a realistic approach have begun to emerge more perceptibly, although this is occurring to a different extent in different states and not in all matters. These manifestations of realism and responsibility are, of course, welcomed by all those who are genuinely striving for the consolidation of peace. It is important only that statements of this kind should be backed up by a readiness to engage in negotiations—from constructive positions—on the settlement of international problems, and that no action should be taken which is at variance with this approach.

It is understandable therefore that when the United States side advances proposals not for granting the Vietnamese people an opportunity to settle the problems of their own internal life without outside intervention, but for consolidating in power in South Vietnam a regime which is alien to the Vietnamese people and is serving foreign interests, the Provisional Revolutionary Government of the Republic of South Vietnam and the Government of the Democratic Republic of Vietnam should regard these proposals as designed to continue the war and should treat them accordingly. No one can expect them to do otherwise.

If the United States wants to get out of Vietnam, why does it not do so? Why does it expand the war, and spread it to Laos and Cambodia? If it really wants peace, why does it not accept proposals for a peaceful settlement?

As for the Soviet Union, our country supports the proposals of the Provisional Revolutionary Government and the Government of the Democratic Republic of Vietnam for a peaceful settlement. In pursuance of its international duty, the Soviet Union is providing and will continue to provide all necessary help to the fraternal Vietnamese people in their just and heroic struggle.

There is no peace in the Middle East either. The situation in this area is still dangerous. Israel has seized Arab territories as a result of aggression and is keeping them under its occupation.

The Soviet Union consistently and resolutely supports the legitimate rights of the Arab peoples, including the Arab people of Palestine.

What is needed in order to change the situation radically and achieve a settlement and normalization in the Middle East?

For this it is essential to ensure the withdrawal of Israeli forces from all the occupied Arab territories. It is essential to reach agreement on the establishment of peace on terms which respect and recognize the sovereignty, territorial integrity and political independence of all states in the Middle East, and their right to live in peace. Agreement on all this, and also on other related questions, must be set down officially in an appropriate document which would have the force of international law. And no one under any pretext whatsoever may encroach on the lawful interests of the Arab states and of the peoples in their territory.

There is no need to deal at length on the importance of the situation in Europe for the cause of universal peace. In the annals of the postwar history of Europe there has been hardly a year without a flare-up of tension. Only by the joint efforts of the Warsaw Treaty states and a number of other European states has it been possible to frustrate attempts to cause trouble and at the same time to lay stone by stone the foundation of a peace in Europe which is in keeping with the spirit of the historic Potsdam Agreement of 1945. The proposals made in this respect by the socialist countries are well known.

Many years of effort in the interests of consolidating peace in Europe are producing their results. Recently there have been tangible signs that the development of events on the European continent has taken a positive turn, and that a tendency towards *détente* has been making itself increasingly apparent in the actions of the governments of European states.

Links and contacts between the socialist countries and the countries of Western Europe have been considerably expanded, and elements of mutual understanding in relations between them are increasing. In this connection I should like to stress the great importance of the development of relations between two Powers on the continent of Europe—the Soviet Union and France—whose co-operation is an essential condition for maintaining peace in Europe and an important factor in strengthening international security. A further important step in the development of this co-operation was taken during the recent visit by the President of the French Republic, M. Pompidou, to the Soviet Union.

What is needed for the European peoples to become confident that their peaceful development will not be endangered? For this it is essential, first, that states should base their policies on European realities as they have taken shape as a result of the war and post-war development, on recognition of the inviolability of the frontiers between all European states, and on observance of the principle of the non-use of force in relations between them.

One fact of great importance is that a more realistic attitude is now being displayed in the Federal Republic of Germany in regard to problems whose solution was previously sought—and not everyone has yet abandoned these methods—by means of aggravating the situation, particularly in Central Europe, by means of a revision of frontiers and by means of a *revanche*. The joint efforts of the Soviet Union and the FRG have resulted in the signature of a Treaty which has been regarded

47

not only in the Soviet Union and the FRG but also throughout the world as an act of great significance.

It is the firm conviction of the Soviet Government that both parties benefit equally from the Treaty, and not only they, but all states interested in the strengthening of European peace, since this is precisely the purpose of the Treaty.

Negotiations are at present being conducted by representatives of the four Powers on the subject of West Berlin. We approach these negotiations in all seriousness and consider that it is possible to reach agreement on the questions arising there. Of course, positive results from these negotiations—and we want such results—depend on the goodwill of all participants.

One important factor for peace in Europe is the German Democratic Republic. Its peace-loving policy is gaining increasingly wide international recognition. There is not a single question in Europe, and no single major international question, to whose solution the GDR could not make its contribution. The question of the admission of the GDR to the United Nations is now fully ripe. The United Nations will benefit from this, as will the cause of peace. Of course, the FGR should also be admitted to the United Nations at the same time.

The positive elements in the development of the situation in Europe are obvious. But it would be very rash to disregard the continuing activities of those forces which are not in favour of *détente* in Europe, and which still cling to their senseless plans for reshaping the map of Europe and link them with the maintenance of tension, the non-settlement of problems, and the activities of the NATO military bloc which has nothing to do with the strengthening of security in Europe.

If all European countries unite their efforts, the problem of securing a lasting peace on that continent is quite open to solution.

In this connection the proposal to convene an all-European conference is meeting with increasing understanding and sympathy in Europe. The practical problems of holding the conference are being actively discussed among the interested parties. A representative forum with the participation of all European states, and also the United States and Canda, could discuss the major problems of the development of co-operation in Europe and take appropriate decisions on them. The conference would be an important step towards the strengthening of security in Europe, and no government should be afraid of this if it is in favour of peace.

The situation in Asia remains tense. However, the peoples of Asia have already had occasion to learn that none of the problems facing them can be solved by unleashing military conflicts. It is therefore natural that the Asian countries should be giving more and more thought to the question of how they can make their continent a region of peace.

The Soviet Union has put forward the idea of creating a collective security system in Asia. It can now be said that the basic approach underlying our proposal—that is to say, the peaceful orientation of an Asian security system and its collective nature, which would provide for the participation of all Asian states in Asian regional co-operation— commands general support.

The United Nations is not dealing with all the problems arising in inter-state relations, and there are reasons for that. But whatever events may occur in this or that part of the world, statesmen and people have a reliable yardstick for assessing what is going on—namely, the purposes and principles of the United Nations Charter.

Of course the United Nations does not and cannot stand above states; it is an aggregate of states and, consequently, the degree of its effectiveness depends on the foreign policies of its member states.

A comparison of all the areas in which the United Nations has achieved success during this quarter of a century with the areas in which it has failed leads to the conclusion that on the whole the balance of its activities has been positive. That is the view of our country, and it was recently expressed by the General Secretary of the Central Committee of the CPSU, Leonid Brezhnev. 'Despite all its shortcomings and weaknesses', he said, 'the United Nations has made a useful contribution to the realization of the purposes and principles proclaimed in its Charter. It has assisted in overcoming a number of acute international crises. We regard this result as a major success for the foreign policy of the Soviet Union, the other socialist countries and all the peace-loving forces on our planet.'

We are not blind to the difficulties encountered by the United Nations. But when we speak of difficulties, we are not inclined to follow the example of those who are ready to fold their arms like an onlooker.

We also disagree in principle with those who put forward proposals for the revision of the United Nations Charter as a means of overcoming the difficulties.

For the purpose of strengthening the United Nations, the Soviet Union considers that the correct road is a different one—to multiply the efforts of all member countries to increase its effectiveness.

Our proposals provide for a whole series of practical steps—from the obligation of states to comply with the principle of the inadmissibility of the acquisition of territory as a result of war, to the cessation of all military and other action for the suppression of the liberation movements of the colonial peoples and the acceleration of work on drafting a definition of aggression. Taken together, those measures can considerably improve the international situation.

It is particularly important to note that in regard to one of the concrete measures—the holding of periodic meetings of the Security Council, the importance of which is underlined in the Charter—the appropriate decision has already been taken.

Another measure proposed by the socialist countries for strengthening international security has also been implemented: agreement has been reached on the Declaration of Principles of International Law concerning Friendly Relations and Co-operation among States in accordance with the Charter of the United Nations, and it is ready for adoption.

The Soviet Union is in favour of intensifying negotiations on general and complete disarmament, taking into account the progress made in the field of military technology and the fact that a number of agreements on the limitation of the nuclear arms race have been concluded—such as the Treaty Banning Nuclear Weapon Tests in Three Environments, the Treaty on Principles Governing the Activities of States in the Exploration and Use of Outer Space, including the Moon and Other Celestial Bodies, the Treaty on the Non-proliferation of Nuclear Weapons—and also bearing in mind the experience of the negotiations that have taken place so far. Obligations relating to disarmament questions must, of course, be assured by the maximum possible number of states; and as regards nuclear disarmament, as we have frequently stressed, the participation of all nuclear Powers is an essential condition.

While the Soviet Union regards general and complete disarmament as the ultimate goal, it is, as before, doing everything in its power with a view to achieving agreement on individual disarmament measures and on the limitation of the arms race.

In addition to what has already been achieved in this field, there is now the draft Treaty on the Prohibition of the Emplacement of Nuclear Weapons and Other Weapons of Mass Destruction on the Sea-bed and the Ocean Floor and the Subsoil Thereof.

However, further progress towards measures of actual disarmament is being stubbornly resisted by forces which are intensifying the arms race and whose policies are having the effect of iron weights on the efforts of certain countries in disarmament questions. Even now these forces are trying to involve states in an increasingly wasteful and dangerous rivalry, in the development and production of ever newer forms of armaments. It is worth while to mention this once again from the rostrum of the present session of the General Assembly.

In the Soviet Government's view, agreement should be reached in the immediate future on the cessation of the production—and on the destruction—of chemical and bacteriological weapons and chemical and bacteriological means of waging war, this most dangerous kind of weapon of mass destruction.

It was with this in mind that the socialist countries introduced for consideration by the Assembly a draft international convention on the subject.

The Soviet Union is proposing other measures whose implementation would be a major step forward in the matter of disarmament. These include the elimination of foreign military bases on the territories of other states, the creation of de-nuclearized zones in various parts of the world, and the discontinuation of underground nuclear weapon tests.

One important sphere of United Nations activity is assistance to people struggling for the elimination of the remnants of colonialism. The peoples of many states represented in this hall, which have become independent during the past ten years, are aware of the importance for their victory of the anti-colonial decisions of the United Nations. However, even now the peoples of a number of territories, especially in Africa, are having to fight for their liberation from colonialist and racist oppression. It is the duty of the United Nations to help them in solving this problem.

Much attention is being paid at the current session of the General Assembly, and in other forums, to the problem of overcoming the economic backwardness of the developing countries and, in this connection, to the question of the Second United Nations Development Decade and the formulation of its strategy. In our view, the idea of formulating such a programme is in principle objectionable. In order to answer its purpose, the programme must provide for political, social and economic measures of a progressive nature.

It is high time to rid the United Nations of the harmful accretions of the past. It is time to turn over the shameful page of interference by the United Nations in the internal affairs of the Korean people, to withdraw from South Korea all foreign forces deployed there under the United Nations flag, and to dissolve the notorious United Nations Commission for the Unification and Rehabilitation of Korea.

The United Nations is based on the principle of universality, and this is of profound significance. If we are guided by this principle—and a departure from it can only weaken the United Nations—there is no justification for the fact that the People's Republic of China has hitherto been deprived of its legitimate place in the United Nations.

The Soviet Union, as one of the founders of the United Nations, approaches with a full sense of responsibility its obligations under the Charter of the United Nations; and it is firmly resolved, in co-operation with other states, to strive for the realization of the exalted purposes and principles of the United Nations.

From a statement at the 25th session of the UN General Assembly, 21 October 1970

The 24th Congress of the CPSU. 3 April 1971

The successes of the Soviet people over the past five years have been most eloquently presented in the report of the CPSU Central Committee delivered by Leonid Brezhnev, General Secretary of the Central Committee of our Party.

This report contains a profound Marxist–Leninist analysis of the internal problems of communist construction and the present international situation.

It sets forth the principles underlying the Communist Party's policy and substantiates these principles theoretically, having regard to the vast experience accumulated by the Party and the nation in the course of the fulfilment of our internal plans and also having regard to world developments since the 23rd Congress of the CPSU.

There is yet another striking feature in Leonid Brezhnev's report. This is the confidence that we are moving in the right direction and healthy, well-founded optimism. It expresses the optimism of our people, of our social system, and of our short- and long-term views. The same may be said of the congress as a whole and of the atmosphere in which it works.

The labour efforts of the working class, the collective-farm peasants, and the intelligentsia have still further increased our country's might.

Peace and our country's security are today safeguarded more dependably than ever before. We know this, and our friends know it. Our adversaries also know it. The Soviet Union's position on the international scene has grown firmer, and our foreign policy enjoys enhanced prestige.

In the report this has been stated to the whole world on behalf of the Communist Party, on behalf of the entire nation, and the Soviet people are proud of this.

Further headway has been made in consolidating the socialist community, in promoting the political, economic, and defence links between its member-states. The close, all-sided co-operation among the countries of the world socialist community is gaining new experience and strength. This has been stated eloquently and convincingly by leaders of fraternal countries attending this congress as guests.

The role played by the fraternal countries in the struggle for peace, to avert war, was shown strikingly and faithfully in the report. These countries have been and are a dependable barrier to any aggressor. Those who have in one way or another tried to test the strength of the Warsaw Treaty member-countries' frontiers found that the socialist countries give serious attention to the defence of these frontiers, as of their socialist system.

A few words about the part played by socialist states in defending other countries of the world against aggression.

Nobody can make the peoples of Asia, the Middle East, Africa, and Latin America forget the steps that our country and its allies have time and again taken jointly in defence of victims of aggression. The peoples know and have seen for themselves that our policy and our determination to defend peace can be relied upon.

Our relations with most of our neighbours and, for that matter, with most countries of the world are shaping up well. This is our great and valuable foreign policy asset.

The following statistics are likewise indicative of the scale of our activity in foreign policy.

Today the state interests of the USSR abroad are represented in the political sphere by 144 embassies and consulates. The Soviet Union is a member of over 400 international organizations. Our country has signed more than 7,000 operating international treaties and agreements.

No question of any importance is today resolved without or despite the Soviet Union. If anybody were to try to prove that it is possible to settle these questions without the Soviet Union he would be regarded as a crank.

Furthermore, it is our proposals for strengthening peace, European security, an end to the arms race, the struggle against colonialism, and the settlement of many other questions which are in the focus of political discussions and which help find the needed solutions. This is acknowledged by everybody, including our political and ideological adversaries.

What gives Soviet foreign policy its force of attraction? Not only the fact that it is backed up by might. Everybody knows that some other powers likewise have considerable economic and other potentialities. The main thing is that our policy is expressive of the nature of our socialist system, which is the most peaceful in history.

In the USA they publish millions of books lauding imperialist foreign policy to the skies. To this must be added the almost daily official and semi-official pronouncements made in the same spirit, and the similarly stuffed newspapers and magazines with their huge circulations.

The man in the street is constantly deafened with this cacophony. Its purpose is to confuse him. But it has a built-in vice—it is woven of falsehood, for behind it are the class aims of the circles pursuing an aggressive policy.

If in Washington they declare that the USA wants to withdraw its troops from Vietnam, but at the same time commit acts of aggression against Cambodia and Laos as well, then how is this to be called? Whatever colour is used here to embellish this policy, falsehood cannot be given out for truth, and the aggressor cannot be given out for a peace-maker.

There is no dearth of examples of this kind.

The strength of our foreign policy lies in its veracity. That is why accounts of the report of the CPSU Central Committee at this congress were flashed to all parts of the world, to all capitals with the speed of lightning. As we already know, it has been received with immense interest as an event of exceptionally great significance.

The governments, leaders, and the people draw their conclusions from the report and from the proceedings at the congress in general. The friends of peace applaud us. Those who pursue a different course in international affairs find themselves with new worries. But their worries are not our concern.

Integrated in our foreign policy are its revolutionary character, consistency in upholding the cause of peace, firm defence of the state interests of the Soviet Union, and true internationalism.

Soviet foreign policy is honest and open in everything, including its aims.

The call for peace was inscribed on the banner of the Soviet Republic on the day it was born. Our country follows that course to this day. Every year and, one can say, every day it is winning new friends in the world.

Small wonder that in the farthest places, say Africa, people who still cannot show where this or that country is situated on a map because the colonialists did not wish them to know this know that in the world there is a land that condemns racial inequality, denounces wars of aggression, and stands for the freedom of all peoples. That land is the Soviet Union.

We have no territorial claims on any country of the world, and no intention of prejudicing anybody's legitimate rights and interests. But we demand the same attitude towards ourselves.

c

Those who are indeed prepared to reach agreement with us on problems requiring a settlement will always find the Soviet Union a serious partner with a sense of responsibility. Those who are out to encroach upon our interests and security or upon the interests and security of our friends and allies invariably find themselves pursuing an abortive policy.

The complexity of the present situation makes it necessary to see and accurately mark out the basic orientations of international developments, to see the class significance of what is taking place. 'Marxism', Lenin wrote, 'requires of us a strictly exact and objectively verifiable analysis of the relations of classes and of the concrete features peculiar to each historical situation. We Bolsheviks have always tried to meet this requirement, which is absolutely essential for giving a scientific foundation to policy.' (V. I. Lenin, 'Letters on Tactics', *Collected Works*, vol. 24, p. 43.)

Guided by this proposition, the Party has always set Soviet foreign policy the task of ensuring the most favourable conditions for the building of socialism and communism, of averting the danger of another world war. All its efforts are aimed towards carrying out this task.

Equally, it is alien to our nature to yield to the threats of the imperialists or show a fancy for ultra-revolutionary verbiage. In either case it would mirror an underestimation of the strength and potentialities of the socialist countries, the international working-class movement, and all other forces of progress. In short, cowardice or the inability to keep one's nerve in collisions with imperialism, as well as ostentatious, theatrical ultra-radicalism are not Marxism–Leninism and are emphatically condemned by our Party.

The USA and some of its allies in aggressive military blocs have recourse to diverse methods of camouflaging their course in international affairs. At the same time they seek to cast aspersions on the Soviet Union's foreign policy and misrepresent its content and aims.

Day after day the US propaganda machine—official and semi-official—goes to any length to distort the facts. In the USA they do not stint funds for this. The forces engaged in this activity would like to erase undeniable facts from the memory of nations.

Here are a few examples.

What was the main decision adopted jointly by the Great Powers, who were allies in the war, to bring lasting peace to Europe and uproot aggression for all time? This was the Potsdam decision, adopted immediately after Nazi Germany was defeated. But instead of following a course of collective security and co-operation with the Soviet Union on the basis of Potsdam, the Western powers split Europe into military blocs and pursued a policy of sustaining tension in Europe.

The purpose of the 1954 and 1962 Geneva Agreements was to bring peace to Indo-China and ensure the independence of the peoples of Vietnam, Cambodia, and Laos. The USA took part in drawing up these agreements and accepted them. However, this did not in the least disconcert the policy-makers in Washington when they decided to unleash aggression in that region, to begin the most dangerous and most sanguinary military conflict since the Second World War.

Without direct support from the USA, Israeli aggression against its Arab neighbours would have bogged down at once or, rather, it would not have been started. Without that support the Israeli extremists would not have ventured to flaunt their refusal to fulfil the UN resolution on the liberation of occupied Arab lands.

These examples speak for themselves. Whatever span of time is taken, short or long, it shows who has historical truth on his side. In our policy we have to take all this into account, all the moves and methods of those who in international affairs pursue a policy alien to the interests of peace.

Our Party distinguishes clearly between the ideological struggle, which must be waged unremittingly and in which there can be neither peace nor an armistice, and our relations with capitalist countries founded on the principles of peaceful coexistence laid down by Lenin.

The Soviet Union and its allies are offering to settle all outstanding international issues by peaceful means, by negotiation. For our part, we are doing our utmost to reach such settlements.

This is the only realistic way of conducting affairs, and it is constantly in the armoury of our Party, the CPSU Central Committee, the Politburo, and the Soviet Government.

If we take only the foreign policy aspect of the Politburo's work, it must be said that this leading organ—this must be stated plainly at the Party's highest forum—should have and has enormous energy and experience in order to cope with the complexity of the tasks before it.

Moreover, this is an organism that must function continuously and smoothly. That is precisely how it functions. You will appreciate that the international situation never freezes, that it never goes, as, say, people go on leave either for a month or for a single day, even when it is shaken by fever. From this one clearly sees how important is the task of building everything in such a way as to worthily safeguard the nation's highest interests, the interests of its security, and the common interests of the socialist countries. The Politburo gives serious, day-to-day attention to questions of foreign policy, ensuring the timeliness and prescience of its decisions.

At plenary meetings, which have time and again considered questions of foreign policy, the Central Committee has invariably approved the foreign policy work of the Politburo. At these plenary meetings the atmosphere was always one of firm confidence that affairs were being conducted beneficially and correctly. This means that the decisions of the 23rd Congress of the CPSU have been carried out properly—consistently and fundamentally.

In the totality of steps which the Soviet Union is taking on the international scene, a large and vital place is held by the actions, the steps taken by the Supreme Soviet of the USSR. This is a useful and effective line of foreign policy activity.

The addresses and statements of the Supreme Soviet of the USSR on major questions of foreign policy, which have always had wide international repercussions, the many-sided work of its Presidium, the work of the Foreign Affairs Commissions and the Parliamentary Group, and the relevant visits, talks, and exchanges of delegations are considerably enriching the foreign policy work of our country and serving the cause of peace.

The Soviet Government—the Council of Ministers of the USSR—gives day-to-day attention to foreign affairs in accordance with the guidelines set by the Central Committee and the Politburo. This activity, and it covers not only policy but also extremely important and voluminous work in the fields of economic relations and trade, scientific and technical co-operation, and cultural relations with other countries, is linked with the participation in it of a large number of ranking representatives of our country, specialists, and so on. It may be said that the representatives of the government have uninterrupted dealings with more than a hundred states, daily reflecting in practice our policy and, to use the accepted term, the directives of the Centre. The hub of that Centre is the will of the Party, expressed above all in the decisions of its congresses.

Taken altogether, thousands of people, including members of the Central Committee, members of the Government of the USSR, and deputies of the Supreme Soviet are in one way or another drawn into all the complex, major steps in the field of our country's foreign policy. Of course, the leaders of our Party and Government are in the front rank of this work, which is enormous in scale and importance.

In conducting its policy our country attaches considerable significance to quests for agreement even with states pursuing a different policy.

It is sometimes asked: how far is this dependable and what is the actual significance of agreements with certain countries if these countries do not always abide by those agreements? This question is sometimes asked in a different, or to put it bluntly, provocative way, when any agreement with capitalist states is said to be almost a 'conspiracy'.

Naturally, nobody can guarantee that a concluded treaty is always carried out meticulously by our partners. Here, too, there is frequently a struggle. In such cases the Soviet Union invariably acts from a position of strict observance of international treaties and agreements.

As regards the 'conspiracy' accusations I have mentioned, they are in all probability disbelieved even by those who make them.

The foreign policy pursued by our country after the 23rd Congress of the CPSU has considerably enhanced the hopes of the peoples for peace. In Europe our relations with France are developing successfully. There has been considerable progress in our relations with Italy. Even outside the socialist community millions of people see the treaties signed by the Soviet Union and Poland with the FRG as a success for them too, as a tangible contribution to the normalization of the situation in Europe. The coming into force of these treaties, the settlement of the problems existing in the relations between the FRG and the socialist countries of Europe, the holding of a European conference on security, and the successful consummation of the talks on West Berlin are important steps that have to be made on the road from a Europe of conflicts to a Europe of lasting peace. They must be realized in parallel, without waiting for one to be completed before passing to another.

These are only some of the problems that can and must be resolved. The Soviet Union will work with unrelaxing vigour to resolve the other problems and tasks that have been clearly formulated in the report of the CPSU Central Committee.

Colonial empires, the huge dismal edifices of which seemed to have been built by oppressors for eternity, collapsed under the onslaught of the peoples. But not all the colonial prisons have been demolished.

The part played by the Soviet Union in carrying out this important international task is exceptionally great not only because our practical political steps are of immense significance but also because the policy of national and racial oppression is perhaps most effectively undermined by our world outlook, by the example of our multinational state.

A major gain of socialism's foreign policy and of all forces for peace is that today the vast majority of countries regard peaceful coexistence as the sole reasonable alternative to war. Our Party and our country are doing everything to assert this principle more broadly and firmly in international relations.

In this context, as before, the question arises of our relations with the United States of America. Our guideline in this question has been stated repeatedly. It has been distinctly and precisely enunciated in the report of the CPSU Central Committee at this congress. In Washington they must seriously weigh everything that was said by the General Secretary of the CPSU Central Committee in his report on behalf of our Party and country.

The Soviet Union wants normal relations with the USA. It believes that Soviet–American relations can be improved. But Washington's statements in favour of talks must be backed up with practical actions. The American side does not always, to use an understatement, show readiness to do this. We are not proponents of talks that have the appearance of fencing. We want serious talks. We want the participants to desist from tripping each other, we want them to look for agreement in the true sense of the word.

In this context much could be said about what is taking place at the talks on West Berlin, in the course of which there have been more than enough of the zigzags so aptly mentioned by Leonid Brezhnev when he spoke of our relations with the USA. The same may be said of the talks on convening a European conference, on the Middle East, and on curbing the strategic arms race.

If the American side earnestly intends to help achieve agreement, then who is preventing it from showing that intention?

At its congress our Communist Party is giving further evidence not only of the strength of our foreign policy but also of the profound humanism and nobility of our ideology in all its manifestations, including in areas that are in one way or another concerned with foreign affairs. All this must be actively brought home to people, particularly in the context of tasks relating to nuclear weapons and their prohibition, and also other kinds of weapons of mass destruction.

As you all know, considerable significance has been and is attached by the Party and the Government to questions concerning our relations with China. Our policy is framed in the report. It has been stated by Comrade Brezhnev convincingly and with the great force of logic. He has shown lucidly how the peoples of the Soviet Union and China would benefit by an improvement in Soviet–Chinese relations; also, he has shown that this would be immensely important for our common struggle against imperialism and aggression. The direction in which relations between the Soviet Union and the People's Republic of China develop depends on China's leaders, on the Chinese side.

The Soviet Union is a peace-loving country. It is proving this both in words and in deeds.

At the congress delegates spoke convincingly and with every justification of the good moral atmosphere that has been established in our Party and country as a result of the work accomplished by the Central Committee. With similar justification we can say that in the world as a whole the Soviet Union has created an atmosphere of profound confidence in itself. This moral and political atmosphere is a major factor on the scales of international politics.

Today, while this congress is in session, millions upon millions of people abroad are watching and meditating on what is taking place in the Kremlin.

This is being done by our friends, and it is being done by our political adversaries.

Everybody knows that important matters of internal development and foreign policy are being discussed and decided here, that the colossal strength of our development plans and of our foreign policy of peace radiates from here, from the Kremlin.

Along with the entire Soviet people, we Communists express deep satisfaction over the impact of our achievements, of the successes of our policy of peace, and of our immortal communist ideas that we are spreading throughout the world with our deeds and by our example.

Every machine-tool, every ton of metal, every new computer, and every *centner* of grain produced in our country is a contribution not only to the upsurge of our economy and living standards but also to our foreign policy.

Important and difficult tasks confront our country on the international scene. Much will have to be done, and this will entail hard work. In order to carry out these tasks it will be necessary to continue surmounting the opposition of the forces of aggression. But we are confident that in the coming years our country will cope with its historic mission as the bulwark of socialism, the freedom of nations, and peace.

From a speech at the 24th Congress
of the CPSU, 3 April 1971

Ratification of the Treaty Banning the Siting of Weapons of Mass Destruction on the Sea-bed. 28 June 1971

The treaty banning the siting of weapons of mass destruction on the sea-bed is another important step towards the limitation of arms. It was not easy to reach this agreement.

It is the result of persevering efforts on the part of the Soviet Union and other socialist countries in maintaining our initiative. As we saw it, it was in the interests of the security of our country, of the socialist community, and of all other states and peoples to erect a barrier to the spread of the arms race to a sphere of our planet where the military activity of different countries had not reached a large scale—to the bed of the seas and oceans.

Of course, it was also taken into consideration that with the development of science and technology, of man's ability to penetrate vigorously into the depths of seas and oceans the arms race might embrace that sphere as well. Needless to say, this would not benefit the cause of peace and international security. On the contrary, it would only be prejudicial to that cause.

Acting on these considerations, the Soviet Union proposed the conclusion of an agreement that would completely, I repeat, completely, ban military activity by states on the bed of the seas and oceans. As you all know, we submitted the draft of the relevant treaty to the Geneva Disarmament Committee. The conclusion of that agreement encountered difficulties in the face of the attitude of some Western powers.

In order to find a way out of that situation and break the deadlock the Soviet Union agreed, since this was a major part of our proposal, to conclude, as a first step, a treaty banning the siting of weapons of mass destruction on the sea-bed and its soil. The treaty under consideration is the result of the talks on that basis.

Although this is the first, it is at the same time a substantial step towards the demilitarization of the sea-bed, for it is a question of excluding the possibility of using it for the siting of the most dangerous kinds of weapons.

In conclusion, permit me to stress once more that the treaty submitted for ratification is an agreement aimed at improving the international situation. Its signing and ratification by the Soviet Union conform to the immutable Leninist guidelines of the Soviet Union's foreign policy of peace.

From a speech at a sitting of the Presidium of the USSR Supreme Soviet on the question of ratifying the Treaty Banning the Siting of Nuclear Weapons and Other Kinds of Weapons of Mass Destruction on the Sea-bed and the Soil Thereof of 11 February 1971

Ratification of the USSR–India Friendship Treaty. 13 August 1971

Conclusion of the Treaty of Peace, Friendship and Co-operation is an outstanding event in the history of relations between the Soviet Union and the Republic of India. It is also a big international event. It may be said without any exaggeration that the close friendship between the Soviet Union and India is one of the main pillars of peace on the Asian continent and one of the cornerstones in the edifice of international peace, for it is a friendship between two large states with an important and active part in world affairs.

Good Soviet–Indian relations, now crowned by the Treaty of Peace, Friendship and Co-operation, are natural and suit the interests of the two nations. We are brought together by our common stake in safe-guarding and consolidating peace. We have a common interest in repulsing the forces of imperialism and aggression.

Faithful to Lenin's course, our country has always supported the people of India in their bid for freedom and independence, and a quarter of a century ago welcomed the birth of the Republic of India. Ever since then we have based our relations with this new state not simply on mutual understanding, but also on close co-operation.

The Republic of India has never failed to take a constructive stand on important international issues, and has invariably backed Soviet proposals designed to strengthen peace, eliminate armed conflicts, and reduce international tension.

In the Central Committee Report to the 24th Congress of the CPSU, Leonid Brezhnev took special note of the fact that 'the Indian government's pursuit of a peaceful, independent line in international affairs, and the traditional feeling of friendship linking the peoples of the two countries have all helped to strengthen Soviet–Indian co-operation'.

Expansion of mutually beneficial economic, commercial, cultural, scientific and technical ties has also been highly useful to both our countries. The people of India are hard at work building a developed national economy to meet the needs of the country's teeming millions. And the Soviet Union, faithful to its internationalist duty, is giving India substantial practical assistance in this most difficult national aim.

Trade between our two countries is growing steadily. Soviet people have gained increasing opportunities to acquaint themselves with the treasures of Indian national culture, one of the world's oldest and richest. And the people of India, especially intellectuals, show a deep interest in the cultural and scientific achievements of our country.

The Treaty of Peace, Friendship and Co-operation provides a still more dependable political and legal foundation for all these friendly ties. It is a treaty between equal partners who deeply respect one another. It is directed to furthering our friendship and co-operation on the basis of respect for the independence, sovereignty and territorial integrity of the two nations, non-interference in one another's internal affairs, equality, and mutual advantage.

The Treaty specially notes that the Soviet Union respects India's policy of non-alignment, which is an important factor in international security and *détente*. For its part, the Republic of India respects the Soviet Union's Leninist foreign policy of peace.

The Treaty reflects the interest of both sides in safeguarding and consolidating peace. It is imbued with the deep interest both countries have in Asian and world security, which is especially important in the light of the present international situation and, in particular, in the light of the situation shaping to the south of the Soviet Union.

Special importance attaches here to the commitment to consult one another in the event of an attack or threat of attack on one of the parties to the Treaty. If one of the sides becomes an object of attack or threat of attack, the two sides must immediately open mutual consultations with the purpose of ending this threat and taking appropriate effective measures to safeguard peace and the security of their countries. This provision has captured attention in many capitals, and due conclusions are being drawn.

The Soviet Union and India attach great importance to close co-operation on the international scene and have agreed to maintain regular contacts to consider important international problems of concern to both countries by means of meetings and exchanges of opinion between their leading statesmen, visits of official delegations and special envoys of the two governments, and through diplomatic channels.

The Treaty specifies that the sides will co-operate with one another and with other countries in dealing with crucial international problems, such as ending the arms race, securing general and complete disarmament under effective international control covering both conventional and nuclear arms, and furthering complete and final eradication of colonialism and racism.

Peaceful co-operation between the two countries is served by the Treaty provisions that neither side will participate in military alliances against the other side or make commitments incompatible with the Treaty or commitments that may be militarily prejudicial to the other side. At the same time, the Soviet–Indian Treaty is not directed against any third country and is not intended to prejudice anybody's lawful interests.

Though only a few days have passed since the signing of the Treaty, it has already become an important part of the fabric of present-day international relations. No longer can anyone formulate policy—either towards the Soviet Union or India—without taking this Treaty into account.

Conclusion of the Treaty, which India has already ratified, is welcomed by the Soviet people, by the people of India, and by all those who cherish peace and progress. On the other hand, it came as an unpleasant surprise for those who seek complications in Asia, and not only in Asia, nursing plans that may, if carried out, lead to new tensions. To be sure, no other reaction could have been expected from these quarters.

From a speech at a sitting of the Presidium of the USSR Supreme Soviet on ratification of the Treaty of Peace, Friendship and Co-operation between the USSR and India of 9 August 1971

Ratification of the USSR–FRG Treaty. 31 May 1972

The Soviet Government has submitted for ratification to the Presidium of the USSR Supreme Soviet the Treaty between the Soviet Union and the Federal Republic of Germany signed on 12 August 1970. The main thing about this treaty is that it marks an end to a long period of tension in Soviet–West German relations caused by the policy of the ruling element in the FRG, and that it provides a political and legal foundation for neighbourly relations and peaceful mutually beneficial co-operation between the Soviet Union and the FRG in the interests of their peoples and of European peace.

The treaty is one more proof of the vitality and effectiveness of the Soviet policy of strengthening international security and expanding European co-operation, as charted by the 24th Congress of our Party and reaffirmed and projected by the Central Committee Plenum of a few days ago.

The purpose and aims of the treaty are clear. They have been put down in precise terms, leaving no room for misinterpretation. Special importance attaches to the commitments concerning the existing frontiers in Europe, the key question of European security. The Soviet Union and the FRG have declared that they consider 'inviolable now and in the future the frontiers of all European states as they are demarcated on the day of the signing of the present treaty', and that they will make 'no territorial claims on anyone'. It is the first time since the war that the western border of the Polish People's Republic and the border between the GDR and FRG are designated in a treaty with a major capitalist state, moreover a state that is one of the legal successors to defeated Nazi Germany. This is unquestionably of prime importance for the consolidation of the western frontiers of the socialist community and for strengthening the security and international positions of our two fraternal allies. These provisions are the heart of the treaty. They repose on existing territorial and political realities that have resulted from the Second World War and post-war developments.

The European nations know from their own experience that an aggressor's encroachments on the borders of other countries and attempts to shift border markers in Europe have time and again led to armed conflict costing millions of lives and causing untold destruction of property and cultural values. All European countries, big and small, are entitled to safe and secure frontiers.

Inviolability of frontiers, a principle clearly reflected and secured in the Moscow treaty, accords with the wishes of all European nations and all peaceful countries. Faithful to Lenin's ideas of the peaceful coexistence of states with different social systems, of friendship and co-operation among nations, the Soviet Union has always promoted and will continue to promote this highly important principle of international law, and will always strive for strict adherence to it.

Under the treaty both sides are committed to renouncing the use of force in mutual relations and in settling international issues. The pertinent articles in the treaty refer to the fact that its provisions repose on the inviolability of the existing frontiers and rule out any and all territorial demands. Renunciation of the use of force in Soviet–West German bilateral relations will help further this principle on a European scale and strengthen confidence and mutual understanding.

We wish to stress that the treaty of 12 August 1970 is not directed against third countries and does not prejudice agreements earlier concluded by its signatories. Its provisions are aimed at strengthening European security and creating a climate of *détente* and co-operation in Europe.

These aims are also served by the accords reached during the Moscow negotiations on the intentions of the two sides, recording the existence of mutual understanding on some vital aspects of European politics.

Of fundamental significance here is the intention of normalizing relations between the FRG and GDR in accordance with accepted international norms. Recently the GDR and FRG came to terms on certain aspects of relations and signed corresponding agreements—the first since the two German states came into existence. This shows that relations between the FRG and GDR can be normalized only on a basis of complete equality and of recognition and respect for the rights of the GDR as an independent state. It is an imperative imposed by the course of European events to end any and all discrimination against the GDR on the international scene, whoever it may come from. Need I say that discrimination against one country by another is incompatible with any improvement in mutual relations.

Among the important practical questions arising now is that of admitting the GDR and FRG to the United Nations. A positive decision without further delay would make it easier to settle many intricate problems involved in improving the situation in the heart of Europe, and would also be in keeping with the universal character of the United Nations.

The understanding that questions related to the invalidity of the

Munich agreement will be settled in negotiations between the FRG and Czechoslovakia is still highly relevant. The settlement of this issue is important for bettering the European climate.

Also to be noted is the readiness expressed by the two sides to do their best for the preparation and successful holding of the European Conference. With the coming into force of the Moscow treaty and in the light of the four-power agreement of 3 September 1971, its preparations will enter the concrete, practical stage so that the Conference could be held very soon.

The West German Parliament has ratified the FRG treaties with the Soviet Union and the Polish People's Republic. This is important for the outlook of Soviet–West German relations and for Europe as a whole. And it came as no surprise that this approval by the parliamentary bodies of the FRG elicited a broad and positive reaction all over the world. It was a victory of reason and showed that most people in the FRG want a new policy, one of mutual understanding and neighbourly relations with other peoples and states.

The fight over the ratification of the treaties showed, however, that revenge-seeking forces are still at work in the FRG and that they are trying to obstruct European *détente*.

This plainly untenable line, which is out of step with life and current trends in Europe, naturally failed to win the support expected both inside and outside the FRG by its practitioners. The CDU/CSU opposition, which had been putting spokes in the wheel of the ratification process for a long time, was finally compelled to reckon with this. Within its ranks, too, it began to sink in at long last that shelving the treaties would irreparably injure the state interests of the FRG and counterpose it to the socialist countries and, for that matter, to the other countries of Europe. As a result, a considerable majority of the CDU/CSU faction in the Bundestag gave up the tactic of rejecting the treaties out of hand.

We are about to see important positive changes in our relations with the FRG. The important thing now is to make the provisions of the Moscow treaty fully effective in the practical day-to-day effort of furthering diverse co-operation between our two countries. It stands to reason that the agreed text and nothing but the agreed text can be the starting point in interpreting the treaty or defining its scope of action and the extent and meaning of the commitments contained in it. This means the treaty and nothing but the treaty. In the new situation created by its conclusion strict observance of its letter and spirit is the surest way of building confidence and improving relations between our two countries. The Soviet Union is ready to follow this way. Of course, we expect the same approach to the treaty from the FRG.

Ratification of the treaty of 12 August 1970 will open up good prospects for closer relations between the USSR and FRG in the political, economic, scientific, technical, cultural and other fields. It will help to expand spheres of mutually beneficial co-operation. The main areas of co-operation have already been defined during General Secretary Brezhnev's meeting with Federal Chancellor Willy Brandt at Oreanda in September 1971. The extensive opportunities created by the treaty will be facilitated by contacts at government level, regular exchanges of opinion and consultations at different levels on bilateral relations and international problems, by parliamentary ties, and contacts between public organizations.

The Moscow treaty creates the requisite conditions for relations between the USSR and FRG to enter a new stage of truly constructive co-operation based on the principles of peaceful coexistence. Besides, it obviously helps, and will continue to help, to stabilize the situation and strengthen peace in Europe.

> *Speech at a sitting of the Presidium of the USSR Supreme Soviet on ratification of the Treaty between the Soviet Union and the Federal Republic of Germany of 12 August 1970*

The 27th session of the UN General Assembly. 26 September 1972

The Soviet State will soon celebrate its fiftieth anniversary as the Union of Soviet Socialist Republics. The Leninist formula of the state unity of the peoples of the Soviet Union contains a powerful potential for building peace. A profound interest in peace is organically inherent in the voluntary and equal union of socialist republics which have joined efforts in a constructive endeavour for the good of their peoples. Predatory wars and the oppression of other peoples are organically alien to such a union.

For the Soviet Union the policy of peace is a true reflection, in the sphere of external relations, of its internal social nature. In the decisions of the Twenty-fourth Congress of the CPSU, our country put forward a programme of peace and international co-operation which, as is universally recognized, reflects not the narrow interests of any state or group of states but the aspirations of all peoples, of all mankind. Every step taken to implement it has a constructive influence on international development as a whole.

'Our policy of principle', as L. I. Brezhnev said, 'is the active defence of peace, freedom and the security of peoples. We are pursuing it together with our friends and allies, co-ordinating our steps in the international arena.'

If aggression is committed, the Soviet Union always sides with the victim of the aggression. If trouble threatens our allies and friends, we always come to their aid. And when we sign treaties, we implement them and fulfil our obligations.

The objectives for which the Soviet Union and all the countries of the socialist community have been tirelessly struggling for many years have taken concrete form in the positive changes which have come about in the international situation. Together with our allies and friends we shall continue to struggle for peace, freedom and the progress of the peoples.

In the interests of peace, we are prepared to co-operate and we do co-operate with all states which are also prepared to do likewise.

In the past, post-war periods have always turned out to be mere respites between wars. In the present circumstances real possibilities exist for a fundamentally different development, namely, a transition to a system of stable peace. It was to ensure this that the United Nations was established.

This transition requires the solution of problems engendered by the Second World War and the special features of developments during the subsequent quarter of a century. If we tried to express in the most general form the essence of the changes that have taken place, we should say that it lies in the fact that there is now a possibility of solving some of these problems, while constructive work has begun with a view to settling others.

The territorial realities that have arisen in Europe, the continent where both World Wars originated, are gaining universal recognition and being formalized under international law. The entry into force of the well-known treaties concluded by the Federal Republic of Germany with the USSR and with the Polish People's Republic confirms the inviolability of European boundaries, including the boundary between the German Democratic Republic and the Federal Republic of Germany and the western boundary of Poland.

The conclusion of the agreement on West Berlin eliminates a chronic source of friction between states in the very centre of Europe.

On the whole the 'cold war' is being replaced by recognition of the truth that in the nuclear age there is no other basis for relations between states having different social systems but peaceful coexistence. More and more often this is taking the form of binding international legal documents.

The prerequisites for many-sided equal co-operation among states, in the political and other fields, are multiplying.

We are now on the eve of an all-European conference on questions of security and co-operation. Preparations for such a conference are to enter the practical phase very shortly. The great importance of this planned meeting of states lies in making Europe genuinely peaceful and in transforming relations among states on the European continent on the basis of mutual understanding and trust; we are in favour of such a policy and such a course of action in European affairs.

In the well-known Prague Declaration, the European socialist countries have already put forward their suggestions as to how, in their view, a system of security in Europe should be built up. Many other states have also expressed their views on this score. This is a great and extremely important task and the all-European conference is expected to make an important contribution to its solution.

In Asia, too, the idea of ensuring security, which is equally in the interests of all Asian states, is also beginning to gain ground. The Soviet Union considers the question of security in Asia to be an important task also. Those who, for some reason, are not now in sympathy with it should understand that the countries of Asia are no less interested than the Soviet Union in strengthening peace in that area.

Although there has been noticeable progress towards a relaxation of international tension, it is hardly likely that anyone would dispute the fact that so far only a beginning has been made and that much more remains to be done.

Some of the problems awaiting solution within an international framework affect the interests of practically all states. If we consider the substance of any of the problems leading to international complications and if we focus our attention on what directly generates the danger of war and the unleashing of military conflicts, we can only come to the conclusion that it is the use of force by some states against others for the purpose of territorial annexation and for the purpose of subjugating peoples and establishing domination over them, in other words, for predatory purposes.

That is why progressive political leaders, for almost as long as states themselves have existed, have recognized the need to eliminate the use of force from relations between states. But mere understanding of this is, of course, not sufficient. Practical efforts by states are required. This is all the more necessary now that the presence and stockpiling of nuclear weapons in the arsenals of states have radically changed the concept of the consequences which military conflicts can have for the peoples of the world.

Although varying views can be held as to the likelihood that this or that crisis or conflict will develop into a nuclear confrontation, as long as nuclear weapons exist, the possibility does exist. No state, no government can ignore this. Our country believes that it is possible to eliminate or, at least, to reduce drastically the danger of a conflict between states provoking a nuclear catastrophe. That can be done if renunciation of the use of force in international relations is elevated to the level of international law and if at the same time—I repeat, at the same time— the use of nuclear weapons is prohibited.

The Soviet Government is convinced that serious consideration of these questions cannot be put off any longer. The conditions for this are already more favourable now than before and the possibilities for adopting positive decisions are broader.

For these reasons, and because it is aware of its responsibility as a permanent member of the Security Council, the Soviet Union has submitted for consideration at the twenty-seventh session of the United Nations General Assembly the item entitled 'Non-use of force in international relations and permanent prohibition of the use of nuclear weapons'.

Many reasons can be found for the ineffectiveness of the decisions adopted by the United Nations on these questions, but one of the most substantial is unarguably that they were considered and decided upon by the United Nations in isolation from one another.

When the question of prohibiting the use of nuclear weapons was raised, several states had doubts as to the possibility of taking such a step if the use of force was not precluded in relations between states.

At the same time, when the question of prohibiting the use of force was considered, the significance of any decisions adopted proved to be limited in the absence of agreement concerning nuclear weapons, that is to say, the most powerful weapons of mass destruction. The separation of one question from the other introduced a certain lack of understanding and suspicion and weakened the effectiveness of the best decisions of the United Nations. Furthermore, their effectiveness was further restricted because they were all in the form of recommendations, or, at best, declarations of intent. They were not given the force of law.

The Soviet Union's proposal envisages the adoption of the most realistic and effective decision possible in modern conditions. It is precisely such a decision which is in the interests of all states, regardless of their social systems, the size of their territory and population, or whether or not they possess nuclear weapons.

It goes without saying that the obligation of states to renounce the use of force, including nuclear weapons, can in no way impair their right to individual and collective self-defence as laid down in Article 51 of the United Nations Charter. On the contrary, such an obligation would reinforce the right to self-defence against aggression and the right to struggle to eliminate the consequences of aggression in cases where it has already been committed and the aggressor seeks to benefit from it.

No one can challenge the inalienable right of states and peoples subjected to aggression to repulse it by employing all possible means so long as the aggressor continues to use force, encroaches upon their freedom and sovereignty and tries to retain territories seized by force. It will suffice to refer to the examples before everyone's eyes: Indo-China and the Middle East. Who would dare to contest the incontestable fact that brute force has been and still is being used against the peoples of Indo-China and against the Arab states and that they are entitled to use all the necessary means to rebuff the aggressor?

Renunciation of the use of force in relations between states in no way limits the right of the peoples of colonial countries to fight for their freedom and independence using any means which may be necessary in that struggle. This right is recognized by the United Nations as being a legitimate one.

The adoption of a decision on non-use of force and the permanent prohibition of the use of nuclear weapons would thus be beneficial to all. But this also makes it necessary for all states, particularly all those Powers which possess nuclear weapons, to participate in its elaboration and adoption.

We appeal to all states represented in the General Assembly to study carefully the draft we have submitted and, on the basis of it, to adopt unanimously a resolution which will reflect the firm will of this world organization to put an end to any use of force in relations between states in violation of the United Nations Charter and to eliminate the threat of nuclear war.

The task of building a lasting peace requires the adoption of effective measures to prevent and avert military conflicts in the future. But it is no less important to put an end to the conflicts which are poisoning the international atmosphere now and to put out the military fires in areas where the right of peoples to be masters of their own destinies is being encroached upon.

The position of the Soviet Union concerning the war against the Vietnamese people is known to all. The continuation and expansion of the United States intervention in Vietnam and other countries of Indo-China provoke indignation and condemnation.

One can only wonder why the only correct conclusion has not yet been drawn: namely, that the Vietnamese people cannot be defeated. Their resistance will not be broken either by heavier bombing, the blockading of ports or damage to hydro-technical installations. The

Vietnamese people are fighting heroically against aggression and fighting for just aims, in order to be master in their own country. They cannot allow anyone from outside to prescribe a political and social system for them or to impose puppets who uphold interests that are foreign to the Vietnamese people.

A way out can be found, but only through serious negotiations, for which a constructive basis has been provided by the well-known proposals contained in the statements by the Provisional Revolutionary Government of the Republic of South Vietnam of 11 September 1972 and by the Government of the Democratic Republic of Vietnam of 14 September 1972.

A solution to the problems of the Middle East must be found. Recent events linked with the new criminal acts of aggression by Israel against Arab countries, including Lebanon, show how serious is the danger and how far the Israeli leaders are going in their reckless policy.

The responsibility which rests with the aggressors is shared by all those who protect them and whose support enables Israel to defy the United Nations and its decisions regarding the elimination of the consequences of the aggression and the restoration of peace in the Middle East.

Only a long-term and just settlement in the Middle East in accordance with the well-known decisions of the United Nations can ensure the peace and security of all—we repeat, all—states in this region. The Israeli troops must be withdrawn from all the Arab territories occupied in 1967.

We also support the just struggle of the Arab people of Palestine for the restoration of their inalienable rights, which have been recognized by the United Nations.

Peace will not be truly lasting until an end is put to the arms race, which is one of the main sources of distrust among states and of the increased danger of war. The struggle for disarmament has been going on for a long time. The Soviet Union and the countries of the socialist community see in the struggle for disarmament one of the main orientations for their foreign policy activities. And this policy will be continued. Some of the things that seemed almost unattainable even ten or fifteen years ago are now reflected in treaties and agreements that have entered into force. These include some which to a certain extent curb the nuclear arms race and reduce the threat of nuclear war: the Treaty of the Non-proliferation of Nuclear Weapons, the treaty banning nuclear weapon tests in the three environments, and others. In addition, the first agreement in history on the elimination of a type of armaments which falls within the category of means of mass destruction, namely, bacteriological and toxic weapons, has now been concluded.

To the sum total of obligations in the field of the limitation of the arms race and disarmament already assumed by the majority of states one more has recently been added: it concerns those types of armaments which have the greatest destructive force. I am referring to the Soviet–US strategic arms limitation agreements. Limiting to the minimum the deployment of anti-ballistic missile systems, the agreements eliminate one of the main motives for unleasing a competition between offensive and defensive missile weapons, the full consequences of which are difficult to predict. By establishing quantitative limits for strategic offensive arms for the first time, the agreements curb the most dangerous trend in the arms race.

The conclusion of these agreements is an important step which will help to reduce the threat of nuclear war and to curb the arms race and which will open up new prospects for progress towards general disarmament. Both sides have agreed to continue the talks with a view to arriving at further agreements in that direction.

Each successful step in the struggle to limit the arms race is important in its own right and is, at the same time, important as a starting point for further efforts. The possibilities for further progress towards the solution of new problems of disarmament will increase with each new step on which agreement is reached. Our country has always desired this and we shall spare no effort in continuing to work, together with all other states, to relieve people of the burden of weapons.

The Soviet Union favours the earliest possible solution to the question of the halting of the production of chemical weapons and their destruction, negotiations concerning which are being held at the Conference of the Committee on Disarmament in Geneva. It also favours the halting everywhere and by everyone of nuclear weapon tests, including underground tests, the elimination of foreign military bases on alien territory and the establishment of nuclear-free zones in various parts of the world.

The General Assembly will be considering in a specific manner the question of convening a world disarmament conference. Our views on this are well known.

The Soviet Government believes that full advantage should be taken of the opportunities that are now taking shape for the convening of a world disarmament conference. We, for our part, shall continue to do everything in our power to ensure that it is held and is successful.

In international politics it is necessary constantly to take account of the various questions posed by scientific and technological progress and the requirements which such progress is making on an ever-increasing scale in the field of international co-operation. This applies to economic, scientific and technological links, which are becoming ever richer in content. It applies directly to new areas in which states are active, particularly outer space.

It was on the basis of these considerations that the Soviet Union submitted proposals on principles governing the activities of states in outer space, on the conclusion of a treaty concerning the moon and on a number of other matters. At the current session of the General Assembly we are proposing that consideration should be given to the item entitled 'Preparation of an international convention on principles governing the use by states of artificial earth satellites for direct television broadcasting'. Our purpose in raising this question is to link inseparably, from the very beginning, the use of this new type of space technology with the noble purposes of strengthening peace and friendship among peoples.

The United Nations must promptly acquire a genuinely universal character. Universality could lend the United Nations new strength and enable it to consider world problems with greater results. We therefore see no justification for attempts to create artificial obstacles to the admission of new states to the United Nations.

We consider it necessary to ensure the earliest possible admission to the United Nations of the German Democratic Republic, which is fully entitled to be admitted, as is, of course, the Federal Republic of Germany too. This will be in the interests of the further development of co-operation among states and will be in line with the political situation taking shape in Europe.

No one should cast doubts on the legitimate right to membership in the United Nations of the People's Republic of Bangladesh, which has recently gained its national independence. That state has a legitimate right to become a member of the United Nations.

What is necessary for the United Nations to succeed is the readiness and determination of member states to act together in the interests of solving the problems facing the organization. This should make the United Nations a real centre for concerted action by nations to achieve common goals, which is an obligation under the United Nations Charter.

From a statement at the 27th session of the UN General Assembly, 26 September 1972

The Vietnam Peace Conference, Paris. 27 February 1973

To begin with, I want to thank the French Government for its hospitality and for facilitating the holding in Paris of the International Conference on Vietnam.

Like all other peace-loving states, the Soviet Union was deeply pleased with the Agreement on Ending the War and Restoring Peace in Vietnam, which opens a new phase in the country's history. It is a decisive step towards ending one of the longest and cruellest wars of our time.

The Paris Agreement is the result of the difficult and courageous struggle of the Vietnamese people against aggression, and a triumph of justice, realism and reason. It was made possible first of all by the heroic stand of the Vietnamese people, with which all those who cherish the ideals of freedom and independence displayed solidarity. It was this combination of Vietnamese fortitude and international moral, political and material aid that helped bring the war to an end.

The Soviet Union did everything it could to give Vietnam real and effective support, and always stood by the embattled Vietnamese people. In this new stage, too, as in the years of severe trial, it will always side with Vietnam's just cause. L. I. Brezhnev has stressed: 'We have always regarded elimination of the seat of war in Indo-China as one of the central objectives of Soviet foreign policy.'

The experience of the Vietnamese struggle gives us much food for thought. The Paris Agreement was not reached until the only correct conclusion had been drawn, that the people of Vietnam cannot be put on their knees. This is convincing proof that in our day no power on earth can break a people fighting for freedom and independence, and in defence of its inalienable rights. It is graphic confirmation of the vitality and effectiveness of the Peace Programme advanced by the 24th Congress of the CPSU, in which ending the war in Vietnam was set down as one of the most important objectives.

The example of the Vietnam agreement shows that nowadays, in this changed world, the most controversial and difficult problems can be settled at the negotiating table. It also means that a sound and realistic approach is steadily gaining ground in international relations.

The sum total of the documents signed in Paris—the Agreement and the supplementary protocols—have laid the foundation for a political settlement. Their significance and effect go far beyond the limits of Vietnam.

The Democratic Republic of Vietnam has gained the long-awaited opportunity to begin restoring the country, developing and consolidating its economic potential, and raising the living standard of its people, who are labouring as heroically in peacetime as they fought for freedom and independence during the war. The Agreement must logically lead to the establishment and maintenance of relations between the DRV and USA based on the principles of peaceful coexistence.

Complete withdrawal of all foreign troops from Vietnam and US commitments under the Paris Agreement not to interfere in the internal affairs of South Vietnam, to respect the right of its people to determine their political future in truly free and democratic elections—this coupled with the establishment of a national council of concord and reconciliation, with guarantees of basic political freedoms and recognition of the present situation in South Vietnam (the existence there of two zones, two governments, and three political forces), all this, cumulatively, has created conditions for South Vietnam's progress along the road of peaceful construction. It has also created conditions for progress along the road of democracy, independence, and neutrality, and for a final

and just settlement of the Vietnamese problem, for the peaceful unification of Vietnam in accordance with the national aspirations and
traditions of the Vietnamese people.

Peace in Vietnam has improved the chances of settling the other
problems of Indo-China. On a broad plane, the Vietnamese agreement
is called upon to eliminate one of the most dangerous seats of war that
has for many years poisoned relations on a global scale. It will be no
exaggeration to say that the world breathed a sigh of relief when the
Paris Agreement was finally reached. New opportunities have arisen
to further international *détente*, improve the general world situation,
to put new curbs on the arms race, and make new progress towards
disarmament.

Following the settlement in Vietnam, relations between countries
that were in one way or another involved in the Indo-China events can
and must become more productive and, in many ways, follow new
lines.

Soviet people were also gratified to learn that in the wake of the
Paris Agreement an accord on restoring peace and achieving national
concord in Laos was signed in Vientiane, ending all armed actions,
including bombing, and providing for the establishment of a new
provisional coalition government of national unity. This clears the
way for the national aspirations of the Laotian people to build a peaceful, neutral, independent, democratic, united, and prosperous Laos.

The ending of the war and restoration of peace in Vietnam is bound
to have a positive effect on the situation in Asia, the part of the world
with the densest population, where recent decades have been marked
by turmoil, conflict and bloodshed. The sure road to Asian security is
not that of military blocs and groupings, playing off one group of
states against another, but neighbourly relations and collective security
based on such principles as inviolability of frontiers, renunciation of the
use of force, respect for sovereignty, non-interference in internal
affairs, and the broad expansion of economic and other forms of co-
operation on a basis of complete equality and mutual advantage.

The present international situation clearly suggests the targets for
further effort in the name of lasting peace. There is the urgent task of
eliminating the danger of war in the Middle East, fraught, as it is,
with dire peril to peace far outside that region. Here, too, as in Vietnam,

a settlement can be reached and peace restored solely on the basis of justice, respect for the legitimate rights of the victims of aggression, and renunciation of encroachments on foreign land and of territorial annexations.

In Europe, of course, the situation is different. Europe is far away from Vietnam. But the end of the war in Vietnam is likely to have a positive influence on European affairs as well. Here in Europe a start has been made to change course from tension to effective co-operation between states with different social systems. The multilateral consultations in Helsinki in preparation for the Conference on Security and Co-operation in Europe, though they are being unjustifiably dragged out, show that positive processes are getting stronger.

For all its importance, the Paris Agreement is only the first stage in settling the Vietnamese problem. A crucial period lies before us when all sides will have to show goodwill and readiness to implement fully the accords reached.

A month has passed since the signing of the Paris Agreement. There has been tangible progress. Armed operations against the DRV have been stopped. Troops of the United States and its allies are moving out of South Vietnam and war prisoners are being exchanged. Consultations have begun between the two South Vietnamese sides. A mechanism is being set in motion to control observance of the cease-fire terms: joint military commissions and an international control and observation commission have begun operating. This conference, too, was convened at the agreed time.

The crucial thing today is for the sides to carry out the articles and provisions of the Paris Agreement within the specified time. Here it is proper to stress the importance and necessity of ensuring the unintermittent and effective operation of the international control and observation commission, whose functions and procedures are clearly defined in Article 18 of the Paris Agreement and the relevant protocol.

At the same time, we want to note the following. Some have been saying that the control and observation mechanism should be expanded, and even that some new bodies not envisaged in the Agreement should be set up. It seems to us that if this direction is taken, we may stray off course and create difficulties rather than ease fulfilment of the Agreement. A large number of control bodies may only complicate matters in the absence of a sense of proportion. The main thing is for all concerned, without exception, to meet their commitments responsibly and carry them out strictly. This is the main thing. This is what success depends on in carrying out the Agreement on Ending the War and Restoring Peace in Vietnam, which all of us welcome and which, it is safe to say, is applauded by the whole world.

We hold that the conference is largely meant to secure universal respect for the basic national rights of the Vietnamese people, for their independence, sovereignty, unity, and territorial integrity. The very chance of a renewal of outside interference of any kind in the internal affairs of Vietnam must be ruled out. The people of South Vietnam must themselves decide their future. Broad international recognition of the Provisional Revolutionary Government of the Republic of South Vietnam is now an accomplished fact of current international relations. We hope that all participants in this conference are taking this into account and shaping their policy accordingly.

It is easy to see that certain attempts are being made to weaken the positions of the democratic forces in South Vietnam, notably those of the Provisional Revolutionary Government. There have been many, I repeat many, violations of the Agreement by the Saigon authorities. This has got to stop. We must not let the Agreement be torpedoed. And we will be justified in telling those who are trying to undermine the position of the PRG that they will fail. No power on earth can reverse developments in South Vietnam and prevent the triumph of Vietnamese independence, freedom and unity—the triumph of principles that, as all of us know, were once grossly violated.

If we want this conference to adopt decisions in cognizance of the Agreement on Ending the War and Restoring Peace in Vietnam, and to give it still greater force, we must require respect for it and use the weight and influence of the conference as a whole and of each of its participants to secure its full implementation.

The people of Vietnam face the formidable task of bringing life back to normal, raising towns and villages from their ashes, and making good the incalculable damage done to their economy. They have already resumed peaceful and constructive work. All the same, every kind of help is called for as an act of solidarity by peoples and states, irrespective of their social system, so that Vietnam can remove the ravages of war speedily. We would expect this help and assistance to be rendered on a bilateral basis.

This is the Soviet view of the basic aims of the conference. In conclusion, we want to express our trust that common effort will assure the success of the conference and that its decisions will promote lasting peace in Vietnam and the rest of the world.

> *Statement at the International*
> *Conference on Vietnam in Paris,*
> *27 February 1973*

The Helsinki Conference. 3 July 1973

The opening of the Helsinki Conference deserves to remain as a memorable day for everybody who cherishes peace and security in Europe. This is the first time in the continent's post-war history that the European states and USA and Canada have gathered at one and the same table. The very fact that they have unanimously come round to the view that this forum must be held is of great positive significance.

The commencement of the Helsinki Conference has been greeted with profound satisfaction in the Soviet Union. I should like to thank the Government of Finland for its efforts in organizing the conference and for the hospitality shown in Helsinki.

The conference, as its name suggests, has the mission of considering problems of security and co-operation in Europe. For all European nations, despite the social, political, economic, or geographical distinctions between them, there are no closer and more vital problems of an international order.

The Soviet Union has come to the conference with the desire to ensure its success. For us this is a consistent expression of the policy of safeguarding peace, which the Soviet Union and our allies and friends, the countries of the socialist community, pursue in European and world affairs.

For us this is a major orientation in the fulfilment of the Peace Programme adopted at the 24th Congress of the CPSU.

Peace and socialism were inscribed on our banner at the birth of the Soviet state. We remain true to that banner. The Soviet Union has no other foreign policy. It emanates from the very essence of our social system.

At its plenary meeting last April the Central Committee of the CPSU noted that the preconditions had been created for a durable system of security and co-operation in Europe. In this context, it was emphasized that a successful European Conference would be of immense significance.

As the participating nations have agreed, the conference will have three stages. Each is important.

The present stage, the meeting of Foreign Ministers, marks the start of the conference. It is our view that from the very outset its work must be given the correct orientation so that it is conducted in a constructive atmosphere and is permeated with a striving for understanding and agreement.

This also concerns the conference's second stage, in the course of which its working organs will have to work hard on the compilation of the final documents.

Of course, the concluding stage, at which the relevant documents are to be adopted, will be of special importance. Depending on the decisions that will be adopted, it is at that stage the peoples will judge how productive the conference has been. The Soviet Union holds that the third, culminating stage of the conference should be held with the attendance of the highest representatives of the participating states.

In Europe, and not only in Europe, there is a distinct turn towards the consolidation of peace, the relaxation of tension, and the settlement of outstanding issues by peaceful means. In this sense, the conference is on the main road of the present evolution of the international situation.

The war in Vietnam, whose flaming breath was felt here, in Europe, thousands of kilometres away, has ended. Much remains to be done to implement all the provisions of the agreements signed in Paris and ensure a life of peace to the peoples of Indo-China, but the decisive step has been taken. The restoration of peace in Vietnam has released, as it were, additional energy for further progress in the matter of world *détente*, Europe included.

Some indications favourable to peace are to be observed also in other continents.

Some headway has been made in recent years in curbing the arms race.

Most countries have signed the Treaty on the Non-proliferation of Nuclear Weapons, although not all have ratified it. In accordance with an international agreement bacteriological and toxic weapons have been banned and are subject to destruction.

As a result of an understanding between the Soviet Union and the USA, certain limits have been placed on the development of the most formidable kinds of weapons—on strategic arms. In the course of the recent Soviet–US summit a further important step has been taken in that direction: the basic principles for negotiations on a further limitation of strategic offensive arms have been worked out, and the imposed restrictions may concern both the quantitative and qualitative aspects of these arms.

On the agenda are some urgent measures in the field of disarmament, including the fulfilment of the UN resolution on the convocation of a World Disarmament Conference, the artificial obstruction of which cannot be justified.

The Soviet Union attaches great importance to the talks on reducing armed forces and armaments in Central Europe that are to begin on 30 October of this year. For us it is a matter of fulfilling one of the provisions of the Peace Programme. If all the participants in the talks formally abide by the principle of non-prejudice to the security of the states participating in the talks, we are convinced that mutually acceptable results will be forthcoming.

The principles of peaceful coexistence and co-operation between states with different social systems are asserting themselves ever more broadly in the world. These are precisely the kind of relations that have taken shape between the Soviet Union and practically all its neighbours belonging to a different social system. It is particularly important that the principles of peaceful coexistence should be applied in full in Europe, in which a visible line runs from north to south between the two social worlds. These principles have been firmly established in the relations between the Soviet Union, on the one hand, and France, the FRG, Italy, and many other West European countries, on the other.

PLATE 1. Gromyko as a child: with his parents, Andrei Matveevich and Olga
Yevgenevna, and sister, Yevdokia Andreevna.

PLATE 2. The Soviet delegation to the Dumbarton Oaks Conference, 1944. Gromyko is in the light suit, in the middle of the front row.

PLATE 3. The Yalta Conference, February 1945. Facing the camera, from the left, Stalin, Maisky, Gromyko, Leahy, Stettinius, Roosevelt and Bohlen. Churchill is on the right, turning towards the camera.

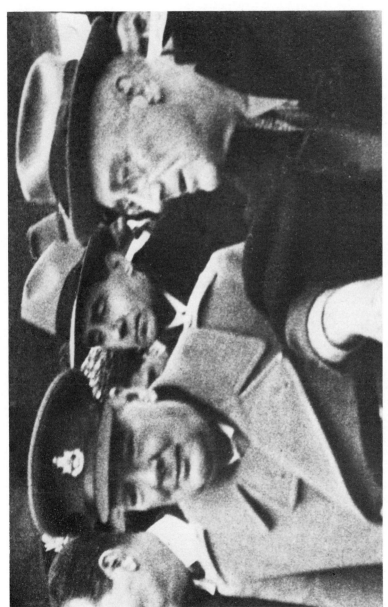

PLATE 4. The Yalta Conference. Churchill and Roosevelt at Yalta, with Gromyko between them.

PLATE 5. The Yalta Conference. At the aerodrome: Gromyko is second on the left, facing the camera. On his left are Harriman, Stettinius, Molotov and Eden.

PLATE 6. The Potsdam Conference, July–August 1945. Stalin sits on the left. Next to him are S. A. Golunsky, Gromyko, Leahy, Burns and Truman.

PLATE 7. The Potsdam Conference. Stalin, Truman, Gromyko, Burns and Molotov.

PLATE 8. The Potsdam Conference. Stalin and Truman, with Gromyko behind Truman's left shoulder.

PLATE 9. The United Nations Charter. Gromyko signing the UN Charter in San Francisco, 26 June 1945.

PLATE 10. Receiving the British Ambassador. In the Kremlin following the presentation of his credentials by Sir David Kelly, British Ambassador to the Soviet Union. Gromyko is second on the right. The year is 1949.

PLATE 11. Receiving state award. Receiving the Order of Lenin from
M. I. Kalinin, 18 April 1945.

PLATE 12. Receiving an award from K. E. Voroshilov, 1957.

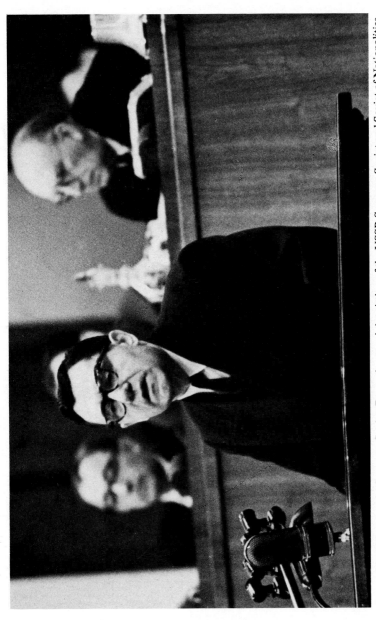

PLATE 13. Addressing the Supreme Soviet. Reporting to a joint sitting of the USSR Supreme Soviet and Soviet of Nationalities on the Geneva talks, 1962.

PLATE 14. With Sir Alec Douglas Home. Gromyko in Moscow with the British Foreign Minister, 1963.

PLATE 15. With Harold Wilson. During the visit to Moscow of a Labour Party
delegation headed by Harold Wilson, 1964.

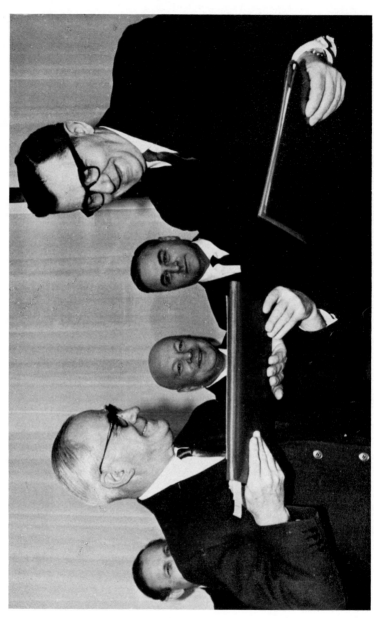

PLATE 16. With Michael Stewart. Exchanging documents with the British Foreign Minister following the signing of a consular convention, Moscow, 1965.

PLATE 17. With Kurt Waldheim.

PLATE 18. With Henry Kissinger.

PLATE 19. Receiving an honorary Doctor of Law degree. The degree-conferring ceremony at Charles University, Prague, 1975. Gromyko is in the front row of the podium, fourth from the left.

PLATE 20. Gromyko giving his address following the conferring of the degree.

PLATE 21. Gromyko in his office at the Ministry of Foreign Affairs, December 1975.

The relations between the Soviet Union and the United States of America are being placed on a foundation of peaceful coexistence more and more confidently and firmly with, needless to say, full respect for the rights and interests of all nations. One can appreciate the significance of this for further *détente* on a world and a European scale. Evidence of this is the exceptionally broad positive response throughout the world to the talks between General Secretary Brezhnev and US President Nixon. The agreements and understandings resulting from these talks reinforce the confidence of the peoples that peace and security are growing more stable for everybody, and therefore for Europe as well.

When the USSR and the USA sign an agreement not only to prevent nuclear war between them but also to do everything in their power to prevent nuclear war generally, this is in the direct interests of all nations and, needless to say, of Europe, where a nuclear conflict would have the most disastrous consequences. That is why this agreement is everywhere regarded as being of historic significance.

In the resolution of the Politburo of the CPSU Central Committee, the Presidium of the Supreme Soviet of the USSR, and the Council of Ministers on the results of L. I. Brezhnev's visit to the USA the confidence is expressed that readiness on the part of other states to subscribe to the principles, jointly recorded by the USSR and the USA, underlying the renunciation of the use of force and the adoption of resolute measures to prevent a nuclear war would be of immense importance in ensuring universal security and lasting peace in the world.

In short, the developments in Europe and the world over the past few months give grounds for believing that the Helsinki Conference is commencing its work in an international climate that has changed perceptibly for the better.

However, there are still regions where, far from diminishing, tension is increasing. As a result of Israel's aggression against its Arab neighbours a dangerous flashpoint still remains in the Middle East, on the southern threshold of Europe. Its earliest damping would serve the interests of all nations.

Soviet foreign policy is aimed at sustaining and consolidating the present tendency towards the restructuring of international relations on

D

the principles of peace. Our point of departure is that this tendency will prevail.

This is supported by the aspirations of all nations for peace. It is supported by countries for which the consolidation of peace is the prime aim of foreign policy. Lastly, it is supported by the consciousness, which is steadily gaining ground among realistically thinking circles in different countries, that no other alternative exists to a nuclear war.

If one considers the significance of the changes taking place in international affairs and ponders over their orientation one will inevitably come round to the conclusion that today the foundation is being laid for new peaceful relations between nations in the foreseeable future.

The Soviet Union holds that the advantages of one social system or another should be proved in peaceful competition and co-operation, and not in war. A contribution, and an effective one at that, can be made to these processes by the Helsinki Conference.

In the course of its long history Europe has given the world unfading and universally recognized achievements of human genius in the most diverse fields. But it has also been the scene of devastating conflicts, collisions, and wars.

There is no place in Europe that does not have a monument to the millions who died in two wars in the lifetime of a single generation.

In our country death for millions of people and destruction had on both occasions come across the western border. The Soviet Union suffered the largest losses in the terrible, gigantic clash with fascism.

I believe we are understood correctly when we say that we shall do everything in our power so that the sacrifices made for the sake of victory should not have been in vain, so that the results of the war, which, together with their allies in the anti-Nazi coalition and many other peoples made victims of fascist aggression, the Soviet people had fought with such strain and self-sacrifice, are not undermined, so that this is the last war not only for the Soviet Union but also for all the other peoples of Europe. This is our great duty to the fallen, to the living, and to the unborn.

The war-time co-operation among the powers of the anti-Nazi coalition might have been an effective factor in a genuinely peaceful arrangement in Europe. Such was the spirit and letter of Potsdam.

All of us remember that immediately after the war developments took a different turn. The long and tense period of the cold war began in Europe. The cold war led to the nurturing of forces of revenge, the arms race, and the rupture of traditional economic and cultural relations. In Europe *détente* was held up for at least two decades.

I should not like to talk about this today. In the final analysis nobody has power over the past; history cannot be remade. But what we can and should do is to draw conclusions from it for the present and the future.

Expressing the feelings and will of the entire Soviet people, Leonid Brezhnev has said that we urge the surmounting of Europe's past record of bloodshed not in order to forget it but that it should never be repeated.

What sort of Europe should we like to see in future?

Above all, a Europe of peace, a continent where aggression is excluded for all time from the life of nations. It is our aim that confidence and understanding should gradually lead to an end to the continent's division into military–political groups. The relations between all European nations must be relations of peaceful and mutually beneficial co-operation.

We are convinced that the creation of that sort of Europe would be consonant with the underlying interests of all the nations participating in the Helsinki Conference, and to put it more broadly—of all countries and peoples.

This is the sort of Europe the Soviet Union and the other countries of the socialist community want.

We believe that however they may differ in other respects, the governments and political parties and organizations that are aware of their responsibility for the cause of peace hold identical views on this question.

The participants in the Helsinki Conference have gathered at one table precisely in order to consider and settle fundamental and most urgent issues on the agenda of European politics. Security and the promotion of co-operation in Europe are a collective matter, and we are convinced that each of the countries participating in the conference, whether it is large or small, can make a valuable contribution.

To work out collectively the principles on which European security and co-operation and the relations among the European states will rest and to formulate these principles in jointly adopted documents means giving long-term orientations to peaceful development in Europe. This, we are convinced, should be the basic political significance of the decisions passed by the Helsinki Conference.

Needless to say, the edifice of this sort of Europe is not built on barren ground. It grows out of the actual situation that took shape on the European continent as a result of the Second World War and post-war development. That is why the Soviet Union has always felt that it may be built up only on the basis of universal recognition of and respect for the existing territorial and political realities.

The basic cause of the international complications and crises that have been precipitated in Europe time and again since the war, regardless of their form, has been that these immutable realities were questioned.

Today there is growing understanding of the fact that in Europe peace can be consolidated only on the basis of the actual state of affairs and not of dangerous illusions.

The contours of normal relations between European countries with different social systems have appeared in recent years. The Helsinki Conference can draw much that is useful from what has already been accomplished in improving the situation in Europe.

First and foremost, I refer to the treaties concluded between the USSR and the FRG, Poland and the FRG, and the GDR and the FRG. The signing of these treaties was not a simple matter for any of the nations that took part in these significant acts. It involved the breakdown—sometimes a painful process—of the notions that had been formed over the years. Tribute must be paid to the sense of realism and political courage displayed by those who understood that there was no other way out of the impasse.

These treaties are now being complemented with a treaty between the FRG and Czechoslovakia, which puts an end to the disgraceful Munich deal.

One of the most significant changes was the abandonment of the former policy of boycotting the German Democratic Republic. It took years, but finally recognition was won by the obvious fact that affairs in Europe cannot be conducted seriously without taking the GDR's interests into account or to the detriment of these interests.

The German Democratic Republic and the Federal Republic of

Germany are shortly to be admitted to the United Nations. The Security Council has already declared itself in favour of this.

The four-power agreement on West Berlin has removed tension in the heartland of Europe. All the conditions now exist for this question to cease being the bone of contention it has been for nearly a quarter of a century.

In the establishment of neighbourly relations between the European states the tone has in many ways been set by Soviet–French co-operation. We highly value the fact that the steps towards *détente* in Europe began largely with the improvement of relations between the Soviet Union and France. For a number of years Soviet–French relations have been developing along an ascending curve. They have acquired stability and scope. This has been reiterated at the recent meeting between L. I. Brezhnev and the French President Georges Pompidou.

Within the short span of only two or three years following the signing of the Moscow treaty much headway has been made in the relations between the Soviet Union and the Federal Republic of Germany.

The visit to the FRG by General Secretary Brezhnev and his talks with Chancellor Willy Brandt showed convincingly that despite the bitter past the two countries have earnestly embarked upon peaceful and mutually beneficial co-operation on a new foundation. Hardly anybody doubts that this is benefiting not only the peoples of the Soviet Union and the FRG but also Europe in the broadest sense of the word.

On the whole, bilateral relations between European states with different social systems are developing steadily. The Soviet Union is actively contributing to this.

The Helsinki Conference has laid the foundation for consolidating the turn from cold war to peace and co-operation. Positive experience of *détente* and relations of peaceful coexistence has been accumulated in and outside Europe. It should be taken into account fully in the conference's decisions.

However, to approach matters realistically means to understand that what has been accomplished is only the beginning. That positive changes have taken place in Europe is obvious to everybody. But can we consider that the security of the European peoples is dependably safeguarded? We are not fatalists and by no means believe that another war is inevitable in Europe simply because that was where the two previous wars broke out. However, nobody can close his eyes to the fact that Europe remains the region with the highest concentration of the most diverse weapons, including the most destructive. It is here that the armies of the military–political groups are in direct proximity to each other.

If all the participants in the Conference are agreed on the main thing, namely, that they should continue *détente* and strengthen security and co-operation in the continent by collective effort, the question arises of what their first joint steps should be. In other words, how to translate the striving of the European peoples for lasting peace into the language of the Conference's decisions?

The prime objective is to reach agreement at the Conference on the principles that should underlie security in Europe and to express the determination of the participating nations to respect and observe these principles in their mutual relations.

This could be one of the key results of the Conference. It seems to us that on this score a sufficiently high level of mutual understanding was achieved during the preparations for it.

The basic norms of peaceful and equal relations between nations have crystallized in the long practice of international relations. In normalizing and expanding their relations, many countries with different social systems have lately found that it was particularly vital to underscore the principles by which they would be guided.

The treaties signed by socialist countries with the Federal Republic of Germany, the Principles of Co-operation between the USSR and France, the Basic Principles of Relations between the Soviet Union and the United States, and some other documents synthesize the benefits and healthy atmosphere emanating from *détente* and establish important landmarks for the development not only of bilateral relations but also of the European and international situation as a whole.

Europe's past and present European reality suggests what the policy of states should be based on in order to avoid conflicts and live in peace.

More than anybody else, the Europeans have learned from bitter experience that wars begin with territorial claims by one country on another. This must be excluded in the future. There must be no ambiguity on this question. Each country, naturally, regards its terri-

92

torial integrity as its prime prerogative. In order to learn to live in peace the principle of the inviolability of frontiers must be unconditionally recognized. This by no means belittles the significance of other principles that are universally recognized norms of relations between states and, at the same time, reflect the concrete political situation in Europe.

These principles are:

—sovereign equality;

—renunciation of the use or threat of force, thus outlawing war as a means of settling international disputes;

—territorial integrity of all European states in their present boundaries;

—peaceful settlement of international disputes;

—non-interference in internal affairs, which signifies respect for the political, economic, and cultural foundations of other states;

—respect for human rights and basic freedoms, including freedom of religious belief;

—equality and the right of nations to decide their own destiny, to establish whatever social system and choose whatever form of administration they consider necessary;

—co-operation between states with the purpose of maintaining international peace and security, and the promotion of relations between them in the economic, cultural, and other fields on the basis of sovereign equality and non-interference;

—conscientious fulfilment of commitments under international law.

Each of these principles is of paramount importance and is significant in its own right. The reason it is suggested that each should be recorded is that each should be strictly observed equally in all fields of relations between states.

The proclamation by the participants in the Helsinki Conference of collectively worked out principles of European security and of their mutual relations will in itself be a great advance; it will help to build up trust in Europe and fortify the confidence of Europeans in the future.

But it would obviously be insufficient to limit matters to this proclamation. It would be useful to reach agreement at the Conference on some measures to ensure the efficacy of the principles that are to be adopted.

To this end the Soviet Union suggests, in particular, that the decisions of the Conference should mirror the readiness of states to reach a settlement, in a corresponding manner, of the disputes existing between various countries as early as possible.

The disputes that may arise between European states in future should be settled exclusively by peaceful means, including negotiation, mediation, arbitration, or other means chosen and agreed upon by the two sides.

We feel that this meets with the wishes of a number of countries, including the neutral states in Europe.

Moreover, it would be important to arrive at the common view that the states participating in the Conference would abstain from extending political, military, economic, or any other assistance or support to any country or countries that commit acts jeopardizing international peace and security.

This would demonstrate the concern of the participants in the Helsinki Conference for strengthening peace not only in but also beyond Europe.

Under conditions of peace expanding political consultations and exchanges of information between the states in Europe would help to promote co-operation. When countries consult each other in order to have a better understanding of their corresponding positions and to draw them closer together, this increases the possibilities for strengthening peace.

The Soviet Union and other socialist countries consider that it would be useful if political *détente* were accompanied by a relaxation of tension in the military field.

We are in favour of the countries concerned mutually notifying each other, in keeping with agreed procedures, about major military exercises in specified regions and inviting observers to exercises of this kind on mutually acceptable terms.

Such are the Soviet Union's thoughts on the political content of the questions that naturally rank first at the Helsinki Conference, namely, the questions of peace and security in Europe.

In line with these considerations the Soviet Union submits to the Conference a draft of the final document on the first point of the agenda.

In our view, the form that this document will have is of no little significance. The Conference must explicitly state the decisions it is adopting.

We consider that in the main final political document it would be expedient to combine the basic provisions and principles of European security and co-operation. This document could be called the General Declaration on the Foundations of European Security and the Principles of Relations between Countries in Europe.

We feel that the constructive views of the other countries participating in the Conference, as they were stated in the course of the preparations for it, are taken into account in our draft.

We trust that the Soviet draft contains nothing that is unacceptable to the participants in the Conference, for the Soviet Union does not seek unilateral advantages.

We do not suggest that any state should modify its social or political system, or ideological outlook—whatever our attitude to them may be—or break off existing links with allies or friends, or renounce commitments entered into earlier.

However, the adoption of a common and agreed document by the states participating in the Conference would show that despite all the distinctions between them they have common interests in important matters. In the final analysis, this could be expressed in the words 'peace and co-operation'.

The solemn adoption by the Conference of a document on the foundations of European security and the principles of relations between states in Europe would be of exceptionally great international importance. It would signify that a set of key provisions for European peace have been worked out and adopted, that all the participants in the Conference pledge to maintain and consolidate peace in Europe by their practical actions.

Who can lose by this? Nobody, or, to be more exact, only those, whether they are near or far from the European continent, who count on sustaining tension and preserving flashpoints of military danger, and endeavour to prevent *détente* between countries of East and West.

The beneficiary would be the peace and security of the peoples of regions adjoining Europe and of a wider area. The consolidation of peace in Europe can and should serve international security in Asia, Africa, and the rest of the world.

In the view of the Soviet Union, the discussion of the question of promoting economic, scientific, technical, and trade relations on a basis of equality should give an impetus to the development of these relations.

In this context I should like to emphasize the following: the establishment of long-term co-operation in Europe and the determination of the basic orientations for the development of economic, scientific, and technical relations for years ahead enter into the Soviet Union's intentions.

The introduction of greater stability into economic and trade exchanges between countries with different social systems has been a characteristic feature of recent years. The next step is to try to elicit new forms and potentialities for co-operation in these fields.

Close bilateral relations, which, needless to say, are not losing their value, would be complemented and enriched by multilateral relations involving the participation of several and, in some cases, perhaps all the European states.

We should like the existing international division of labour to be taken into maximum account. Back in 1921 Lenin said that there were 'no reasons why a socialist state like ours cannot have unlimited'—I emphasize, unlimited—'business relations with capitalist countries'.

The Soviet Union has no intention of fencing itself off from the rest of the world. There is no doubt that large-scale and long-term economic, scientific, and technical co-operation would be a kind of material foundation for security in Europe, giving it an additional reserve of stability.

The Soviet Union expects tangible results from the Helsinki Conference also as regards the expansion of cultural co-operation and contacts between organizations and people.

To a large extent peace and security in Europe depend on the degree of trust between nations, on whether goodwill and mutual respect or, on the contrary, suspicion and hostility take root in the relations between them.

In the multinational Soviet Union immense significance is attached to equality and friendship among nationalities. We believe that the ideals of peace, the equality of all nations, and neighbourly relations should be increasingly asserted in international association. There should be no room for the propagation of hatred, aggression, militarism, the cult of violence, racial or national superiority, or other goals incompatible with the spirit of *détente* and co-operation between nations, with the UN Charter, or universally recognized moral norms.

Cultural co-operation, contacts, and exchanges of information should obviously be promoted strictly in accordance with the principles regulating the relations between the states participating in this Conference. I refer above all to respect for the principles of sovereignty and non-interference. Any departure from this would be justifiably assessed as an attempt to encroach upon the affairs of others. We must avoid this, and put an end also to the psychological effects of the cold war. This means strictly respecting each other's laws, customs, and traditions. This will be the Soviet Union's point of departure.

For a number of years there have been between the Soviet Union and many Western countries fairly broad cultural relations that are contributing to the mutual cultural enrichment of nations. Tourist exchanges are proceeding, and contacts have been established between public organizations, young people, and representatives of kindred professions.

Considerable potentialities exist for a further expansion of contacts in diverse fields. A large contribution to this could be made by the Helsinki Conference.

If the Conference is regarded not as a single act but as the commencement of serious collective work, a bridge should perhaps be thrown across to possible subsequent European meetings. We hope that it will be possible to reach a common view on the organizational forms in which this could be embodied.

The countries represented at this Conference have some experience of multilateral political co-operation. The preparatory consultations for the Conference that were held here, in Helsinki, have accomplished useful work. Representatives of more than thirty countries stated their views and it was evidently not simple to bring them to a common denominator. Nevertheless, mutually acceptable decisions were found, and this, too, is an encouraging sign.

At the multilateral consultations recommendations were worked out for the governments of the participating states on some questions of the Conference's further work. On the whole these are reasonable and balanced recommendations.

The Helsinki Conference is beginning its work in a good, business-like atmosphere.

The Soviet Union considers that the second stage of the Conference, when the Co-ordinating Committee and commissions begin to function, should also be conducted efficiently and smoothly. They could, in our opinion, begin their work soon after the completion of the first stage and carry out their tasks without unnecessary delays.

All the possibilities are on hand for the work of the Conference, including its third stage, to be completed within the shortest span of time, before the end of this year, i.e., 1973.

The level on which the final stage of the Conference is conducted should conform with its great international significance. This is the Soviet Union's firm conviction. All the indications are that many other states agree with us.

We are convinced that the decisions the Conference adopts at its final stage will be, one can say without exaggeration, historic for the peoples of the European continent and that they will have a broad positive response from throughout the world. Their weight and prestige will be increased by the fact that they will be adopted at the final stage by summit-level representatives of states.

Unremitting effort by all countries, political realism on the part of statesmen, and the ability to see far into the future will be needed in order to justify the hopes that the peoples link with the Helsinki Conference.

By living under conditions of lasting peace Europe could be a living and attractive example of peaceful coexistence for all the other continents and fulfil its role as an unfading centre of world civilization.

*Speech at the Helsinki Conference
on Security and Co-operation in
Europe, 3 July 1973*

The 28th session of the UN General Assembly. 25 September 1973

The past year has been crowded with major international events. Some of them, even if viewed individually, represent historic milestones. However, what chiefly characterizes this entire set of events is the development and strengthening of the shift from an extended period of tension in the world to *détente* and business-like co-operation. From this standpoint, the past year can in a sense be described as having marked a turning-point.

The war in Vietnam was brought to an end. The flames of one of the most dangerous breeding grounds of war were stamped out. The just cause of the Vietnamese people gained a major victory.

In Southern Asia, steps are being taken to bring about a further easing of the tension which several times in the past has led to open hostilities.

The positive changes in the situation in Europe are even more clearly apparent. The task of normalizing relations between the states of Eastern and Western Europe is virtually complete. We hope that no one will create artificial obstacles to the completion of this process. The convening of the European Conference in Helsinki marked the opening of a new and extremely important stage in the work of guaranteeing security and organizing peaceful co-operation on a continent-wide scale.

The danger of a global clash between the two world-wide social systems which would inevitably result in a terrible catastrophe for all mankind has been lessened. That is how the entire world views the Agreement between the USSR and the USA on the Prevention of Nuclear War, which was concluded during the visit to the United States of L. I. Brezhnev, the General Secretary of the Central Committee of the CPSU.

Today, the principle of peaceful coexistence is not only recognized as the only possible basis for relations between the socialist and capitalist countries but is increasingly being given practical effect and embodied in treaties and agreements. The process of *détente* is a broad and deep one which is involving an increasing number of states and affecting more and more important areas of the relations between them.

This gives us reason to hope that, as Leonid Brezhnev noted in a

99

recent statement, 'the present *détente* is not a temporary phenomenon but the beginning of a fundamental reorientation of international relations'.

The changes for the better in international affairs arouse particular satisfaction in the Soviet Union. Not, of course, that other peoples are any less interested in peace than the Soviet people. It is just that to us the increasing trend towards *détente* and co-operation is also confirmation of the correctness and consistency of the foreign policy pursued by the Soviet Union.

Peace and friendship between peoples have always been the watchword of Soviet foreign policy and its unchanging goal. That goal was defined by V. I. Lenin, the founder of the Soviet Socialist State and head of its first Government. It has been and continues to be the basis of the foreign policy guidelines laid down at all Congresses of the CPSU. Our country has taken this position under all circumstances, regardless of the configuration of the international situation.

The shift in the course of international events in the last few years indicates clearly that ensuring a lasting peace on earth is not simply a noble but remote ideal; it is, rather, a completely attainable goal of practical politics.

Another fact is no less obvious. The positive results that have been achieved up to now did not come about of themselves.

Obviously, there is no Government that will not say it wants peace, lasting peace, indeed eternal peace. If such pronouncements are not to remain an idle dream, however, they must be backed up by unremitting efforts that go on day after day.

The Soviet Union exhorts its allies as well to follow this course. Indeed, we go beyond exhortations; acting in close co-ordination and in the light of international developments, we take concrete initiatives. At the recent Crimean meeting of leaders of the Communist and workers' parties of the socialist countries, it was emphasized that all the states concerned must now join efforts in consolidating the favourable changes that have come about in international affairs, must consistently give practical effect to the treaties and agreements that have been concluded and must advance steadily towards the main objective, which is that of ensuring a lasting peace.

It is a secret to no one that *détente* has its enemies whose resistance must not be underestimated. There is also a certain inertia to be overcome. After all, what we are trying to do is to solve problems that have built up over a period of years or even decades.

However, the supporters of *détente* are more numerous, and what matters is that their efforts should increase and not slacken.

In a number of capitalist countries, a trend towards broader cooperation with socialist states has emerged and is becoming increasingly apparent. Far-sighted political figures in those countries, taking a realistic, responsible view of the world situation, show a willingness to join efforts in working out solutions which give equal weight to the interests of all concerned. It goes without saying that this benefits not only the states directly concerned but the entire cause of peace.

One sometimes hears it said that now that the Soviet Union and the United States are improving their relations and concluding important agreements which help to lessen international tension, there is nothing left for other states to do but to stand by passively. Some go further than that and try to foster the false notion that all of this damages the interests of other countries.

Apart from the fact that such assertions, whether intentionally or unintentionally, distort the actual state of affairs, their practical effect can only be to paralyse initiative and hamper *détente*.

Yes, the situation in the world has definitely improved in the past year. It is incomparably better than five or ten years ago. But does that mean that all is bright on the international horizon? No, not by any means.

Again and again we find ourselves returning to the situation in the Middle East, which, it must be stated bluntly, presents a danger because of the continuing Israeli aggression.

The Soviet Union remains convinced that the Middle East problem can be solved. The basis for a solution exists in the form of the well-known Security Council resolutions, which—as was confirmed once again by the recent discussion of the Middle East question in the United Nations—are supported by an overwhelming majority of member states of our organization. The aggressor is becoming increasingly defiant in his refusal to agree to a settlement.

Every effort must be made to see that Israel and the countries and circles that support its present policy understand at long last the need for a more sober approach and that they truly set out on the path leading to a solution of the problem.

As far as the Soviet Union is concerned its position is clear: the situation in the Middle East must be resolved on the basis of the complete—I repeat, complete—withdrawal of Israeli troops from occupied Arab territories and of respect for the independence and inalienable rights of the states and peoples of the area, including the Arab people of Palestine. Our main, decisive interest in the Middle East is to promote the achievement of a just and lasting peace. The Soviet Union wishes to state this once again from this rostrum in the most categorical terms.

The biggest problem is that of the continuing arms race. The development of techniques of mass destruction and the stockpiling of weapons have long since gone beyond the point where using them becomes an absurdity, for, as Lenin foresaw half a century ago, this process is 'undermining the very conditions for the existence of human society'. It must be obvious to all how ruinous it is to go on replenishing the arsenals. Yet, only in recent years has it become possible to take the first step towards limiting the arms race.

It would be wrong to underestimate the importance of the measures that have already been taken. These measures serve to impede to some extent the unrestrained proliferation of armaments, particularly the most destructive types.

Just recently, an important frontier was crossed when, as a result of agreements reached between the Soviet Union and the United States, mutual limitations were imposed on strategic arms and principles were formulated for negotiations on further such limitations. In conjunction with the historic conclusion of the Agreement between the USSR and the USA on the Prevention of Nuclear War, these accords contribute significantly to an improvement in the international atmosphere.

However, further efforts are needed, and they cannot, of course, be confined to two nuclear Powers, even though those two may be militarily the mightiest in the world. We would, in particular, find it gratifying if other states were willing to adhere to the principles jointly laid down by the Soviet Union and the United States for renunciation of the use of force and for decisive action to prevent the outbreak of nuclear war; that would be of exceptional importance in ensuring lasting peace throughout the world.

Today, we all have more experience in settling international problems than we had yesterday. And it suggests to us that even in the field of disarmament real progress can be achieved in some areas. All that is needed is to follow in practice a truth which in theory is certainly recognized by all: not to proclaim 'all or nothing', but to single out one after another those problems on which agreement can be reached even at the present stage, and then solve them. Experience has shown that this approach can prove its worth even in matters as vital to the security of the state as that ultimate weapon, the nuclear missile. Is that not demonstrated by the Soviet–American agreements dealing with that matter?

Neither can there be any doubt about another matter. Those agreements would not have been possible if they had put either side at a disadvantage, if the principle of equal security had not been scrupulously observed.

But if, on such a basis, two countries have been able to achieve a limitation of arms, then why cannot, say, five Powers act similarly, provided, of course, that there will be no threat to the security of any of them? And if that can be done, what is there to prevent such a method from being applied to a wider range of countries? The greater the number of states that participate in a practical solution of the disarmament problem, the more tangible will be the benefit for the security of all peoples.

Furthermore, we believe that the successes achieved on the path towards *détente* already make it possible for considerable additional resources to be made available to assist the developing countries.

In view of all these considerations, the Soviet Union wishes to propose that the question of the reduction of the military budgets of permanent members of the Security Council by ten per cent and utilization of part of the funds thus saved to provide assistance to developing countries should be included in the agenda of the twenty-eighth session of the UN General Assembly as an important and urgent item.

In our view it would be appropriate to take as the starting-point for the proposed reduction the level of military budgets for the current year, 1973. That proportion of the funds made available by such a reduction which would be used to benefit the developing countries could, for example, amount to ten per cent.

Needless to say, such a step would require the participation of all the permanent members of the Security Council without exception. It would also be desirable for other economically and militarily powerful states to reduce their military budgets.

We suggest that the funds made available for economic assistance to the developing countries should, first of all, be granted to those countries of Asia, Africa and Latin America which have experienced great difficulties this year because of grave natural disasters such as drought and floods.

The United Nations has laid the groundwork for fruitful activities on behalf of peace in a number of important fields.

Specifically, at last year's session the General Assembly voted by a large majority in favour of the settlement of two major problems: the non-use of force in international relations and permanent prohibition of the use of nuclear weapons, and the question of a World Disarmament Conference.

The Soviet Union believes that the earliest possible implementation of the solemn declaration of the General Assembly, speaking on behalf of the members of the United Nations, concerning their renunciation of the use of force in international relations and the permanent prohibition of the use of nuclear weapons, would be an effective means of ensuring that one of the principles of the United Nations Charter was laid down as a law of international life. To that end, a forceful decision in the matter must be taken by the Security Council.

For its part, the Soviet Union is ready to negotiate and to formalize reciprocal undertakings with all—and I stress, all—the nuclear powers on the non-use of force, including, at the same time, prohibition of the use of nuclear weapons.

The time has come to undertake practical preparations for the convening of a World Disarmament Conference. Arrangements must finally be made so that the Special Committee provided for in the General Assembly resolution relating to preparations for that Conference can carry out the functions entrusted to it. There is no need to prove how desirable it is for all the nuclear Powers to take part in the Committee's work.

Although *détente* and the development of peaceful co-operation are measured, not in decades, but merely in years, into this short period of time there have been compressed events which are significantly changing the face of the world.

The Soviet Union and France have been dealing with each other in a consistent and serious manner for a number of years. Both countries have acquired useful experience and are using the favourable trends of *détente* to develop both their bilateral ties and political co-operation in international matters, and especially European matters. The Soviet Union values that important achievement.

The radical changes achieved by the Soviet Union and the Federal Republic of Germany in their relations demonstrate that the two states are guided not by considerations of expediency, but by the long-term interests of their peoples and the interests of peace in Europe. A spirit of realism has also prevailed in the approach of the FRG to questions which had long divided it and the Polish People's Republic and the German Democratic Republic. Many obstacles to the establishment of normal relations between the FRG and the other socialist countries of Europe have been removed, although in the FRG itself, from all indications, such a policy is not to everyone's liking. The influence of forces clinging to old, outworn policies can still be felt there even today.

A few days ago the General Assembly congratulated the representatives of the GDR and the FRG, two independent sovereign states, on their countries' admission to membership in the United Nations. This is one of the most important indications of the changes which are taking place in the world.

In a mere eighteen months or two years an enormous distance has been covered in relations between the Soviet Union and the United States. As a result of Soviet–American talks at the highest level—during the visit of President Nixon to Moscow in May of last year and the visit of the General Secretary of the Central Committee of the CPSU, Leonid Brezhnev, to the United States this year—a firm basis has been laid for the development of relations between the two countries in a way which is fully in keeping with the principle of peaceful coexistence and which opens up vast possibilities. A number of agreements in various fields have been concluded. All these agreements have been made public; they speak for themselves. And they have not remained mere pieces of paper; much work has been done to give them concrete expression.

It is of fundamental importance that the improvement in Soviet–American relations is being achieved on the basis of mutual recognition of the opposition between the two states' social systems and ideologies, and on the understanding that the rapprochement between the USSR and the USA is directed against no one and threatens no one's interests.

The Soviet Union is convinced that if both sides unswervingly carry out all the obligations they have assumed, including the strict observance of a basic principle in international relations, that of non-interference in each other's internal affairs—a principle on which our whole approach is based—then Soviet–American relations will be a permanent favourable factor promoting international peace—a point which is of historic significance.

Relations between the Soviet Union and Japan are not at a standstill. The Soviet Union intends to continue to work to ensure that these relations become relations of genuine neighbourliness and co-operation. That is quite feasible if both countries constantly bear in mind the fundamental long-term interests of peace and security in the Far East.

The Soviet Union is ready to expand its relations of mutually advantageous co-operation with all countries of Europe and the other continents which so desire it, whether in the search for solutions to current international political problems, wide-ranging economic agreements, joint efforts to use the benefits of scientific and technological progress or the exchange of spiritual values.

On the first day of the present session of the General Assembly the second phase of the Conference on Security and Co-operation in Europe began. This is a great and unprecedented endeavour. For the first time all European states, together with the United States and Canada, have sat down at the same table in order to jointly determine measures that would help to assure the peoples of Europe a peaceful future for as long as can be foreseen.

The Soviet Union views the prospects for the work of the Conference with considerable optimism. Its participants have already to a certain extent found a common language; there are, at least, no differences between them in agreeing that the Conference faces tasks of great importance which will require business-like and constructive consideration. If such an approach prevails to the end, the participants in the Conference will be able to place their contribution to the strengthening of general peace on the scales of history with a sense of satisfaction. That will benefit not only states directly concerned with European affairs, but all peoples of the world.

There is a possibility of achieving a good and, in terms of its potential consequences, even an historic success as a result of the Conference. All that is necessary for this is for all participants to display a responsible and serious approach to the problems before them. Nobody should yield to the temptation to teach others how to manage their internal affairs. It must be admitted that some would like to try to impose their own internal practices on others. No, internal practices, internal laws, represent the line before the threshold of every state at which all others must stop.

Meanwhile, some in the West are not averse to launching noisy propaganda campaigns and even to resorting to methods of blackmail in order to cover up their own attempts to interfere in the affairs of other countries. Matters have gone so far that they are attempting to arrogate to themselves the right to dictate right and left by whom and how the question of emigration from this or that country should be handled, how many emigrants there should be and when and just where they should go. In doing so, they do not hesitate to praise to the skies those who represent no one but who, whether voluntarily or inadvertently, are merely an unwitting weapon in the hands of the forces opposed to the relaxation of tension in the world.

The Soviet Union decisively rejects such an approach and condemns it. We will not allow anyone to interfere in our internal affairs.

The question that inevitably comes to mind is this: do the organizers of these campaigns seriously think that only the Soviet Union, only the socialist countries, are interested in international *détente* and in the development of trade, scientific and technical and other forms of co-operation and that others are merely doing them a great favour by agreeing to hold talks on these matters?

The main thing now is not to let the basic, truly important problems facing states be overshadowed by a poisonous atmosphere deliberately created over trumped-up questions.

The Soviet Union considers it desirable to supplement political *détente* in Europe with military *détente*. This cause may be served by yet another major undertaking by a number of states: the talks opening on 20 October 1973 on the mutual reduction of armed forces and armaments in Central Europe.

As a result of the positive changes in the international situation, it is also becoming possible to view the situation in Asia in a new light.

In Asian affairs, as in international affairs in general, the policy of the Soviet Union is a policy directed towards peace, security and co-operation. The Soviet Union extends its hand to any state which shares these goals. A shining example of this is the uninterrupted development of relations between the USSR and India, a great, peace-loving Asian Power. It is further demonstrated by the history of friendly relations between the Soviet Union and many other Asian countries. Our fundamental belief is that there are no problems in relations between the Soviet Union and the states of Asia which could not be solved at the negotiating table.

The Soviet Union is the initiator of the concept of collective security in Asia. This idea is constantly gaining strength; scepticism is being dispelled and unfounded suspicions are disappearing.

In a recent speech in Alma-Ata Leonid Brezhnev said that we support collective security in Asia because 'we are seeking to eliminate war, armed conflicts and imperialist aggression on the continent of Asia; we want the conditions for unhampered development and national revival to be guaranteed for every country and people; we want a spirit of trust and mutual understanding to prevail in relations between the countries of Asia'.

The Soviet Union is in favour of equitable participation in the system of collective security by all Asian countries, without any exception. Any intention of directing collective security in Asia against any state is totally alien to us, despite allegations to the contrary.

The positive changes which have recently become apparent on the Asian continent also include the emergence of new, constructive factors in the situation on the Korean peninsula and this is, first and foremost, to the credit of the Democratic People's Republic of Korea. That being so, it would be all the more inadmissible for new, artificial obstacles to the peaceful and democratic unification of Korea to be added to the old forms of outside interference in the internal affairs of the Korean people.

There is, of course, no need to recall in detail in this Assembly the consistent support which the Soviet Union has given and continues to give to the developing states of Asia, Africa and Latin America. On more than one occasion the United Nations has been the arena for fierce political battles with colonialism of every kind, and the Soviet Union has always resolutely defended oppressed peoples and given all possible support to their struggle for national liberation.

We are well aware that this is a difficult and grim struggle, and some very recent events remind us yet again that it may take tragic turns.

In Chile, as we know, the lawful government has been overthrown. The elected President, Salvador Allende, his country's most outstanding patriot, has been killed. The forces of reaction have struck a blow at the Chilean people's desire for true independence and freedom.

There was serious provocation of another Latin American state, Cuba, whose embassy and one of whose ships were fired upon. Surely the heads of the military junta realize that such acts can only be described as international brigandage and acts of aggression?

An anti-Soviet campaign has been stirred up in the country; there are instances of arbitrary and violent action against Soviet institutions and citizens who were sent to give friendly assistance to the Chilean people at the request of the lawful government of the country.

What can one say about this? There can be no doubt that history will bring to account those who attempt to prevent the peoples from breathing the air of genuine independence or to drown in blood their right to national freedom.

For its part, the Soviet Government could not remain indifferent to the intolerable situation that was developing and took the decision to break off diplomatic relations with Chile, or, more precisely, with the military junta.

There is no doubt that the just cause of the Chilean people will triumph in the end, despite the current tragedy.

States which have embarked on the course of political independence have always found and will continue to find in the Soviet Union a friend ready to aid them in consolidating their economic self-sufficiency, to share its knowledge and experience and to assist them in their moments of difficulty. Expansion of co-operation with developing countries is an integral part of the foreign policy of the Soviet Union.

It is our conviction that the relaxation of international tension is conducive to a situation where young states can, in peace, devote all their efforts and resources to economic and social progress, to raising the living standards of their people, and to shaping their own future without fear of outside interference.

The healthier the over-all world atmosphere becomes, the more anachronistic are the remaining vestiges of colonialism and reserves of apartheid and racial discrimination, the stronger is the condemnation they merit and the more vigorous must be the struggle to bring about their complete elimination. It is the clear duty of the United Nations to contribute to the speediest possible elimination of these shameful survivals of colonialism wherever they still exist, be it in Angola or Mozambique, Bissau or Southern Rhodesia, South or South-West Africa.

It is our aim that the voice of the fighters should be clearly heard here, within the walls of the United Nations, that the Declaration on the Granting of Independence to Colonial Countries and Peoples adopted by the fifteenth session of the UN General Assembly should be fully implemented and that the racists and colonialists should be finally deprived of the opportunity to receive support from outside, in particular from certain members of the United Nations, something which is still a feature of current international life.

Those who struggle against colonialism and racism for their national liberation and for their inalienable human rights and dignity enjoy the unwavering support of the Soviet Union. Let there be no doubt that the Soviet Union will continue to do its utmost to ensure that this struggle ends in a decisive victory.

In the struggle for peace, the Soviet Union and the countries of the socialist community are one with the developing states and we value this highly. With some of these countries we have well-established relations; with others relations are only now beginning to develop. But apart from this the platform of the struggle for further *détente* offers ever-greater opportunities for co-operation. We believe that the fullest possible advantage should be taken of them.

Throughout its history the United Nations has operated in varying

110

political weather, and so far the fine days have been far fewer than the bad ones. What has enabled it not merely to survive but also to do many useful things? The fact that it was founded for the purpose of maintaining international peace. And this task remains permanently relevant. From another point of view, the United Nations Charter contains adequate provisions for the fulfilment of the organization's lofty mission.

The United Nations has demonstrated its strength in those cases where the purposes and principles of its Charter have been strictly observed, and its weakness where departures from the Charter have been permitted. What matters is that this world organization should remain in the mainstream of international politics, contributing to the solution of crucial problems.

This does not in any way imply that the Soviet Union is inclined to neglect any other aspect of the diversified activities of the United Nations, whether of an economic, social, cultural or humanitarian nature. It actively assists in putting into practice everything of value that the collective wisdom and experience of states can produce.

Indeed, a few days ago, the Presidium of the Supreme Soviet of the USSR ratified two important international legal instruments pertaining to respect for fundamental human rights and freedoms and the protection of human dignity and the interests of society as a whole. These documents were carefully and thoroughly elaborated in United Nations bodies and were subsequently approved by the General Assembly. I am referring to the International Covenant on Economic, Social and Cultural Rights and the International Covenant on Civil and Political Rights. These two Covenants do not merely contain wishes or recommendations of a declaratory nature, but provide for quite specific obligations on the part of states that are party to them. We appeal to countries which have not yet signed or ratified these Covenants to follow our example and to take steps to ensure that they come into force as soon as possible.

The peoples of the world expect from the United Nations measures which will contribute to a further improvement in the international situation. With favourable changes taking place in the world, opportunities are increasing for the United Nations to make its own major contribution to the consolidation of *détente* and to making it stable and irreversible.

For its part, the Soviet Union is sparing no effort for the triumph of the cause of peace on earth. This is the essence of its peace-loving policy and its peace programme, launched by the Twenty-fourth Congress of the CPSU. Every state, every statesman can be confident that he will continue to find in the Soviet Union a faithful partner at all times and in all cases where action is taken to prevent the danger of war and contribute to peace.

From a statement at the 28th
session of the UN General
Assembly, 25 September 1973

The Geneva Peace Conference. 21 December 1973

The convocation of this conference has been met with profound satisfaction in the Soviet Union. Though this is the first step, it is an important one towards a political settlement of one of the most acute international problems. For a quarter of a century it has been a constant source of tension not only in the Middle East but also far beyond its boundaries.

From time to time—and we are all witnesses of this—tension in that region erupts into open military collisions. World peace is endangered every time. Such was the case six years ago. Such was the case only recently, in October last, when the hostilities were particularly savage, despite the fact that they were of relatively short duration.

There is hardly any doubt that there will be further bloodshed in the Middle East if the basic causes of the tension reigning there are not removed. This is the inevitable conclusion of anyone who is in any way familiar with the actual situation and assesses that situation objectively.

The intolerable situation created in the Middle East by Israel's policy cannot continue any longer. We should like to hope that this is realized by the participants in this conference and that they have come here with the firm intention of laying the beginning for a just, peaceful settlement.

For the peoples of the region and for the peoples of the whole world there is no acceptable alternative to such a settlement. This is irrefutably demonstrated by the entire course of developments, including recent developments.

Today it is obvious to everybody that the Arab states will never reconcile themselves to the loss of the lands seized from them in the summer of 1967. This position has the complete understanding and support of the Soviet Union. In their just struggle the Arab states rely on the support of the overwhelming majority of countries of the world. On their side they have the growing solidarity of the Arab world.

It is hopeless to count on holding the occupied territories by force. The need for a different, realistic approach to the question of war and peace in the Middle East, a need the Soviet Union has always spoken about, has become pressing.

The vast majority of states have in one form or another shown quite distinctly that they do not wish to see the perpetuation of a hot-bed of tension in the Middle East. To ignore this means to go against the clearly expressed will of the people of the world.

The positive changes towards *détente* that have taken place in the world in recent years are also clearing the way for a dependable settlement in the Middle East. Some difficult international problems, including those which seemed to be unapproachable, have been resolved in many parts of the world. Suffice it to recall the termination of the war in Vietnam or the settlement of acute, important post-war problems in Europe, and the significant turn towards normalization and improvement in the relations between countries with different social systems on the basis of peaceful coexistence and through the conclusion of international treaties and agreements.

In the context of the Middle East, too, a tangible indication of the positive changes was the initiative of the Soviet Union and the United States that found expression in the well-known resolutions of the UN Security Council. Against this background the continued Middle East conflict, even if hostilities have ended, is an impermissible anomaly.

I should not like to repeat who is to blame for this. We know who it is and believe that not only we know. Today, when matters have begun to move towards a settlement, the important thing is something else, namely to determine what should be done in order to establish a peace in the Middle East that will be durable and just for all the states and peoples of that region.

The Soviet Union is firmly convinced that first the fundamental principle of international life that no territory can be acquired by war should be observed rigidly.

In this lies the key to the entire problem. If the participants in the conference really wish to deliver the Middle East from the danger of further conflicts it is necessary to remove the prime cause of the crisis— the continued occupation of Arab lands seized more than six years ago. All of them must be returned to their rightful owners. We are convinced that there will be no peace in the Middle East as long as there are Israeli troops in these territories.

Any document adopted by this conference should clearly and distinctly define Israel's obligation to withdraw troops from all territories occupied in 1967.

Without agreement between the two sides on this fundamental issue we do not see how a settlement can be reached that would conform to the interests of the Arab states, Israel, and international security. On the other hand, if an understanding is reached on this basis many other aspects of the settlement would unquestionably be settled much more easily.

Moreover, it is necessary to ensure respect for and recognition of the sovereignty, territorial integrity, and political independence of all the Middle East states, their right to live in peace. This also concerns Israel. Our stand has been clear and consistent from beginning to end— we are for the peace and security of all the peoples of that region. Of course, this implies that justice is assured for the Arab people of Palestine. Their legitimate rights must be protected. Needless to say, the Palestine problem cannot be considered and settled without the participation of representatives of the Arab people of Palestine.

You all know that very nearly the main argument in favour of the occupation of foreign territory is that Israel is allegedly denied the right to exist. This argument holds no water. This right was assured to Israel by the very fact of that state's creation by decision of the United Nations. It was backed up by the establishment of diplomatic relations with Israel by many countries, including the Soviet Union. Israel's Arab neighbours have declared that they are prepared to reach an understanding on a settlement in keeping with the known Security Council resolutions, which distinctly record the principle that all countries drawn into the conflict have the right to exist.

However this cannot be a unilateral right. It is inconceivable without respect for the sovereign rights of other states and peoples. One's own right to exist should not be used to the detriment of the interests of others. Only mutual and equal obligations and the readiness to strictly carry out these obligations can ensure the normal development of inter-state relations in the Middle East.

This applies fully also to the principle of the inviolability of frontiers. As in other regions of the world, dependable frontiers are, above all, frontiers of peace, giving confidence that they will not be violated. It is naive to think that one's own frontiers can be made secure by seizing foreign territory. The only secure frontiers are legal frontiers recognized by those who are on either side of them. In the case of the Middle East these are the lines of demarcation existing on 4 June 1967.

Such is the Soviet Union's stand on the most fundamental aspect of a Middle East settlement. It is entirely consistent with the letter and spirit of the resolutions passed by the United Nations from 1967 to the present time. I refer notably to the Security Council resolution No. 242 of 22 November 1967.

The Soviet Union firmly maintains its course towards a radical improvement in the situation in the Middle East. It has not retreated and does not intend to retreat from that course.

We hold that to this day the above-mentioned 1967 resolution of the Security Council retains its significance as a realistic and substantiated approach to the problems existing in the Middle East and to their settlement.

This is not only our belief. It is shared by practically all UN members, who have time and again expressed it in and outside the United Nations.

Of course, it is one thing to recognize resolutions in words, and another to carry out their provisions in practice. If this were done the problem of a Middle East settlement would have been removed from the agenda long ago. But to this day the smell of gunpowder and burning wafts over the Sinai and the Golan Heights, while the pain of terrible wounds does not abate in the hearts of thousands of Arabs and Israelis.

The practical objective of the conference is to work out a concrete and realistic programme for the fulfilment of all the provisions of the above-mentioned Security Council resolution.

This is made binding also by the resolutions passed by the Security Council during the recent hostilities. They linked the cease-fire in the Middle East with the immediate commencement of talks with the purpose of achieving a lasting settlement of the Middle East problem.

As we see it, the understanding that will be reached by the sides concerned relative to such a settlement will be formalized at the conference in the relevant documents. It is important that these should be weighty documents, that they should be mandatory for all sides subscribing to them. In other words, they must have the force of law.

This would give a solid foundation for peaceful coexistence, for neighbourly relations between all the states and peoples of the Middle East.

Obligations undertaken by the two sides under international law would be the best guarantee of their mutual security, which can be provided only on the basis of confidence and co-operation between states, of the strict fulfilment of signed treaties and agreements, and not by the seizure of foreign territory.

If the need arises for giving the understandings additional weight, the Soviet Union would, in accordance with the wishes of the interested sides, be prepared to accept the relevant obligations together with the other powers concerned. The UN Security Council could also bring its influence to bear. The main thing is that a political settlement in the Middle East should indeed be lasting.

Some other steps could be taken in this direction. I have in mind, in particular, a demilitarized zone in some sectors on the basis of reciprocity and the temporary stationing of international personnel in individual areas. Understandably, in each case this must be specially stipulated and, what is more important, decided on principles acceptable to all the sides concerned.

We believe that given agreement on the main problem, which we have already mentioned, questions of this kind will not be an obstacle to a general settlement.

Despite all the difficulties the Middle East problem can be resolved. We have stated this before, and we state it now from the rostrum of

116

this conference. But we have warned of something else, namely that the flames of war in the Middle East may spread at any time. A dangerous situation exists in the region to this day. Further procrastination over a peace settlement harbours grave danger. We hope that this is fully appreciated by everybody in this hall.

Immense responsibility devolves on the participants in the conference. Their joint efforts can and should bring lasting peace to the peoples of the Middle East.

The Soviet Union considers that one of its immediate tasks is to help abolish the Middle East hot-bed of tension. We continue to support the Arab peoples in their efforts to establish a durable and just peace in the Middle East. At this conference we shall do everything in our power to help achieve the necessary understandings in order to allow such a peace to materialize.

The Soviet Union feels no hostility towards the state of Israel as such. A policy of annexation and the flaunting of norms of international law and UN resolutions were what earned Israel universal condemnation, including condemnation by us. Israel came even to this conference without having fulfilled the Security Council's resolutions Nos. 338 and 339. The situation can change only when Israel confirms by its actions that it is prepared to reach an honest and mutually acceptable settlement.

The urgent, paramount task today is to settle the question of an effective disengagement of troops.

Genuine peace would conform with the vital interests of all the Middle East states. The advantages of peace would enable their peoples to switch their effort from confrontation, which dissipates the human and material energy of both sides, to the solution of the problems of social and economic progress.

This would also benefit many other states and peoples, who, on account of circumstances everybody knows about, feel the negative effects of the Middle East conflict. These effects are today felt, and quite tangibly at that, by countries situated in close proximity to the Middle East and by countries situated many thousands of kilometres away from it. International economic co-operation, trade, and shipping—if we take only that aspect—would have incomparably more favourable conditions.

One can only imagine how much healthier the entire international atmosphere would be and how the process of *détente* would advance with the settlement of the Middle East conflict. This would have a most beneficial impact on the situation in the entire Mediterranean basin, in Europe, in Asia, and everywhere else in the world.

The peoples of the Middle East, and of the whole world, expect practical steps aimed at achieving a lasting peaceful settlement in that region to be taken. The Soviet Union will do its utmost to enable the work of the conference to proceed precisely in that direction, to make it business-like and constructive.

Statement at the Peace Conference
on the Middle East in Geneva,
21 December 1973

The 6th special session of the UN General Assembly. 11 April 1974

For the first time in the history of the United Nations the General Assembly has been specially convened to consider questions of international economic relations. This aspect of relations between states is in itself of great significance. Since the time of Lenin, the Soviet State has been in favour of broadening business-like co-operation among all countries and making it truly democratic. Such co-operation is also called upon—today even more than yesterday—to serve as an important instrument in the strengthening of universal peace.

The questions of raw materials and development, which are on the agenda of the session, would appear to be matters of a purely economic nature. But it can hardly be doubted by any of the authoritative representatives of states who are present here that these questions should be examined in the light of politics. This also applies fully to those phenomena in international economic relations beyond the bounds of the socialist system which have recently become exacerbated.

In our view, the special session will fulfil its task if, through the combined efforts of its participants, it can contribute to the working out of political approaches to the pressing problems of economic interrelationships and to the discovery of ways to solve them. The Soviet Union is prepared to take a constructive part in this work.

The very fact that questions of economic development have been submitted to broad international discussion is indicative of the deep-rooted changes which are taking place in the world today. Would it have been conceivable for a forum like the present one to have been held successfully against the background of the bombings in Vietnam or under the conditions of a direct confrontation between states with different social systems when the threat of a wide-scale military conflict at times came so close to mankind?

It is the change towards *détente* and the improvement in the international political climate which are creating a favourable environment for the normalization of economic relations. The restructuring of relations in the world on the basis of the widely recognized principles of peaceful coexistence has really only just begun, but in this sphere, too, it is already yielding tangible results.

The basic conditions for economic, scientific, technological and other kinds of co-operation between countries are improving, and such co-operation is on an increasingly large scale. As *détente* is becoming more extensive, further opportunities are opening up for the social and economic progress of those countries which have fallen behind in their economic development through no fault of their own, as we all know.

We are convinced that a fundamental solution of the questions under discussion at this session can only be found in the mainstream of these major positive processes of the present time. In other words, such solutions should correspond to the interests of the further improvement of the international situation and the development of equitable and mutually advantageous co-operation.

It was the developing states which took the initiative in convening this special session, and the People's Democratic Republic of Algeria which showed particular initiative in this respect. We understand the motives which prompted them to do this. We well understand the situation of those countries which were formed as a result of the disintegration of the colonial system and the powerful impact of the national liberation movement.

Our country especially sympathizes with the desire to overcome the grim legacy of the past as rapidly as possible and to accelerate sharply

E

the pace of economic development. The Soviet Union has itself travelled the road of transformation from an essentially agrarian country into a major industrial Power. We have discovered from our own experience how complicated and arduous this road is.

The basic causes of the persistence of economic backwardness and low living standards in Third World countries have already been identified correctly.

Indeed, this question cannot be avoided by under-statements and half-truths. The crux of the matter is that many developing countries remain to this very day the object of exploitation by monopolistic capital.

Many fundamental problems concerning relations between developing countries and monopolistic capital, which is often backed by official policy, are, as it were, concentrated in the questions which are under consideration at this session.

They include the international division of labour imposed on economically backward countries, as a result of which the former colonies are still on the periphery of economic life. They also include the continuing control by foreign monopolies of the major sectors of the economies of those countries. For example, can we disregard the fact that more than half of the world's trade in raw materials is to this day controlled by foreign, and above all multinational corporations?

The export of profits to the metropolitan countries—although they are now described as former metropolitan countries—continues as before; in this way, the already limited resources of the newly liberated and economically weak states are reduced. Finally, the former practice of unequivalent exchange—the notorious 'price squeeze'—still operates as ruthlessly as a heavy press.

In recent months, the food situation has become more acute in several regions of the world and the energy and monetary crises have aggravated the difficulties which previously existed.

All these phenomena are not only detrimental to the interests of the developing states; they adversely affect the state of world trade and co-operation among states in general and in many respects poison the over-all international political atmosphere.

The Soviet Union and the countries of the socialist community consider that one of the main ways to solve these problems would be a consistent restructuring of the system of international economic relations, over-shadowed as it is by the weight of the grim past. The vestiges of colonialism and all forms of inequity and unequal rights must be fully eliminated from it.

In practice, this means that in the economic sphere, too, relations between states with different social systems must be imbued with the principles of peaceful coexistence and co-operation based on equality.

Our country was the first in the history of international relations to renounce the advantages arising from inequitable treaties which tsarist Russia had enjoyed. We are still resolutely opposed to more powerful states, on the basis of superiority in their level of development, in practice imposing inequitable co-operation on countries which are less developed economically. There is also no need to dwell on the inadmissibility of applying economic levers in order to interfere in the internal affairs of states or to put political pressure on them. Who can deny with any justification at all that if we were to leaf through the pages of history of the past thirty or forty years alone we would see that many of them prove to be far from clean in this respect?

The spirit and the letter of equality should permeate not only political but also economic agreements. This fully applies both to bilateral agreements and to the multilateral commodity and other economic agreements which are increasingly becoming part of contemporary practice.

Such concepts as international co-operation and discrimination based on differences in social and economic systems are mutually exclusive. Unfortunately, discrimination still occurs in relations between states and such phenomena are to be encountered even today. Such practices date back to the most acute periods of the 'cold war' and the sooner they recede together with it into the past the better.

I should like to mention especially the principle of sovereignty. It is a major theme running through all the discussions and deliberations, both political and economic, in the United Nations and in its specialized economic agencies. This principle presupposes unconditional respect for the sovereign right of each state to dispose freely—I repeat, freely—of its natural resources.

The principles of the inadmissibility of the acquisition of territory by force and of respect for the territorial integrity of all states are directly related to the struggle for the consolidation of the political independence of young states and for the attainment of their economic independence.

It is not just recently that the Soviet Union has started promoting and defending these fundamental principles of relations among states, only a few of which I have mentioned. Most of them, as applied to questions of trade and economic co-operation, are embodied in such important documents as 'Principles governing international trade relations and trade policies conducive to development'. That document was drafted and approved in 1964 by the United Nations Conference on Trade and Development with the active participation of the USSR and other socialist countries.

Last December, during the twenty-eighth session of the General Assembly of the United Nations, in a joint statement, the delegations of the socialist countries, including the Soviet Union, reaffirmed their dedication to the policy of developing equal and mutually advantageous co-operation and promoting the social and economic progress of all countries.

Of course, it is important to have good principles. But this is by no means all that is required. Another major way of solving problems of economic development is to institute all-round co-operation among the states of the world in full conformity with the principles which have been enunciated, in other words, to translate the principles which have been proclaimed and recognized into practical policies.

As far as the Soviet Union is concerned, it is making every effort to this end.

The Soviet Union advocates the expansion of trade and economic ties with the developed capitalist states based on the complete renunciation of any form of discrimination and the removal of artificial barriers. Without this, the development of genuinely equal and just world trade and economic relations is hardly feasible. Along with political *détente*, business-like co-operation between East and West is also advancing step by step, though there is still much to be done.

For more than half a century, the Soviet state has been pursuing a policy of supporting the struggle against colonialism, co-operating with liberated countries and rendering them all possible aid and assistance. We pursued this policy at a time when we ourselves were in need of even the most basic essentials. We are firmly adhering to it today.

122

The Soviet Union's co-operation with the developing states has gone far beyond the bounds of purely commercial relations, although such relations do continue to play an important role. In recent years our trade turnover with this group of countries has increased several times over; moreover, along with increasing imports of traditional commodities, the proportion of manufactured goods from the young national industries supplied by these countries to the Soviet Union is growing.

The reason why this has become possible is that the Soviet Union is carrying out a whole series of measures for the benefit of the developing countries. As far back as 1965 we abolished customs duties on their products—and did so unilaterally.

Incidentally, we are hoping that all the developing countries will take a similar approach to the creation of favourable conditions for trade with the USSR. Scarcely anyone could question the legitimacy of such a wish.

It would probably be difficult to express in figures the extent of the economic, scientific and technological assistance rendered by the Soviet Union to other countries. I will only say that with our help about 1,000 industrial and other major projects have been built or are under construction in the developing countries. They include such gigantic projects as the Aswan dam in Egypt and the Bhilai project in India.

Such projects are, at the same time, a real school of advanced technological experience, a school for the training of hundreds of thousands of qualified experts both on the actual site of the project and at enterprises and in educational establishments in the Soviet Union.

Our assistance is aimed primarily at building an industrial base with its key branches in the young states. This is surely the basis for solving major economic problems and overcoming backwardness—and consequently for strengthening economic and political independence.

All the projects constructed become, without exception, the national property of the developing countries. Any export of profits is completely ruled out in relations with those countries.

Another important aspect of our co-operation is the fact that it is conducted on a planned basis and is adjusted to domestic programmes for the long-term development of young states. In that way, not only their current needs but also their basic long-term interests are taken into account.

We shall continue to co-operate with the states of Asia, Africa and Latin America and to give them all the aid and assistance we can in the most varied ways—from extending long-term credits to providing access to advanced technological knowledge, and from training national personnel to sharing experience in economic planning. The aim is precisely to provide aid and assistance in accordance with the wishes of individual states.

As in the past, we shall strive for unity of action with those states in the world arena in the interests of *détente* and peace, and together with them promote the solution of urgent international problems and rebuff the encroachments of the forces of reaction on their freedom and independence and on their right to carry out progressive social and economic reforms. This policy has been laid down by the Communist Party of the Soviet Union; it is not subject to the winds of expediency but is a consistent policy, a policy of principle.

As before, our country will oppose attempts to separate the national liberation movement from its natural ally—the community of socialist states. We shall never accept, either in theory or in practice, the fallacious concept of the division of the world into 'poor' and 'rich' countries, a concept which puts the socialist states on the same footing as certain other states which extracted so much wealth from the countries which were under the colonial yoke.

The authors of that concept are not only concealing the basic difference between socialism and imperialism, but at the same time are completely disregarding the question of how and at whose expense the high level of development was achieved. Thus the responsibility of those who for centuries kept many peoples under colonial oppression and who are really to blame for the economic backwardness of the developing countries is, as it were, taken off the agenda. We are not in favour of polemics for the sake of polemics, but in this matter of principle things should be called by their real names.

Recently an acute shortage of fuel and energy raw materials has arisen in a number of countries, including some developing countries. The flashy term 'oil crisis' has come into circulation.

Was the outbreak of this crisis inevitable, predestined, as it were, by the stars? No, mankind is not threatened by extinction through lack of energy—all the experts seem to agree on this. Science has by no means said its final word on the exploitation of new sources of energy. The causes of the crisis are not natural, but social and political. The best proof of this is that the socialist world has hardly encountered it.

Is not the present oil situation in the West the result of a certain policy, a consequence of decades of grasping exploitation, or, to put it bluntly, the plundering of the natural resources of the oil-producing countries? On the other hand, has it nothing to do with the policy of Israel, its annexation of Arab territories and its obstinate reluctance to leave the Arab lands seized by force? Who in this interweaving of politics and economics can separate one from the other?

Of course, one cannot remain indifferent to the fact that aggravation of the oil problem may lead to the disruption of trade and economic ties in a great number of sectors and may provoke a fresh outburst of international tension. But it is important to recognize clearly whose policy is the cause of this phenomenon and who is responsible for it.

We are not in favour of an embargo on oil and oil products for its own sake. We are in favour of a just solution to these problems on the basis of respect for the inalienable legitimate rights of peoples to their natural resources. We are in favour of their sovereignty and its observance. No one can question this right of the states concerned.

The Soviet Union advocates a solution to this problem which would in all respects take into account the interests of both the producers and the consumers of oil. In order to achieve this it is necessary that the search for solutions be conducted, not behind closed doors, but with the participation of a wide range of states. Moreover, it is essential that the solutions themselves should conform to the purposes of strengthening international co-operation and consolidating peace. No one country or group of countries can claim the role of arbiter in this respect.

The Soviet Union declares its readiness to participate in both bilateral and multilateral discussions of ways of overcoming the crisis situation in the field of energy, bearing in mind that in this the interests of all states should be safeguarded. In this sphere, as perhaps in no other, there has arisen a pressing need for a restructuring of existing international economic relations and for the affirmation in them of the principles of truly equal and mutually advantageous co-operation.

We support the actions of those countries which see a way out of the crisis through a further limitation of the activities of the foreign oil companies which bear the main responsibility for its outbreak. The intermediary role of the international monopolies—which still largely control the production, refining and sale of oil and oil products and their prices—between oil-producing and oil-consuming countries is becoming an increasingly heavy burden.

At the Conference on Security and Co-operation in Europe, the Soviet Union and the socialist countries are proposing that the European states combine their efforts in executing a number of important long-term projects, some in the field of energy, including atomic energy. The successful conclusion of the Conference would also have the favourable result that it would greatly contribute to the solution of the energy problem as it affects the European continent. It would also represent an important positive contribution to the development of economic co-operation outside Europe.

Even the best organized co-operation in the economic field, or in any other field, can be achieved, as we all realize, only if we keep in mind the main prerequisite—the preservation and strengthening of world peace. Concern for peace is necessarily the primary duty of all states, large and small. However diverse the questions discussed in the United Nations, the main point of the activities of the organization, its principle task, is the maintenance of peace and international security.

That task is no less urgent in the present situation of the beginning of *détente*.

At its twenty-eighth session, the United Nations General Assembly stressed in its resolutions that international peace and security are essential conditions for the social and economic progress of all countries.

It goes without saying that if, in preparing the appropriate final documents of the special session, due importance is attached to the tasks of preventing war and maintaining peace—which are of paramount importance for all mankind—it can only strengthen those documents.

Such is the position of principle, the political approach of the Soviet Union to the questions under discussion. It is precisely in this spirit that we shall act during the subsequent consideration of the various specific aspects of the problem that has arisen.

*From a statement at the 6th
special session of the UN General
Assembly on strengthening the
economic independence of
developing states, 11 April 1974*

The 29th session of the UN General Assembly. 25 September 1974

For more than half a century our country has consistently pursued a policy of peace, a policy of rebuffing aggression and safeguarding the rights of peoples, as that policy was formulated by Lenin. In present-day conditions too the struggle for peace means for us not just an abstract category but is a matter of concrete efforts to give practical effect to the foreign policy guidelines laid down by the Twenty-fourth Congress of the CPSU. It is the expression of the Soviet people's will for peace and uncompromising determination to make it stronger.

Implementation of the Congress's decisions—the Programme of Peace and Co-operation—has already yielded tangible results in the improvement in the international situation. This is clear to any impartial observer. It is equally clear that the current positive changes are to everyone's benefit. Indeed, if there is an area where the fundamental interests of all nations, without exception, do converge, that is the maintenance of peace.

The Soviet Union pursues its policies in close co-ordination with its allies and friends. The socialist community of states unites its participants in a common creative effort—the building of an advanced society which by its very nature rejects war. It is no accident that many major peace initiatives have been sponsored by the socialist countries. The session of the Political Consultative Committee of the member states of the Warsaw Pact last April reaffirmed their joint determination to fight for the triumph of the ideals of peace and economic and social progress.

The general state of world affairs is being moulded by a tremendous number of factors, ranging from political and military to national or even psychological. And it therefore hardly lends itself to one-dimensional assessment. But the main trend of international development arouses no doubts: it is *détente* and the desire for *détente* which are today the predominant features.

For the first time, international *détente* has gone beyond good wishes and verbal assurances. It is a term that has now found a place for itself in the political vocabulary precisely because it is backed by some very real content—the positive changes in reality itself. From the vantage point of recent years one can distinctly see how much has been done in this respect.

Through joint efforts by many states it has become possible to reduce the risk of armed conflict between the two social systems. But of special significance are the well-known agreements of 1972–74 between the Soviet Union and the United States. This applies above all to the Agreement on the Prevention of Nuclear War. The two major Powers undertook to make efforts to preclude entirely the risk of military conflict, including that involving nuclear weapons, between the Soviet Union and the United States, or between either of the parties and other states. At the same time, they agreed to refrain from the use of force against each other and against other countries in circumstances which might endanger international peace and security.

Not long ago there was bitter fighting in Indo-China, in the Middle East, and in South Asia. And these were not the only areas where events took a dangerous turn. Now several international conflicts have, to a certain extent, been channelled in the direction of political settlement.

It is well known that on more than one occasion tensions in Europe have risen to an alarming level. There were no military clashes, but if the total damage inflicted by the 'cold war' and its tensions were estimated, it would prove enormous from all standpoints. Nowadays the political development of the European continent is ever more steadily taking a different course. Not only have the acute problems of the territorial and political arrangements arising out of the Second World War been solved, but also prospects for a safer, peaceful future for Europe have been opened up.

Alongside this there is another major asset of *détente*—the development of bilateral relations between states with different social systems. In the past there were periods when it was possible to organize business-like co-operation between the different systems. But the experience of decades has shown us that that was the exception rather than the rule. Now peaceful coexistence is increasingly becoming the law of contemporary life. And the very nature of these relations is changing in many ways as they become steeped in the spirit of peaceful co-operation.

Finally, it was precisely *détente* that put on the agenda the question of restructuring economic relations in the world. The point of this was to eliminate inequality and discrimination, and to ensure in practice the sovereign right of states to dispose of their natural resources. The recent special session of the General Assembly of the United Nations called severely to task those who for centuries have been exploiting the labour and resources of others, and indicated ways of eliminating economic oppression. The Soviet Union supports the just demands of the developing countries.

On the whole, it can be stated with confidence that international events are now taking a course closer to peace. However, one should also see one other thing clearly: the movement towards peace does not always follow a straight line, and difficulties along this road will not necessarily decrease with each passing year. In a certain sense the problems which have to be dealt with today are not simpler but are perhaps even more complicated than those of yesterday. And there is more to it than just objective causes.

In the final analysis the solution of these accumulated problems is hampered by the deliberate opposition of those forces whose interests are associated with policies contrary to the policy of *détente*. A closer look will reveal behind each instance of aggravation—whether caused by encroachments on the freedom and independence of nations, by the stepping-up of the arms race, or by attempts to test the durability of existing international treaties—the overt or covert activities of these forces. And when at times you hear people say that *détente* is a purely temporary phenomenon or allege that it has exhausted itself, you can recognize without fail from what quarter these statements come.

The Soviet Union counters them with its own motto, which is not to slacken efforts to ensure that the healthy processes which have now been embarked upon should become irreversible and consolidated. As Leonid Brezhnev stressed recently: 'If you want peace, pursue a policy of peace and struggle for that policy!' We are convinced that in our time the complete elimination of the threat of war is feasible—albeit not close at hand—provided active and persistent efforts are made to that end.

The fact that the world is still far from what the peoples would like it to be is demonstrated by the tragedy which has afflicted the Republic of Cyprus. Some may have the impression that this is an event of local significance. The Soviet Union takes a different view.

Before the eyes of the world the force of arms is being used ruthlessly to trample on the independence and territorial integrity of a sovereign member state of the United Nations, a participant in the non-aligned movement. The fact that this is a small country presents developments in a special light. Another hot-bed of tension has appeared in the eastern Mediterranean, and unless urgent measures are taken no one can guarantee that the situation will not deteriorate even further.

From the very beginning the Soviet Union came out in defence of the inalienable rights of the state of Cyprus. It has been resolutely calling for an end to outside interference in the affairs of Cyprus, for the withdrawal of foreign troops from its soil, for the restoration of constitutional order, and for the Cypriots to be given a chance to decide their destiny for themselves. That is the only way to radically remove the tension. The demand that the Charter of the United Nations be observed should not be an empty phrase—as those responsible for events in Cyprus would like to see it. It must be complied with in the case of the Cyprus tragedy too.

The Cyprus problem must be brought out of the impasse resulting from NATO attempts to solve it *in camera*, in political darkness, and according to the narrow interests of militarist circles. This goal—that is, a just solution to the Cyprus problem—is promoted by the Soviet Union's proposal to convene an international conference on Cyprus within the framework of the United Nations. The decisions of such a conference, adopted with the direct participation of representatives of the Republic of Cyprus and aimed at ensuring the country's independence, sovereignty and territorial integrity, could be effectively guaranteed by the permanent members of the Security Council, for, under the

Charter of the United Nations, it is precisely they who are entrusted with special responsibility for maintaining international peace and security.

Indo-China is situated on the other side of the planet, and the situation there is different. But the underlying reasons why the guns are still firing and blood is still flowing in some parts of the region are the same as in Cyprus. It is all due to the stubborn reluctance of foreign-backed reactionary forces to respect the legitimate rights of the peoples.

The comprehensive assistance and support given by the Soviet Union and other states of the socialist community to the Vietnamese people have helped them to achieve victory in the long and heroic struggle against aggression. The Soviet Union will continue to support the Vietnamese people in peacetime too. The aspirations of the patriotic forces of Indo-China for freedom and independence will always meet with our understanding and solidarity.

For almost thirty years now the Middle East has been in a state of fever. Over this period wars have broken out there time and time again. In fact, the last one was only a year ago. This should be enough to convince anyone that the Middle East problem must be solved, and solved justly, with the interests of all the peoples of the region being taken into account.

What does that imply? First of all, the withdrawal of Israeli forces from all the Arab lands seized by them in 1967 and the implementation of the legitimate national rights of the Arab people of Palestine. Otherwise there can be no stable peace in the Middle East. It does not need a prophet to foresee a new flare-up of hostilities if the Middle East settlement is reduced to half-measures, no matter how well advertised they may be.

There are increasing signs that Israel regards the disengagement of forces in the Sinai and the Golan Heights not as the first step towards a general settlement—which is what it should be—but as a manoeuvre intended to freeze the situation. The obvious unwillingness to leave the occupied Arab territories and, moreover, a desire to consolidate Israel's hold on them are quite evident. What other explanation can there be for the militarist intoxication which has again overcome Israel and for the attempts to exert military pressure on the Arab states? Unless this stops, the disengagement of troops may prove to be a mere regrouping of forces prior to a new clash.

The Soviet Union believes that there must be no delay in implementing measures leading to a political settlement in the Middle East, and this means prompt resumption of the Geneva Peace Conference, the most appropriate forum for considering the Middle East problem in all its complex totality and for finding solutions satisfactory to the parties involved in the conflict. Naturally, this fully applies also to the Arab people of Palestine, whose representatives must take their rightful place at the Conference.

We believe that the time has surely come to address ourselves earnestly to the problem of Palestine. A wider approach is required here, one which would open the way to ensuring not only in words but in deeds the legitimate national rights of the Arab people of Palestine, and that is why we favoured including the question of Palestine on the agenda of this session of the General Assembly as a separate item.

There are some who try to represent the Soviet Union's position as one-sided and only serving the interests of the Arab states. Yes, indeed, we do support and will continue to support the legitimate demands of the Arabs. But it would be wrong to see only this particular aspect in our position. When we insist that territories acquired by force should not become a prize for aggression, the implications of our demand go well beyond the limits of the Middle East. It reflects intolerance of aggression in general. What this involves, therefore, is a major international principle and the question of consistency in policy.

Furthermore, the Soviet Union is in favour of Israel's existence and development as an independent sovereign state. We have said so many times and we affirm it once again. Real, not illusory, progress towards a Middle East settlement will create prerequisites for the development of relations between the Soviet Union and all the states of the Middle East, including Israel.

The scope of the policy of peace and *détente* is broad. It is important not to lose momentum in any field and, above all, wherever serious work has already begun to build more stable relations between states on the basis of the observance of the principles of peaceful coexistence.

In this context, the Soviet Union attaches primary importance to the successful conclusion of the Conference on Security and Co-operation in Europe. This is question number one in European political life today. An objective assessment of what has already been done at the Conference prompts the conclusion that, on the whole, the results are impressive.

The Soviet Union is convinced that the opportunity is there to conclude the Conference at an early date by adopting weighty decisions in the interests of security in Europe. In saying this we not only properly appreciate the collective work that has already been done; we also proceed from the premise that solutions to the problems still outstanding can be found if all the participants display the necessary political will and realism.

Naturally, it would not be right to expect the Conference to settle at one fell swoop all the questions accumulated over the long years of tension and mistrust. But it is equal to the task of achieving agreements on crucial problems which can determine a stable peaceful development in Europe for the foreseeable future. It will also be easier to tackle other outstanding issues in an atmosphere of *détente*.

It is also important to achieve results at the Vienna talks on the reduction of forces and armaments in Central Europe. The key to this is strict observance by all of the rule of undiminished security for each side. Agreement on the questions under discussion would in practice supplement political *détente* in Europe with military *détente*.

The conversion into a practical proposition of the idea of consolidating peace in Asia through the joint efforts of states should not, in our opinion, be a matter for the distant future. No doubt the situation there remains complex. There is no small number of trouble spots, conflicts and international disputes on the continent of Asia.

Political thought in Asia, too, is switching more and more to the search for ways of securing peace and stability. And surely this is demonstrated by the efforts of India, Pakistan and Bangladesh to normalize relations on the Indian Subcontinent and by the idea of converting the Indian Ocean into a zone of peace.

We note with satisfaction the growing interest in the Soviet Union's initiative concerning the establishment of a collective security system in Asia. More and more states in Asia are supporting it. The Soviet–Indian Declaration, signed as a result of the visit of Leonid Brezhnev to

India in November 1973, contains important principles, which can serve as a basis for the development of an effective system of relations between states in Asia.

The establishment of peace and co-operation in Asia meets the fundamental interests of all Asian people. The achievement of this goal is a matter which concerns every country of that continent.

The agenda of this session includes an item which has a direct bearing on the improvement of the situation in Asia. This is the proposal by thirty-two states, including the Soviet Union, on the withdrawal of all foreign troops stationed in South Korea under the flag of the United Nations. The presence of those troops, which have now been there for more than two decades, represents a source of constant military and political tension in the Korean Peninsula. Their presence is still more inappropriate under present conditions when, on the initiative of the Korean People's Democratic Republic, efforts are being made to bring about the peaceful reunification of Korea.

If we analyse the reasons which have so often caused acute tensions in the world, and which even now frequently lead to dangerous situations, we shall easily see that in many cases this was the result of the armaments race. It is indeed a fact that immediately after the Second World War some states embarked upon a course of building up armaments and setting up military bases on foreign territories, thus making the creation of tension and sabre-rattling their policy. It is a secret to no one that it was precisely that policy of theirs which at times brought the world to a very dangerous brink.

Facts must be faced. So far it has not proved possible to stop the arms race. Indeed, today the arms race absorbs more money than ten or twenty years ago. It has been estimated that the world annually burns in the furnace of armaments over $250 billion. This is more than the entire national income of the developing states of Asia and Africa. One can only imagine what benefits these resources could yield if they were used for peaceful purposes, for development, to combat hunger, poverty and disease.

And so a paradoxical situation develops. The peace movement has never had such momentum as it enjoys today, and never has the world produced such quantities of arms as it does today. On the one hand, there is the longing for peace on the part of hundreds of millions of people who realize the grim danger of the arms race, but, on the other hand, there is the increasing avalanche of armaments.

What is the matter? Maybe some forces which have got out of human control are at work? Certainly not. The reason is policy. And if it is policy, well, one may ask, whose policy?

If it all depended on the socialist countries, the arms race would have been eliminated long ago. No one has tabled more specific proposals on disarmament than they. Ever since the non-aligned countries moved into the forefront of international affairs they too have been actively working in favour of disarmament. Voices of reason are to be heard in other countries too, and they resound with ever greater confidence both in parliaments and in broad public circles.

Military–industrial circles that profit from the arms race oppose its cessation. Those politicians who are linked with these circles have long since placed their narrow interests above the aspirations of the peoples. The influence of these circles has had a telling effect on all disarmament negotiations.

As positive changes make their way in the world, so objective prerequisites for finding real agreements in the sphere of disarmament improve. It is noteworthy that the largest number of agreements of this kind have been reached in the last few years. Although they do not reverse the arms race, they do curb it in a whole series of ways.

In one case, it takes the form of limiting the further development of nuclear weapons and the creation of new destructive models. The Moscow Treaty Banning Nuclear Weapon Tests in the Atmosphere, in Outer Space and under Water has been serving this end well for over a decade now.

The same objective is served by the recent treaty between the Soviet Union and the United States whereby both countries have undertaken to stop, as of 31 March 1976, underground testing of the most powerful nuclear devices and also to limit underground nuclear test explosions in general. The Soviet Union will strive to see to it that the prohibition of nuclear weapon tests eventually becomes comprehensive and universal.

In another case, it takes the form of a limit on the territorial spread of armaments. Such is the purport of the Treaty on the Non-proliferation of Nuclear Weapons, which has proved its effectiveness. We are in favour of making full use of the possibilities inherent in that treaty and of increasing the number of states party to it. The objective is to make this treaty universal.

A number of agreements exclude the sea-bed and the ocean floor, outer space and celestial bodies from the sphere of possible deployment of nuclear weapons. In accordance with an international agreement bacteriological weapons have been prohibited and eliminated from military arsenals and prospects are emerging for the outlawing of another deadly means of warfare, namely, chemical weapons.

And what about the agreements on the limitation of strategic arms between the Soviet Union and the United States? I feel that there is no need to explain their unprecedented significance since they are designed to narrow the actual material basis of the nuclear-missile arms race. Quite recently these agreements were supplemented by new important agreements. Last July, the Soviet Union and the United States decided to limit further their anti-ballistic missile systems and mapped out ways of achieving the further limitation of strategic offensive arms in terms of both quality and quantity. The Soviet delegation in Geneva, where talks on these questions were resumed the other day, has firm instructions to seek their solution.

The Soviet Union will continue to work tirelessly to further the cause of disarmament in areas where this is possible. It will look for new fields where concrete results can be achieved through the joint efforts of states.

The Soviet Union took the initiative in placing on the agenda of the twenty-ninth session of the General Assembly as an important and urgent item the question of the prohibition of action to influence the environment and climate for military and other purposes incompatible with the maintenance of international security, human well-being and health.

What is the motive for this?

The achievements of scientific and technological progress have expanded the possibilities of influencing nature and the climate of the globe and, in a certain sense, of controlling the complex and powerful processes involved. Unfortunately, the latest discoveries can be used not only for creative, but also for military purposes, with extremely destructive consequences for mankind. These are not the conjectures of science fiction writers, but an actual threat that is assuming an ever-more realistic shape. It is in the interests of all peoples to nip this threat in the bud.

The Soviet Union proposes that an international convention should be concluded which will outlaw the military use of the environment. Compliance with the provisions of such a convention, a draft of which we are submitting to the Assembly, could be secured through the adoption by each state, in accordance with its constitutional processes, of appropriate measures to prohibit activities contrary to the convention and through consultations and co-operation among states, notably within the framework of the United Nations.

The conclusion of such a convention would prevent the emergence of new means of warfare and, at the same time, would facilitate the solution of a problem common to all mankind—the protection of the environment. We trust that all the participants in the Assembly will fully appreciate the universal significance of this important initiative.

In its attitude in the United Nations, the Soviet Union proceeds on the assumption that the UN can and must play an important part in developing and consolidating the positive processes characteristic of the present-day world situation. We have quite a number of useful resolutions to our credit aimed at strengthening international peace. Now everything depends on their being consistently implemented.

In this regard, I should like to refer especially to some resolutions adopted by the United Nations over the last two or three years by a large majority of votes. In the first place, I have in mind the prohibition of the use of force in international relations, coupled with a permanent prohibition on the use of nuclear weapons. This is an Assembly decision of fundamental importance. It must acquire binding force for all states and, in this regard, the Security Council has an important role.

One cannot say that the United Nations decision on the World Disarmament Conference has not been followed up. A special committee for its convening has even been set up in which, among other states, three nuclear Powers are participating. However, in fact the question is still not really being dealt with. It is time for the Committee to proceed to prepare concrete recommendations on the practical aspects of the convocation of the conference. The boycotting of this important measure by several states is contrary to the clearly expressed desire of the overwhelming majority of member countries of the United Nations. We regard it as a challenge to the world organization.

Through no fault of the Soviet Union, there is delay in the implementation of such a generally useful enterprise as that of reducing by ten per cent the military budgets of the permanent members of the Security Council and the use of a part of the funds thus saved for providing assistance to developing countries. This example belongs in the same category. This action would have a double effect: it would promote the limitation of the arms race and, at the same time, provide additional assistance to states that need it most. The attitudes towards this proposal act as a kind of litmus paper, revealing the intentions of states regarding acute present-day problems.

The further development of bilateral relations between states based on the principles of peaceful coexistence is a vast and far from exhausted reserve for deepening *détente*. On this basis our country is prepared to establish and expand not just normal but, where possible, friendly relations with all states sharing this approach. This has been and remains one of the most important aspects of Soviet foreign policy.

It is our desire to see the consolidation of all the positive results that have been achieved so far in our relations with leading capitalist states on the basis of fruitful efforts on both sides. We want to move ahead and make these relations stable. In this context, the statements by the new leaders of the United States, France and the Federal Republic of Germany about their intentions to continue to move towards *détente* and co-operation have been met in the Soviet Union with satisfaction.

Today economic, scientific and technological links assume an increasingly large role in relations between states with different social systems. If co-operation in these fields is built on respect for the principles of equality and non-interference, it will not only be mutually advantageous but will also promote the establishment of a material basis of sorts for durable peace and good-neighbourliness.

We value highly the good and, in some instances, close relations which have been established between the Soviet Union and many developing countries. The countries of Asia, Africa and Latin America which have embarked upon the road of national independence and the consolidation of economic independence can continue to rely firmly on our support. We were in at the source of their struggle against colonialism, and at each and every stage of it we have supported and will continue to support the developing states in word and in deed. That is our basic principle, and we shall not deviate from it.

The solution of such complex and urgent problems as those of energy and food, which are attracting much attention, particularly in the United Nations, should also be sought on the path of peace and cooperation, of strict observance of the principles of equality and sovereignty, and of the right of states to dispose of their natural resources.

The number of young member states of the United Nations has increased at this session of the General Assembly. We should like to express our particular satisfaction at the fact that the People's Republic of Bangladesh has become a full member of the United Nations and that an end has thus been put to an injustice with regard to that major Asian state.

The Soviet Union, which was one of the first countries to establish diplomatic relations with the Republic of Guinea-Bissau, welcomes its admission to the United Nations with great satisfaction. The Soviet Union also welcomes the admission to the United Nations of the newly independent state of Granada. Soon to come is the proclamation of the national independence of Mozambique. The current attempts to frustrate the process of decolonization that has begun in that country must be most resolutely rebuffed. That of course applies equally and fully to Angola. That will, indeed, be the crowning moment of the armed phase of the struggle for national liberation of the former Portuguese colonies, and will provide even further evidence of the irresistible march of social progress.

The year that has passed since the fascist coup in Chile has revealed the great depth of the tragedy that has befallen the Chilean people. But it has also demonstrated that endless terror and the suppression of elementary human rights cannot break the will of the people of Chile for a free and independent life. The bloody deeds of the junta are in glaring contradiction with the lofty humane principles and purposes of the United Nations, and are a challenge to human honour and decency.

It is no accident that the junta in fact remains in a state of international isolation.

The struggle for national independence and economic liberation and for the elimination of the vestiges of colonial systems has been scoring impressive victories in recent years. But that struggle is by no means ended. The manifestations of economic oppression and inequality and the fact that there are still dark blemishes of colonialism, apartheid and racial discrimination on earth cannot be tolerated. Until they disappear, the peace-loving states and the United Nations as a whole cannot slacken their efforts to eradicate them.

It is always necessary to identify the most topical issues among the great variety of problems posed by the course of world developments. At any given moment the efforts of states should be concentrated precisely upon these issues. It is the opinion of the Soviet Union that some of the high-priority tasks of today are the following:

—to proceed in practical terms to a Cyprus settlement; stop the violence against that country and its people; secure respect for the sovereignty, independence and territorial integrity of that state and, for those purposes, convene a representative international conference on Cyprus within the framework of the United Nations;

—to resume as a matter of urgency the work of the Geneva Peace Conference on the Middle East to solve questions concerning the establishment of a just and durable peace in that area;

—to conclude the Conference on Security and Co-operation in Europe at an early date by adopting, at the highest level, decisions ensuring a peaceful future for Europe;

—to achieve specific agreements in the Soviet–American Strategic Arms Limitation Talks, in the multilateral negotiations on the reduction of armed forces and armaments in Central Europe, and in the Committee on Disarmament;

—to take measures to implement the decisions of the sixth special session of the General Assembly of the United Nations on strengthening the economic independence of developing states.

No one would venture to claim that the solution of all these problems, and of others to which we have drawn the attention of this Assembly, is an easy task. But their solution is necessary and feasible, and all states really interested in developing peaceful and reasonable forms of international intercourse should work towards that end. The Soviet Union will be unstinting in its efforts to promote the establishment of durable and lasting peace on earth.

From a statement at the 29th
session of the UN General
Assembly, 25 September 1974

The 57th anniversary of the October Revolution. 6 November 1974

The Soviet people and all the working people in the world are now marking the glorious anniversary of the Great October Revolution. Fifty-seven years ago, the workers and peasants of Russia, led by the Party of Lenin, took power into their own hands and established the world's first state of working people.

There has been no other event in history which has exercised such a powerful impact on the entire course of world development as the Great October Socialist Revolution. Having radically changed the destiny of nations, it heralded the epoch of transition from capitalism to socialism and pointed the way to peace and progress.

At present, together with the Soviet people, the peoples of the fraternal socialist countries are marching under the banner of the October Revolution. Many of them recently observed notable anniversaries in their new life.

Closely connected with the October Revolution are the successes of the fighters against imperialism and colonial slavery, for freedom and national independence.

The cause of the October Revolution is a living cause near and dear to millions of working people on all continents. The experience of the October Revolution is a priceless treasure of the international working class. The holiday of the October Revolution is a festival of all progressive mankind.

The victory of the October Revolution meant not only a change of social system in one country. It heralded the decline of the entire world system based on exploitation, imperialist oppression, violence and wars. The era of the revolutionary transformations which have radically changed the aspect of the modern world dates from this victory.

At present, the world system of socialism, the international working class and all anti-imperialist forces have become the determining factor of world development. It is completely natural that the present positive changes in the world have become possible, thanks above all to the change in the correlation of forces in the international arena in favour of peace, democracy and socialism.

Karl Marx prophesied: 'In contrast to the old society, with its economic miseries and its political delirium, a new society is springing up whose international rule will be Peace . . . .' A just and democratic peace was the call addressed by the October Revolution, by the great Lenin to all nations and governments.

The Party of Communists carried the banner of Leninist foreign policy through all the difficulties and trials of those years when our country was alone in a capitalist encirclement. We marched with this banner through the fires of the Great Patriotic War, in the course of which the Soviet people and their glorious Armed Forces routed Hitler's military machine and brought the peoples of Europe freedom from fascist tyranny. Loyal to this banner, the Soviet state has firmly upheld the peace and security of nations throughout the post-war period.

Today, just as half a century ago, the foreign policy of the Soviet Union, which sprang from the Proletarian Revolution, is a class internationalist policy by its very nature. It protects the interests not only of the Soviet people and the peoples of the socialist countries but also embodies the interest in peace of the most advanced force on earth— the international working class, all the working people.

Pondering the serious positive changes taking place in the international situation, one may say without fear of exaggeration that in one way or another they are all connected with the implementation of the Peace Programme of the 24th CPSU Congress.

This programme, put forward by Leonid Brezhnev in the report of the CPSU Central Committee to the Congress and unanimously approved by the Congress, a programme we are carrying out jointly with the fraternal socialist countries, is a concentrated expression of the objective needs of social development, the objective needs of international life, the basic aims of the peace-loving policy of the socialist states in the present period. The great positive changes which have become possible as a result of the implementation of the Peace Programme are recognized by all now. And we can claim without reservation that this programme has exerted a profound influence on the entire international situation, inasmuch as it has armed all peace champions with definite ideas and set them definite tasks in the struggle for relaxing international tension and averting the menace of war.

Yet it was comparatively recently, a mere two or three years back, that some personalities abroad predicted the failure of the Peace Programme. Experience has mocked the prophecies of these sceptics.

Of course, an acute political struggle is proceeding in the world arena around the problems and tasks raised in this historic resolution of the 24th Congress. One could hardly have expected anything else. But the main thing is evident: the Peace Programme is being implemented successfully. The external conditions for the Soviet people's peaceful creative work are more favourable now than ever before.

In the struggle for peace and socialism, unprecedented in its scope, we are marching together with the fraternal socialist states, acting from common, concerted positions. The socialist community is an alliance in which the community of advanced ideology, the unity of aims and the working people's internationalist solidarity have merged. History has no other example of such unity!

Helping and supporting one another, the countries of socialism are enhancing the rates of their economic development. It is a well-known fact that the countries affiliated with the Council for Mutual Economic Assistance are the most dynamically developing group of states in the world. Close ties between the countries of the socialist community cover practically all the spheres of their Party and state activities. The Warsaw Treaty is a reliable shield for their security. The fraternal countries' political and military co-operation is being improved within its framework in the name of peace. Organically combining national interests with the interests of the entire community, the socialist states have accumulated valuable experience in the co-ordination of their foreign-policy activities.

The community countries have scored no little success by their joint efforts. One of the greatest achievements is the final establishment of the German Democratic Republic as an independent, sovereign state. The attempts by imperialist circles to hamper the formation of a new society on German soil have failed: for a quarter of a century now the GDR has been a reliable outpost of socialism on its Western frontiers.

This is a great victory for the people of the German Democratic Republic, a common victory of the countries of socialism!

Together with its friends and allies, the German Democratic Republic has marked its 25th anniversary. Present at this great celebration, common for all the socialist community, was our Party and government delegation with Leonid Brezhnev at the head. Together with the GDR leaders, we watched with emotion a grand march through the streets of socialist Berlin of many thousands of young people, of working men and women of the Republic, who demonstrated their loyalty to the ideals of socialism and peace.

We are sure that just as the imperialist policy of non-recognition of the GDR has failed, so the blockade of another socialist country, fraternal Cuba, will also crumble in the end.

The achievements of the countries of the socialist community, including their constant and stable economic growth, are in striking contrast to the present situation in the capitalist world.

Most capitalist states are gripped in the vice of severe inflation which increases as production is curtailed and unemployment grows in a number of countries. Currency upheavals are not subsiding and chaos in the energy field, which is frequently called (not without reason) an energy crisis, is growing in severity. All this is a great burden shouldered by the working sections of the population. Perhaps not since World War II has capitalism met with such economic difficulties.

They are doing their utmost in the West to discover the cause of the increasing phenomena of crisis, to invent a remedy for it. But these attempts are unsuccessful—and no wonder. The bourgeois politicians cannot or, to be more precise, do not want to tell the whole truth about the causes of these phenomena. Nothing is said about the irrefutable fact that the present difficulties are to a great extent a result of the militarization of the economy in a number of large capitalist countries, a result of the swelling of their military budgets. Hence, things hinge to a great extent on the policy of certain circles, a policy of building up armaments.

During the past few years the Soviet Union and the countries of the socialist community, acting in contact and co-operation with all progressive and peace-loving forces, have succeeded in steering the course of events in the direction of strengthening peace and asserting the Leninist principles of peaceful coexistence. There are good grounds for saying that the process of restructuring inter-state relations, which is traceable to the October Revolution, is gaining ever greater momentum in our day.

For understandable reasons better relations between the Soviet Union and the United States of America have special significance. In the course of the three Soviet–US summit meetings much has been done so that peaceful co-operation, and not confrontation and conflict, determines the nature of these relations. The Party is consistently working to make the development and improvement of relations between the USSR and the USA stable despite the opposing natures of the social systems and ideologies of the two countries.

The safeguarding and strengthening of peace is the main area where the interests of the Soviet, American and all other peoples coincide. It is on this basis that our agreements and treaties with the United States rest. This is true, above all, of the agreement on the prevention of nuclear war and the basic principles of mutual relations between the USSR and the USA.

The same holds for the co-ordinated steps of the two states towards the limitation of strategic offensive and defensive arms. Soviet–US talks on this important question are continuing. The Soviet Union seeks to bring about agreement between the two sides to exercise maximum restraint in deploying their strategic weapons. We stand for an agreement which would prevent a further race in these armaments both in terms of number and quality. But, of course, any agreement should accord with the principles of reciprocity and not impair our security.

Leonid Brezhnev and US President Gerald Ford are to meet near Vladivostok on 23–24 November. We think this meeting will be of great importance for the continued development of Soviet–US relations. For our part, we shall work towards this goal.

The Party constantly focuses its attention on questions related to the situation in Europe. Together with the other members of the Warsaw Treaty, we have done a great deal to effect a number of major foreign-policy moves which have led to a considerable improvement in the political climate on the European continent and to the assertion of political and territorial realities in Europe within the framework of the international law which emerged in the wake of the Second World War. Today conditions for co-operation between European states are much more favourable than they were in the past.

Relations between the Soviet Union and France have been on a good level for a considerable period of time. Rapprochement between them rests on a solid basis and is called upon to play an important part in European and world *détente*. Experience has proved on more than one occasion, especially at turning points in history, that the two countries and the two peoples stand in need of friendship and concord between each other. One may rest assured that the forthcoming visit of Leonid Brezhnev to France on 5–7 December will serve these goals.

The Soviet Union attaches great importance to its new relationship with the Federal Republic of Germany. The line adopted by the two states towards overcoming the grievous past and developing co-operation is fully justified from the viewpoint of both the interests of the USSR and the FRG, and the strengthening of peace and security in Europe as a whole. Further evidence of this is provided by the results of the recent talks in Moscow with Helmut Schmidt, Chancellor of the FRG, during which the major issues of the further development of political relations and economic co-operation between the two countries were considered.

As for the Soviet Union, it is prepared to shape its relations with the Federal Republic of Germany in earnest and for a long time.

Our well-established good relations with neighbouring Finland are a fine example of co-operation, which has been successfully advancing for three decades now.

Our country proves by its deeds that it is working for broad co-operation with all European states. We are actively involved in solving pressing political problems, in carrying out large-scale economic projects, and in expanding cultural exchanges and contacts. But the consolidation of the situation in Europe on a peaceful basis necessitates the combining of the development of bilateral relations with efforts aimed at ensuring security on a collective basis.

Above all, this includes the task of bringing the All-European Conference on Security and Co-operation in Helsinki to a successful conclusion. The peoples of Europe expect the conference to adopt at summit level important decisions which will make peace and security law in relations between states. Those leaders in the West who have not yet realized this and who hold petty considerations above lofty goals should give thought to the responsibility they take upon themselves by deliberately hampering the progress of the conference. Its positive outcome will ensure a more favourable atmosphere for the solution of other questions too, including the problem of reducing armed forces and armaments in Central Europe.

Speaking of the favourable changes in Europe in the current year, we note with satisfaction the establishment of normal, one may say friendly, relations with Portugal following the overthrow of the fascist dictatorship in that country.

Our relations with Greece have also changed for the better. The military fascist regime, which for years fettered the Greek people, has been toppled. This is a success for Greece's democratic and peace forces in whom the true friends of the Greek people never lost faith.

The shifts brought by *détente* have also substantially affected the Asian continent. The fraternal Vietnamese people, firmly supported by the Soviet Union, have won an impressive victory in the struggle against imperialist aggression. Our Party and our country have proved in practice their loyalty to internationalist duty. It is important now to bring the political settlement in Vietnam and throughout Indo-China to completion. It is necessary to make the Saigon regime give up its attempts to frustrate the implementation of the Paris Agreements, which should be strictly observed.

That the most acute problems can be solved at the negotiating table is convincingly shown by the continuing normalization on the Indian Subcontinent. The Soviet Union has greatly contributed to this normalization. We express satisfaction with the fact that the efforts of our country are highly spoken of by the states immediately concerned—India, with which our co-operation in the international arena has proved highly important for the cause of universal peace, and

Pakistan and Bangladesh, with which we have also established good relations.

Close friendly relations with India, a great Asian power, have become an important factor of peace in Asia and elsewhere. The range of Soviet–Indian co-operation is very wide. The Soviet state will continue to do everything in its power to make this co-operation grow stronger and expand.

Since Lenin's day firm friendship has linked the Soviet Union and our neighbour, Afghanistan, a state which has been consistently pursuing a neighbourly line with our country and firmly adhering to the policy of non-alignment.

Our country seeks to develop neighbourly relations with Japan not only in the economic, but also in the political field. It is now up to Japan to show its readiness in this matter.

The need for dependable security in Asia through the joint efforts of the countries of that continent is urgently knocking at the door. We are not inclined to play down the difficulties on this road, but life itself demands that the Asian states jointly work out a system of security which will deliver the peoples of Asia from war and aggression.

One of the most distinctive features of the present-day situation is that, through the efforts of the Soviet Union and the fraternal socialist countries, the principles of peaceful coexistence are gaining ever wider ground in inter-state relations. These principles are not only being applied in international practice, but established legally in a whole series of agreements between states with different social systems.

Since Lenin's day our country has waged and will continue to wage the struggle to relieve mankind of the burden of arms. We reject the subtle web of false arguments with which the opponents of disarmament are entangling the people's minds. The success or failure of disarmament depends on the policy of states, and above all on the policy of big powers. But it is known that not all of them come out for an end to the arms race.

The Soviet Union has on many occasions submitted for consideration to the relevant international forums proposals for disarmament, including those for general and complete disarmament.

At the present time the UN General Assembly is considering the new initiative of the Soviet Union as regards the prohibition on influencing the environment for military purposes. This important proposal has already met with extensive international support.

As topical as before is the problem of taking effective steps to prevent the further proliferation of nuclear weapons. The Soviet Union will continue making efforts in this direction.

In the conditions of the continued arms race and the incessant intrigues of the forces of imperialist reaction and aggression, our Party, its Central Committee and the Soviet Government devote and will devote unflagging attention to enhancing the defence might of the Soviet Union. Expressing the will of the entire Soviet people, the Party will continue to do everything to fully and reliably protect the security of our country and that of our friends and allies.

The principled course of the CPSU and the Soviet Government of support for the peoples struggling for national liberation and political and economic independence has been going on since the days of the October Revolution. This policy underlies our co-operation with many developing states of Asia, Africa and Latin America. Where colonialism still manages to retain its position, the peoples fighting against it know that they have the effective support of the Soviet Union.

Co-operation between the socialist and developing states is also growing in the international arena. We act jointly on the majority of important problems. This expands the basis of the common anti-imperialist front in favour of *détente* and opens up better opportunities for the advance of both the cause of peace and the national liberation struggle.

The practice of our days shows numerous examples of the active influence of the developing countries on the solution of international problems. With the support of the socialist states, they are upholding their legitimate rights and interests ever more successfully.

At present it can already be said that the last hour of the last colonial empire has struck. We hail the patriots of Guinea-Bissau, Mozambique and Angola who for many years have been waging a struggle for the freedom and independence of their peoples and who have scored great successes in this struggle. As regards Guinea-Bissau, that country has already been admitted to the United Nations and has met with wide international recognition.

In his recent speech L. I. Brezhnev noted: 'The successes achieved in the struggle for *détente* are undoubtedly considerable, but we must not rest content with that. International life brings forward new problems, while many old ones are far from solved.'

We should not shut our eyes to the fact that there still exist influential forces which would like to turn the world back to the time of the 'cold war'. This is why all who treasure the peace and security of nations should show high vigilance and rally their ranks in the struggle for peace.

Through the fault of the NATO militaristic circles, the destiny of Cyprus has become the object of the military and political machinations of this bloc. On the Cyprus question the Soviet Union and its friends keep to a consistent position which enjoys respect in the world. We are struggling for that state to remain independent and territorially intact and we stand firmly for an end to foreign interference in the domestic affairs of Cyprus, for the withdrawal of all foreign troops from its territory, and for the Cypriots being given an opportunity to solve their domestic affairs themselves.

The situation in the Middle East remains, as before, complicated and dangerous.

With the support of its protectors Israel is trying to retain the Arab lands seized as a result of aggression. Chauvinistic intoxication has apparently not yet passed in Tel Aviv, which is clearly putting its trust in the force of arms. But this is a great miscalculation fraught with grave danger, and not least of all for Israel itself.

The Soviet Union is ceaselessly working for a just and lasting peace in the Middle East. This, however, cannot be achieved as long as Israel holds the occupied Arab territories and the legitimate national rights of the Arab people of Palestine are not ensured. Nobody can deny the Palestinian Arabs' legitimate right to self-determination, including national statehood. The Soviet Union has rendered and will render support to the Arab peoples, the people of Palestine included, in their just struggle. The USSR is for the immediate resumption of the work of the Geneva Peace Conference.

All progressive mankind angrily protests against the atrocities of the Chilean military which conducts a policy of terror against its own people. One may rest assured, however, that the freedom-loving people of Chile have not yet had their last say. On their side is the fraternal solidarity and support of the Soviet people.

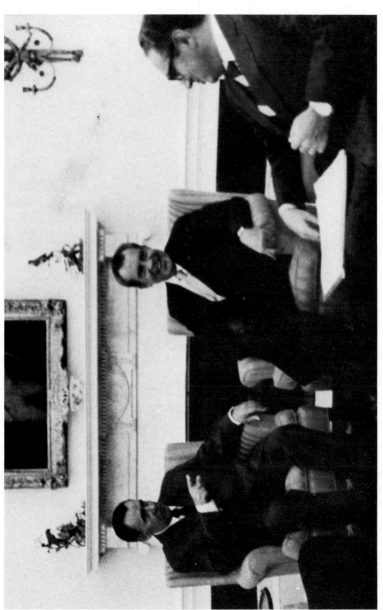

PLATE 22. In the White House: with Richard Nixon and Henry Kissinger, 1973.

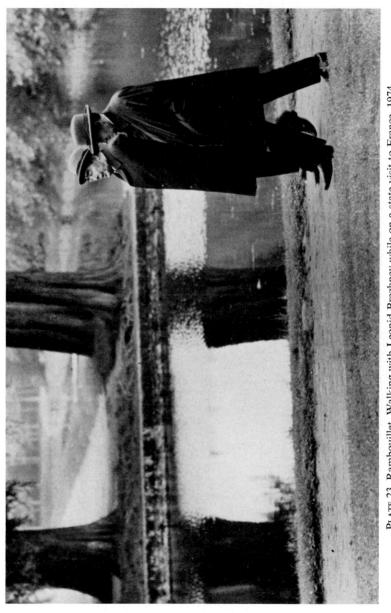

PLATE 23. Rambouillet. Walking with Leonid Brezhnev while on a state visit to France, 1974.

PLATE 24. Arriving in Paris on a state visit. Brezhnev and Gromyko have been met by Giscard d'Estaing.

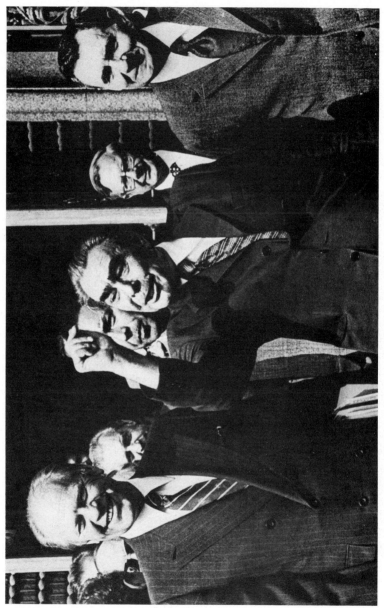

PLATE 25. The Helsinki Conference, July 1973. Gerald Ford, Leonid Brezhnev, Gromyko.

PLATE 26. Kissinger, Brezhnev, Ford and Gromyko at the Helsinki Conference.

PLATE 27. Brezhnev and Gromyko at a meeting with the French delegation to the Helsinki Conference, headed by Giscard d'Estaing.

PLATE 28. Gromyko at the Helsinki Conference.

PLATE 29. The Helsinki Conference. The Soviet delegation: Brezhnev, Gromyko, Chernyenko.

PLATE 30. A visit to Great Britain. Being met by Mr Callaghan on arrival in London, March 1976.

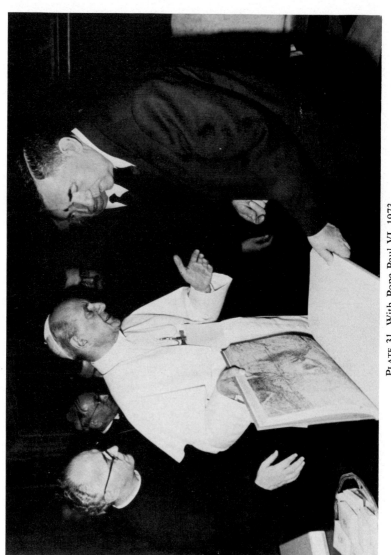

PLATE 31. With Pope Paul VI, 1973.

PLATE 32. A visit to Italy. Gromyko with his wife while on a visit to Italy, February 1973.

PLATE 33. A visit to India: with Morarji Desai, April 1977.

PLATE 34. A visit to West Germany. Arrival at the airport with Leonid Brezhnev for
a state visit to West Germany, 4 May 1978.

PLATE 35. Meeting with Helmut Schmidt during Brezhnev's visit to West Germany, 4–7 May 1978.

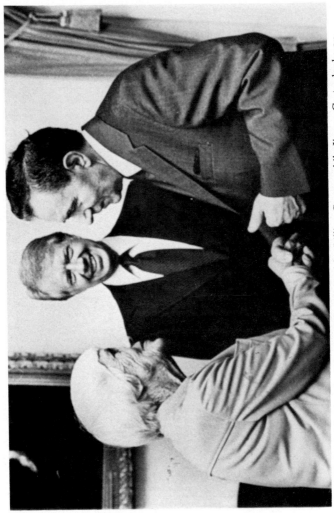

PLATE 36. Meeting the Carters. Being greeted by Lillian Carter, while Jimmy Carter looks on. Washington, September 1978.

PLATE 37. In the White House. Meeting Jimmy Carter.

PLATE 38. With US Secretary of State Cyrus Vance and Leonid Brezhnev.
Moscow, March 1978.

PLATE 39. Gromyko with his wife, Lidia Dmitrievna,
and grandchildren, Andrei and Aleksei.

PLATE 40. With his wife.

PLATE 41. Gromyko with his grandson Andrei.

The Soviet people resolutely demand that an end be put to the bestialities of the junta and that the Chilean patriots languishing in prisons, including Luis Corvalan, a faithful son of the Chilean people, be freed.

The present-day leadership of China has joined the opponents of international *détente*. It has subjugated its policy to the struggle against the Soviet Union and the socialist community, and is trying to interfere with the development of peaceful international co-operation. Our Party has given and will continue to give a rebuff to these actions of Peking aimed at merging with extreme right-wing imperialist reaction. At the same time, we shall, as before, strive for the normalization of Soviet–Chinese relations and do everything possible for the restoration of relations of friendship between the Soviet Union and the People's Republic of China. We proceed from the fact that this meets the vital interests of both the Soviet and the Chinese peoples.

Despite the stubborn resistance of reaction, the revolutionary transformation of the world initiated by the October Revolution is proceeding steadily, is developing and strengthening.

Every day lived by mankind confirms the correctness of Lenin's words to the effect that 'The basic reason for this tremendous acceleration of world development is that hundreds of millions of new people have been drawn into it'.

There is a growing movement of the public forces, classes and parties which are stubbornly struggling for peace and social progress. A vivid proof of this are the class battles which are growing in scale in the capitalist countries.

In the vanguard of this struggle is its tested leader, the world communist movement.

Fidelity to Marxism–Leninism and unity in the struggle against imperialism constitute the invincible strength of the world communist movement.

All this makes us confident of future even greater class victories for the working people of the entire world.

The CPSU, jointly with the other fraternal Parties, is exerting and will continue to exert every effort so that the cohesion of the communist ranks will grow and strengthen on the principled basis of Marxism–Leninism. This is a behest of Lenin, and the Party undeviatingly follows and will continue to follow it.

F

Struggling for universal peace and the security of peoples, the Party fulfils its internationalist duty to the international communist and working-class movement and to the peoples of the whole world. Its profoundly principled and lofty foreign policy is unanimously approved by the Soviet people.

'Along the road of the October revolution—towards new victories for the cause of communism and peace.' From a report at the meeting devoted to the 57th anniversary of the Great October Socialist Revolution, 6 November 1974

Part 3: 1975–78

Ratification of the Convention on Biological Weapons. 11 February 1975

Today the Presidium of the Supreme Soviet of the USSR is examining the International Convention on the Prohibition of the Development, Production, and Accumulation of Stockpiles of Bacteriological (Biological) and Toxic Weapons and on Their Destruction, unanimously approved by the Foreign Affairs Commissions of both chambers of the USSR Supreme Soviet on 3 February of this year.

The question of banning bacteriological weapons has received considerable attention in recent years on account of the enormous danger of these kinds of weapons of mass destruction for human life.

As a result of the tireless efforts of the USSR and other socialist countries an understanding was reached at the talks in the Disarmament Committee on a total ban on bacteriological weapons as the first step towards the final settlement of the problem of chemical and bacteriological weapons. In March 1971 the socialist countries submitted to that Committee a draft Convention on the Prohibition of the Development, Production, and Accumulation of Stockpiles of Bacteriological (Biological) and Toxic Weapons and on Their Destruction. That draft was used as the basis for the convention that was approved by the UN General Assembly in December 1971 and opened for signature in April 1972.

The convention clearly records the commitment of the signatory states never and under no circumstances to develop, produce, accumulate, or in any other way acquire, or preserve microbiological or any other biological agents or toxins, whatever their origin or method of manufacture, of such kinds or in quantities designated not for prophylactic, protective, or other peaceful purposes. The ban thus covers all biological agents and toxins without exception that may be used as a weapon.

The convention is an important step towards the prohibition of chemical weapons as well. In it is formulated the obligation of the signatory states to continue talks on the achievement of an agreement banning chemical weapons in the immediate future in a spirit of goodwill.

The convention now before the Presidium of the USSR Supreme Soviet provides for the total abolition of a weapon of mass destruction, namely the bacteriological weapon. This is its distinction from all the agreements on disarmament signed hitherto.

The conclusion of this convention creates favourable conditions for the signing of further agreements on an effective ban on other kinds of weapons of mass destruction, and for further efforts to relax the arms race and achieve disarmament.

Addressing an election meeting in Moscow's Bauman Electoral District on 14 June 1974, Leonid Brezhnev said: 'We are working tirelessly for real progress in the field of disarmament. The advocates of the arms drive argue that limiting arms, to say nothing of reducing them, means taking a risk. But as a matter of fact, it is an immeasurably greater risk to continue the unrestrained stockpiling of arms. Proceeding from this we have again and again called on all states, all governments to put an end to the arms drive and to begin to advance to the great goal—universal and complete disarmament.'

> *From a speech at a meeting of the Presidium of the USSR Supreme Soviet on the question of the ratification of the Convention on the Prohibition of the Development, Production, and Accumulation of Stockpiles of Bacteriological (Biological) and Toxic Weapons and on Their Destruction, 11 February 1975*

Meeting the voters of the Kaliningrad Electoral District, Moscow. 2 June 1975

Our Party has always given close attention to questions of the international situation and foreign policy. The 24th Congress of the CPSU adopted the Peace Programme, which is historic for the tasks outlined in it.

Throughout the period that has elapsed since then our Party and our country have concentrated their main effort on carrying out this Programme to the fullest extent.

The basic orientation of all the Soviet Union's foreign policy actions is self-evident.

These actions are aimed at one and the same objective, but from different directions. Their purpose is to ensure favourable external conditions for the building of communism in our country, still further consolidate the Soviet Union's international position and the position of our allies and friends, and preserve and consolidate world peace.

By championing peace and pursuing a policy of peace vigorously and consistently we are carrying out a task of world-wide significance, for there is no nation that wants war.

Together with other countries of the socialist community and all the peace forces we are fighting the menace of another war. The fraternal Parties and countries are co-ordinating the main orientations of their foreign policy and their concrete foreign policy initiatives.

The urgent problems of the world situation and our approach to them are systematically discussed at sittings of the Warsaw Treaty Political Consultative Committee and at other meetings of the leaders of the fraternal Parties and states. Every such meeting makes our common policy more effective.

This year, 1975, sees a noteworthy anniversary of the Warsaw Treaty Organization. Twenty years ago the socialist countries of Europe set up a defensive alliance in the true sense of the word and undertook mutual obligations to guarantee the inviolability of their frontiers and territories.

This Treaty's member-states are effectively fulfilling their obligations. The security of each of them and of the alliance as a whole is dependably safeguarded and our people may be certain of this.

It is safeguarded by the economic potential of the socialist community.

It is safeguarded by the armed forces of the fraternal countries, which are protecting the peaceful labour and peaceful life of their peoples.

It is safeguarded by the energetic, firm and, at the same time, peaceful foreign policy of the socialist countries.

Communists and the entire Soviet people have a right to express satisfaction over the fact that our foreign policy, which is a class, principled policy, is assessed highly throughout the world.

Of course, this is not the assessment of those who would like to reverse developments to the days of the cold war, of those who think of international developments in no context other than that of whipping up tension.

It is the assessment of those who are concerned with the destinies of peace.

Our foreign policy is called Leninist precisely because it is permeated with ideas of friendship among nations. For this reason the peoples outside the socialist community regard as their own the aims pursued by the community.

Thousands of kilometres separate us from African countries, most of which have squared their shoulders and won independence only some 15–20 years ago, from Latin American states, and from many states in Asia. But even in the most distant parts of the world our policy of peace, its profound humanism, and its condemnation of the intrigues of imperialist reaction and aggression, have won profound respect for the Land of Lenin, for the Soviet Communist Party.

Only recently our people, the peoples of fraternal socialist countries, and practically the whole world marked the thirtieth anniversary of the defeat of Nazi Germany. Once again Soviet people bent their heads to the memory of the millions of their fellow-countrymen who gave their lives in the battle against fascism.

At the same time, we reaffirmed with redoubled force our determination to do everything in our power to prevent the tragedy of war from ever overcoming mankind again.

Every Soviet citizen, every decent person in the world was stirred by Leonid Brezhnev's speech at the meeting in Moscow to mark the thirtieth anniversary of the Soviet people's victory in the Great Patriotic War. 'The struggle for peace', he said, 'continues, and it should have neither respite nor pause.'

These are fine words and they aptly mirror the essence of affairs, the urgency of the tasks facing us.

Our country marked the thirtieth anniversary of the Great Victory in a situation where the foreign policy efforts of the CPSU and the Soviet Government are yielding tangible results. The most important of these is that this is the fourth decade in succession that the Soviet people have been free of war and have enjoyed a peaceful life, which is the most valuable blessing of man. This is in itself a significant achievement of our Party, of our whole people.

Moreover, it is of colossal international importance because it reinforces the confidence of nations that peace can be successfully upheld, that the threat of another war can be removed from mankind.

Everybody can see the positive changes taking place on the European continent. Together with the fraternal parties of other countries, the CPSU sets the aim of creating a situation of durable and lasting peace in Europe. Step by step we are making quite good progress towards this aim, although many difficult problems remain to be settled.

Among the factors that have led to the changed situation in Europe, a special place is held by the treaty concluded in 1970 by the Soviet Union and the FRG, and the relevant treaties signed with that country by Poland, the GDR, and Czechoslovakia.

The core of these treaties is the principle that the frontiers that have taken shape in Europe as a result of the Second World War are inviolable. There is no need to dwell at length on the significance of this. The recognition of the present political and territorial realities in Europe in international law is an achievement that speaks for itself.

This is a triumph not only of the Soviet Union and other socialist countries, but also of the forces of realism and peace in the FRG, and of all the European peoples who earnestly want peace and genuine security.

We can note with satisfaction that today the Soviet Union's relations with many West European states are developing successfully. In our relations with France the policy of co-operation and accord in the interests of *détente* has for many years been beneficially influencing the situation not only in Europe but also outside it.

Our relations with Britain, Italy, the Scandinavian countries, and some other states in Western Europe are also improving.

The Helsinki Conference has become a major landmark in Europe's conversion into a continent of lasting peace. The Soviet Union and its allies and friends are doing their utmost to bring this undertaking, unprecedented in European history, to a successful conclusion in the common interests, I repeat, in the common interests of peaceful development in Europe.

Soviet people know what significant changes have taken place in recent years in our relations with the USA, and how important these changes are to the Soviet and American peoples, and to the cause of world peace. These changes are the result, above all, of a series of summit talks between the Soviet Union and the United States.

The Vladivostok meeting between Leonid Brezhnev and US President Gerald Ford has been extremely useful from that angle. Important understandings were reached at that meeting on questions of bilateral Soviet–US relations and on some world problems.

The two sides are now working on the fulfilment of these understandings, including, above all, those that concern the limitation of strategic arms.

Much else has been accomplished during these years in the struggle for peace, in extinguishing flashpoints of tension, and in halting aggression wherever it has been unleashed.

Here note must be made, first and foremost, of the great victory of the Vietnamese people, whose courage and staunchness have won the admiration of the whole world. True to its internationalist duty, the Soviet Union has unswervingly given its help and assistance to the just cause of the fraternal Vietnamese people.

Under incredibly difficult conditions the patriots of Vietnam held on high the torch of freedom and independence throughout the period of their struggle for their country's liberation, carrying it through all hardship and privation to final victory.

Significant successes have been achieved in the struggle for peace and *détente*, and the Soviet Union and its Leninist foreign policy have unquestionably played a leading part in this.

The Soviet Union, its friends and allies, and all the other peace forces will have to make a larger effort than ever before to ensure truly lasting peace and make the present positive processes aimed at achieving *détente* and preventing another war ultimately irreversible.

This is a task of immense importance, and it is by no means a simple and easy one. There still are circles who during the long period of the arms race have grown accustomed to the clang of weapons coming off the production line, and who would much rather count the additional billions assigned for military purposes. However, it may be stated quite definitely that the political course steered by these circles conflicts with the dictates of the times, with the just demands of the peoples.

The CPSU and its Central Committee are directing the Soviet people towards greater achievements in international affairs and towards upholding the Soviet Union's interests on the international scene firmly and resolutely.

For us the struggle to end the arms race, reduce military budgets, and use the colossal material and human resources wasted on weapons production for promoting the material welfare of people and building dwellings, schools, and hospitals remains a pressing task in international affairs.

But as long as the arms race lasts and as long as there are forces seeking to bring the world back to the old road of tension—and everybody knows that such forces exist in the West and in the East—the Soviet Union and its Warsaw Treaty allies consider that their sacred duty is to strengthen their defence capability.

Our successes in foreign affairs are achieved not only at the negotiating table with our partners. They are achieved primarily by the workers at the factories, by the efforts of the collective farmers, by the intelligence and knowledge of our scientists, engineers, and technicians, by the labour of all our people, by the might of our socialist economy.

Achievements in communist construction, the ideological cohesion of the Communist Party and the entire Soviet people, the enhancement of the Societ Union's defence capability, and the successful fulfilment of five-year plans are the sure way to success in international politics as well.

Our successes in the building of communism and in foreign policy are due to the titanic creative work of our Party and its Leninist Headquarters (we can use that word in its highest sense)—the Central Committee of the CPSU and the Politburo headed by Leonid Brezhnev.

Everybody knows of the outstanding part played by Leonid Brezhnev in foreign and domestic affairs. Through his many-sided work he expresses the thought and will of our Party and people. This explains the profound respect he enjoys not only from Soviet people, both communists and non-party people, but also from millions upon millions of people abroad.

The Soviet Union will continue pursuing its anti-imperialist policy of safeguarding the legitimate rights of peoples, large and small, its policy of opposing aggression and the threat of aggression, of uprooting the remnants of colonialism and racism.

The Soviet Government will continue its policy of promoting co-operation with all countries with a different social system in keeping with the principles of peaceful coexistence.

As before, in its foreign policy our Party will continue giving priority to consolidating the might and unity of the socialist community, which is the decisive force in the struggle for peace among nations.

Speech at a meeting with electors
of the Kaliningrad Electoral
District, Moscow, 2 June 1975

The 30th session of the UN General Assembly. 23 September 1975

This year will remain in the memory of the peoples as the year of the conclusion of the Helsinki Conference on Security and Co-operation in Europe. The Final Act of the Conference, to which the signatures of the top leaders of 33 European countries, the United States of America and Canada were affixed, is a most outstanding document of our time.

The peoples of Europe to a very large extent pinned on the Conference the hope that the European continent would be able, at last, to break out of the vicious circle of its history, where every post-war period turned into a pre-war period, to be followed by a war unleashed by aggressors. The peoples of Europe expected that the Conference would work out and adopt important decisions in the interests of their security and agree on the main directions for equal and versatile co-operation. Everywhere in Europe people wished the Conference to succeed.

The participants in the Conference succeeded through intense and collective effort in achieving important results, which have been clearly recorded in the Final Act.

This concerns, above all, the political sphere—the working out of principles governing relations among the participating states. Provided they are strictly observed by all states, the threat of war will be excluded from the life of the peoples of Europe and an atmosphere of trust in the peaceful development of each country will come into being on the continent.

This is also true and applicable with regard to the measures for stability and confidence agreed on at the Conference, which are designed to promote a reduction of the risk of armed conflicts in Europe.

A positive role is to be played by the understandings reached at the Conference on co-operation in the fields of trade, large-scale industrial projects, science and technology, and the protection of the environment.

A substantial contribution to the development of co-operation between the states participating in the Conference are the understandings on questions of co-operation in the fields of culture, information, contacts and education, and their significance will be ever increasingly felt as *détente* deepens and develops.

It is not without a sense of satisfaction that I note that the success of the Conference was largely facilitated by the efforts of the socialist countries which invariably seek to switch international relations on to the track of peaceful coexistence. This success became possible also because in Western countries the well-founded conviction is gaining strength that it is necessary to adopt a constructive approach to the solution of problems that arise in Europe instead of aggravating and inflaming the situation, which in the past often reached dangerous levels.

The understandings reached as a result of the Conference are based on the recognition by all its participants of the absolute truth that respect for the sovereign equality of states, the non-use of force, the inviolability of frontiers, territorial integrity, non-intervention from outside in the internal affairs of states, as well as other basic principles, are laws which no one may transgress.

What are the implications of the result of this joint work of thirty-five states for the peoples of Europe and indeed of the entire world?

The answer is provided by the experience of the past, when a desire to seize others' territories and brutal force raised to the level of state policy acquired the character of criminal claims to world domination and developed into the brown plague of fascism, racism, direct aggression and the tragedy of world wars. Now the thirty-five states which took part in the Conference have assumed, jointly and before the whole world, the obligation to build their relations on the principles of peace, and peace alone, and of deeper co-operation.

The results of the Conference constitute a carefully weighed balance of the interests of all its participants, and they reflect generally acceptable understandings and well-founded compromises. We have every reason to state that the experience of the Conference will be used most extensively for the settlement in general of the pressing problems of today.

In short, as was stressed by Leonid Brezhnev in his speech at Helsinki:

'The results of the prolonged negotiations are such that there are neither victors nor vanquished, neither winners nor losers. This is a victory for reason. Everyone has won—countries of the East and of the West, the peoples of socialist states, parties to alliances and neutrals, large and small. This is a gain for all people who hold dear the cause of peace and security on our planet.'

Assessing highly the results of the Conference, the Soviet Union believes that the main task now is to translate the understandings reached into deeds, and to advance towards new milestones in the struggle for a lasting peace. This is the course the Soviet Union follows and will continue to follow, and this is what we also expect others to do.

Who would argue that the year 1975 will go down in history as the year of the triumph of the just cause of the peoples of Indo-China? Triumph crowned their liberation struggle that had been carried on for almost thirty years against colonialists and aggression.

Those people sustained tremendous losses, but their will for freedom was never broken. The victory won by the peoples of Indo-China is above all the result of their own efforts. At the same time, it is also a major and universal success for all the peace-loving and progressive forces which invariably demonstrated their solidarity with the struggle of the patriots of Vietnam, Laos and Cambodia, and provided them with moral and material support.

The Soviet Union—as the whole world knows—has fulfilled its internationalist duty to the Vietnamese people. It has sought persistently the elimination in Indo-China of one of the most dangerous hot-beds of war to have troubled international relations.

The lessons of Indo-China are simple and obvious. The struggle of peoples for freedom, national independence and social progress is invincible. It cannot be destroyed by bullets or fire. The outcome of many years of conflict in Indo-China is a convincing case in point. It is also clear that any attempt to dictate or to impose one's will on other peoples by force of arms is untenable and in the final account doomed to failure.

This is a good lesson, in the sense that the policy of acting from 'positions of strength', which has now been rejected also at the conference table in Helsinki, should be relegated to the archives of history, never to be revived.

The radical change in the state of affairs in Indo-China creates more favourable prerequisites for establishing peaceful co-operation in Asia as a whole. Practical steps in this direction would serve the interests of the settlement of urgent problems and the strengthening of security throughout the continent of Asia, which of course requires, as in Europe, collective efforts by all states concerned, both large and small. And it is through such efforts, and subject to strict compliance with the principles of equality and non-use of force in any guise in resolving disputes between states, that the most effective solution to the problem of Asian security can be found. Let no one think that the Soviet Union would benefit from such a turn of events in Asia to a greater extent than some other states. Not at all; objectively, all countries of Asia are equally interested in this.

The Soviet Union continues to consolidate friendly relations with developing countries with which we are united by a common desire for peace and progress. We have invariably rendered and will continue to render support to the countries of Asia, Africa and Latin America and to the movement of non-aligned states in their struggle to consolidate their national sovereignty and economic independence, to overcome the grim legacy of the colonial past, and against intrigues aimed at undermining their independence and infringing upon their legitimate rights.

Step by step the countries of Asia, Africa and Latin America are freeing themselves of the consequences of the cold war and its political distortions. In this respect the decision of Latin American states to put an end to the policy of boycotting socialist Cuba, a policy imposed upon them, was an important event.

It is quite natural that it should be precisely in the present-day situation that the last pillars of colonialism, built up over centuries, are falling down. Quite recently, Mozambique, Cape Verde, Sao Tomé and Principe, the Comoros and Papua New Guinea have joined the ranks of independent states. Our country welcomes the victory of the just cause of their peoples.

We congratulate the representatives present in this hall of the Republic of Cape Verde, the Democratic Republic of Sao Tomé and Principe, and the People's Republic of Mozambique which have become fully-fledged members of our Organization.

Of course, the completion of decolonization is not proceeding without difficulties. The events in Angola, for example, testify to this. The forces hostile to the liberation struggle of peoples do not surrender their positions without fighting. They sometimes find accomplices also among those who like to pose as zealous champions of the good of oppressed peoples while in practice they are in collusion with the oppressors.

But in spite of all difficulties, the struggle for the elimination of the vestiges of colonialism, for the uprooting of racism, is now closer to final victory than ever before.

The states of Asia, Africa and Latin America constitute a great and active force in world politics, and this imposes on them a grave responsibility for the state of affairs in the world. We view with understanding the fact that these countries, still suffering from the consequences of exploitation, discrimination and economic coercion, are today participating in the work of putting forward and elaborating proposals to establish such international economic relations as would be based on equality and justice.

Thus, the past year has been marked by significant international events of a positive nature. It is not for us, the socialist states, to underestimate the significance of successes in the international arena. Their contribution to the struggle for those successes is common knowledge.

At the same time, one should be clearly conscious of the fact that *détente* is not a process which develops by its own momentum. For *détente* to move ahead, ever new impulses must be given it. A continuous day-to-day struggle must be conducted for it in international forums and from parliamentary rostrums. Each state, each Government, should realize that it can and should make its own contribution to *détente*.

We deem it necessary to state this from the rostrum of the United Nations because, as facts prove, it would be wrong to underestimate the resistance of the enemies of *détente*. Designs dangerous to the cause of international co-operation continue to originate in their camp. And in this connection no small arsenal of means is put into action, ranging from the direct use of force against other countries and peoples to demagoguery which exploits the tenacity of the cold-war dogmas and sows doubts as to the benefits of *détente* for all peoples.

The same forces which once in the past sought to thwart the convening of the Helsinki Conference, and later on tried to prevent it from succeeding, attempt to question the effectiveness of its results. However, the problem does not only lie in tendentious propaganda campaigns against *détente* and international actions aimed at deepening it; what is even more dangerous is the continuous policy of interference which endangers the independence of states, even though such a policy may be camouflaged by words in defence of the ideals of freedom and democracy. Two years ago this policy paved the way for the bloody fascist coup in Chile. Today almost the same methods are used to exacerbate the situation concerning some other countries.

The world is deeply concerned over the blatant attempts to bring outside pressure to bear on Portugal, clearly made with the intent to compel the Portuguese people to abandon their chosen road of free development. In the interests of solving the complex political and economic problems faced by Portugal a calm situation with regard to that country is required. No one can be allowed to flout the inalienable right of the Portuguese people to determine their destiny independently and without outside interference. Such is the position on which the Soviet Union has proceeded and will continue to proceed.

All participants in this world forum of states would probably agree that one of the main tasks in the international sphere remains the elimination of the hot-beds of armed conflict. One need not dwell on the gravity of the threat when in this or that hot-bed the conflict suddenly flares up and again produces a crisis. The world has repeatedly faced such a turn of events and knows full well how hard it is to put out the flames of war.

This, above all, concerns the Middle East, where a dangerous situation has persisted for many years.

To establish a just and lasting peace in the Middle East in the interests of all the states of the area and peoples inhabiting it, it is necessary that Israeli forces be withdrawn from all the Arab territories occupied by them in 1967; to ensure the legitimate rights of the Arab people of Palestine, including their right to establish their own state; to guarantee the rights of all the countries of the Middle East to independent development.

The main problems of the Middle East are still awaiting solution. The appropriate machinery for their examination is there—the Geneva Peace Conference. The Soviet Union stands for the reconvening of the Conference with the participation of all—and we stress 'all'—parties concerned, including representatives of the Palestine Liberation Organization. It will be recalled that the twenty-ninth session of the General Assembly reaffirmed by an overwhelming majority the right of the Arab people of Palestine to self-determination and national sovereignty. The solution of the Palestine problem is an integral part of an over-all settlement in the Middle East. Today this is axiomatic and politicians cannot pretend that they do not see it.

The Soviet Union is ready to continue to do everything so that the Middle East may become an area of lasting and durable peace. That is what we want to see above all in the Middle East, an area adjacent to the southern borders of our country.

The Soviet Union consistently pursues a policy of friendship with the Arab countries, which are defending a just cause. This friendship is deeply engrained and we do not believe that anyone will succeed in undermining it. The Soviet Union will continue to do everything in its power to consolidate this friendship on the basis of justice and principle.

The Soviet Union has consistently come out in defence of the independence and the territorial integrity of the Republic of Cyprus, for the withdrawal of all foreign troops from the island, and for the settlement of the internal matters of their state by the two communities, Greek and Turkish, themselves. In other words, we are for the implementation of the well-known United Nations decisions on Cyprus. It is only on such a basis that a just settlement of the Cyprus problem and the elimination of this hot-bed of tension will be possible.

The precarious state of armistice obviously does not ensure the stabilization of the state of affairs on the Korean peninsula. The need to create conditions for establishing durable peace on the Korean peninsula and speeding up the peaceful reunification of Korea has long been pressing. Those goals would be served by the cessation of outside interference in the internal affairs of the Korean people and, in the first place, the withdrawal from South Korea of all foreign troops stationed there under the United Nations flag, as well as by the conclusion of a peace treaty. It is the duty of the United Nations to assist in every possible way in taking such steps.

Hardly anyone would dispute the fact that everything that has been achieved in the field of disarmament so far represents but the first steps. Indeed, mankind so far has been unable to check the arms race or even substantially to slow down its pace. It goes on in the direction both of developing ever more destructive means of warfare and of building up the total volume of armaments.

The Soviet Union is convinced that in the situation of a relaxation of tensions in the world the prerequisites have been created for the implementation of effective measures which would end the arms race. In other words, it is now not only necessary but also possible to supplement political *détente* with military *détente*. The states participating in the Helsinki Conference unanimously pronounced themselves in favour of this in the Final Act.

The Review Conference of the Parties to the Treaty on the Non-proliferation of Nuclear Weapons held last May in Geneva came out for the implementation of broad measures for the limitation of the arms race and for disarmament. It is precisely such specific steps towards easing the burden of armaments that become the touchstone for testing the genuine readiness of states and governments to pursue the course of peace.

The struggle for disarmament has always been and continues to be an integral part of the foreign policy line of the Soviet Union. The USSR is a permanent and active participant in negotiations on various aspects of the disarmament problem.

We attach great importance to the lessening of military confrontation in areas where it is especially dangerous. Now, following the conclusion of the Helsinki Conference, one of the primary tasks is to find ways towards agreement on the reduction of armed forces and armaments in Central Europe, without infringing the security of anyone. The Soviet Union will contribute in every way to the success of the talks on this problem currently under way in Vienna.

Within the framework of the United Nations we have on more than one occasion already stated in detail our position on disarmament questions. And we have not merely stated it. The Soviet Union has put forward a large number of specific proposals many of which have formed the basis of important decisions adopted by the United Nations. We have consistently supported their implementation. This applies in particular to the resolution of the twenty-seventh session of the General Assembly on the non-use of force in international relations and the simultaneous permanent prohibition on the use of nuclear weapons.

Another question raised by the Soviet Union—the reduction of the military budgets of permanent members of the UN Security Council—also retains the utmost importance.

We consider it important to conclude speedily an international convention on the prohibition of military or any other hostile use of techniques to influence the environment.

In the field of disarmament, as in other matters, the Soviet Union adopts a realistic approach. It is constantly seeking areas of disarmament and arms-race limitation in which it is feasible to find commonly acceptable agreements.

At the same time, we have never overlooked the main objective—general and complete disarmament. We are of the view that this problem should be in the forefront of attention of a world disarmament conference. The United Nations has already approved the idea of convening it. In that forum all countries of the world could, on an equal footing and freely, set out and compare their positions and outline ways and means of limiting and arresting the arms race.

The USSR is a consistent champion of the use of science exclusively for peaceful purposes and in the interests of mankind and is prepared for wide, large-scale co-operation in the sphere of science and technology with all states interested in this.

However, the experience of the past shows that achievements in science and technology can be used for dangerous, even criminal purposes.

With today's rapid development of science and technology in various countries new types and new systems of weapons of mass destruction could emerge in various places. One can assume with a high degree of certainty that they would be even more ominous than those existing at present.

None of this can be ignored. Further, it is well known how difficult it is to withdraw from the arsenals of states any weapon that has already been developed, and consequently how much safer and more reasonable it is to prevent its emergence in advance. If things are viewed from that angle, the need for, the urgency of, effective measures to prohibit the development of new types and new systems of weapons of mass destruction should become absolutely evident.

Proceeding from this, aware of its responsibility as a permanent member of the Security Council, the Soviet Union proposes placing on the agenda of the current session of the General Assembly as an important and urgent matter an item entitled 'Prohibition of the development and manufacture of new types of weapons of mass destruction and of new systems of such weapons'.

The draft agreement which we submit to the General Assembly is worded in such a way that, while banning the development of new types and new systems of weapons of mass destruction, the agreement would not at the same time impede the economic, scientific and technical development of signatory states and would not infringe their right to make use of scientific research and discoveries for peaceful purposes, for the benefit of people and without any discrimination.

In submitting our second proposal we were moved by the same concern, that of delivering mankind from the danger of war; by the desire to curb the race in the most pernicious weapons at present in the arsenals of states, nuclear weapons. Its purpose is to end completely nuclear weapons tests and thus radically limit the practical possibilities for perfecting them further.

In line with this approach, the Soviet Union has already proposed the inclusion in the agenda of the thirtieth session of the General Assembly of an important and urgent item entitled 'Conclusion of a treaty on the complete and general prohibition of nuclear weapons tests'.

In accordance with the draft treaty which is submitted for the consideration of member states of the United Nations, its adherents would undertake from now on not to manufacture nuclear weapons and to prohibit and prevent any test explosions of nuclear weapons in any environment, including the underground environment. Such an obligation must, of course, be assumed by all states, including all nuclear Powers.

While outlawing all nuclear weapons tests, the treaty must not at the same time deny access to the benefits of the peaceful uses of nuclear explosions for both nuclear-weapon and non-nuclear-weapon countries.

The lofty purposes and principles proclaimed in the Charter are an embodiment of the collective quest of the peoples for peace and progress. They were born out of the flames of the greatest tragedy that has ever befallen mankind. Celebrating this year the thirtieth anniversary of the end of the Second World War, the peoples look to the future with hope.

The greatness of the exploits performed in the struggle against fascism and aggression by the peoples of the Soviet Union and the peoples of all countries who, during the years of war, combined their efforts in the name of victory and founded the United Nations, setting themselves the task of saving present and succeeding generations from the scourge of war, will never fade.

In the three decades since the end of the Second World War a great distance has been covered in the struggle for international security. Particularly impressive are the successes achieved in recent years, which graphically prove that the prevention of war between states is not a utopian but an attainable goal. However, that must not be a source of complacency. There is still much to be done to achieve a truly stable peace on earth.

As for the Soviet Union, we wish to see no stops on this road, no zigzags and, above all, no U-turns. Substantial steps in that direction can be made here, at this General Assembly of the United Nations, and we are willing to take a most active part in this common endeavour.

From a statement at the 30th session of the UN General Assembly, 23 September 1975

Receiving an honorary degree from Charles University, Prague.
27 September 1975

I should like first to express my heart-felt gratitude to the Academic Council of Charles University for this great honour, the conferment upon me of the scientific degree of honorary Doctor of Law.

In accepting the diploma of honorary Doctor, I am particularly moved by the fact that this title has been conferred upon me by one of the oldest universities in Europe.

One of its first rectors was the legendary Jan Hus, and in the course of its history of over six hundred years your famous university has given the world such outstanding scientists as Jan Essenius, Jan Purkinje, Jaroslav Heirowski, and Zdenek Needly.

Among its students there have been many renowned sons and daughters of the Czechoslovak people who inscribed not a few vivid pages into the history of your country: Bogumir Smeral, one of the founders of the Communist Party of Czechoslovakia, the ardent patriot and anti-fascist Julius Fučik, and others.

I regard the conferment upon me of the scientific degree of honorary Doctor of Law as recognition of the services of the Communist Party of the Soviet Union and the USSR in the promotion of science and the contribution of Soviet scholars to the theory and practice of international relations.

Soviet foreign policy, engendered by the new, socialist social system established as a result of the victory of the Great October Revolution, expresses the nature and character of that system.

It is profoundly scientific, rests on the objective laws of social development—on Marxism–Leninism—and is based on scientific analyses of the development and cycles of modern society, on analyses of the processes taking place in it and of the changing international situation.

Soviet foreign policy and diplomacy were created and fathered by Lenin.

The founder of the Soviet state developed the propositions of Marx and Engels on the international policy of the proletariat and its communist vanguard, and not only worked out the principles of socialist foreign policy but also charted realistic ways and means for asserting these principles and determined the tactics of Soviet foreign policy and the ways and means of achieving its aims and tasks.

'Lenin', Leonid Brezhnev noted, 'was the first in human history to combine the theory of scientific communism with the practice of conducting state foreign policy. From this durable alloy of the thought and actions of Lenin sprang the principles and methods of socialist policy on the world scene, by which we, his pupils and followers, are and shall always be guided.'

Socialist diplomacy emerged on the world scene as a new and powerful factor in inter-state relations. It broke in upon the sphere of the exploiting system's customs, norms, and traditions that held unchallenged sway in the world prior to the October Revolution.

With a sense of pride in our workers' and peasants' state, and in the Communist Party, Lenin said: 'The Bolsheviks are moulding entirely new international relations that are giving all oppressed nations the possibility of delivering themselves from imperialist oppression.'

In international relations the diplomacy of socialism has established and is establishing new, progressive, and genuinely democratic norms for relations between states.

In keeping with its class nature, socialist diplomacy is successfully carrying out the important tasks springing from the role of the world socialist community as the principal motive force of the revolutionary process today. It is making every effort to achieve the great ideals of peace, democracy, and socialism.

In conformity with the changing situation in the world, the CPSU creatively develops Lenin's extremely rich legacy and is guided by his immortal teaching.

From the first foreign policy act of the Soviet state—Lenin's Decree on Peace—to the Peace Programme adopted by the 24th Congress of the CPSU, the Communist Party and the Soviet Government have maintained a continuity in the main orientations of the struggle for peace and the freedom and security of nations.

The face of our planet has changed fundamentally since the October Revolution. The Soviet Union has become a mighty world power. The world socialist community has come into being and is steadily gaining strength. Socialism has grown into a force that is increasingly determining international developments.

174

On the world scene today the Czechoslovak Socialist Republic and other countries of the socialist community act together with the Soviet Union. Their close, all-round co-operation and mutual assistance, their unity and common, harmonized, and well-co-ordinated guidelines in questions of world politics, and their consistent struggle for peace are bringing mankind tangible positive results. We are proud that the policy of peace pursued by the socialist countries is consistent with the aspirations of all peoples.

This is what explains the magnetism, the attractive force of our concerted actions on the world scene directed towards ensuring the dependable security of nations.

I should like particularly to emphasize that it is due to the efforts of the countries of the socialist community that the peoples of Europe are living in peace for the fourth decade and that the process of *détente* is steadily gaining ever greater momentum.

The long years of effort by the countries of our community, on whose initiative the Helsinki Conference on Security and Co-operation in Europe was convened, has been crowned with success. This year will remain in the memory of nations as the year when that Conference was consummated. Almost all the speakers at the current session of the UN General Assembly noted that the Conference was a major achievement in the drive for lasting peace in the world.

With this Conference the peoples of Europe linked many of their hopes that the European continent would at last break out of the vicious circle of its history when each post-war period became a pre-war period, when the striving to conquer foreign territories turned into claims to world supremacy, into a brown plague of fascism, racism, and undisguised aggression, and the tragedy of world wars.

By collective efforts the countries participating in the Conference achieved important results, worked out the basic principles of relations between states in Europe, co-ordinated the main orientations of their equal co-operation, and thereby created an atmosphere of confidence in peaceful development.

These results are recorded in the Final Act, which may justifiably be called one of the most outstanding documents of our time.

Needless to say, we are aware that it is one thing to formulate principles, even the very best, even the finest, and formalize them with signatures, and another to carry out the understandings that have been reached, to give them a concrete material content, and move to new landmarks in the struggle for lasting peace. In order to achieve this much still remains to be accomplished. We shall have no shortage of desire, patience, or determination to make a tangible contribution to the fulfilment of the obligations undertaken by states under the Final Act.

Today when the process of *détente* has become the predominant factor in international relations, we feel that there are favourable conditions for reinforcing political *détente* with military *détente* and, in particular, for taking effective steps to limit the arms race and achieve disarmament. The road to this is neither short nor easy, but we, the socialist countries, including my country, the USSR, will work in that direction perseveringly and energetically.

I should like to mention briefly yet another aspect of socialist foreign policy—its humanitarianism.

All of us know how much those who chart the foreign policy of the leading countries of the other social system like to talk about freedom, human rights, and various humanitarian problems.

But here are a few characteristic examples. Socialism proposes that an end should be put to the use of force in international relations and that the relevant agreement envisaging, at the same time, the banning of nuclear weapons should be signed.

Who objects to this? Those who shape the policy of the countries I have mentioned. Where, one can ask, is the humanity in this?

Socialism proposes an end to nuclear tests. Underground tests have yet to be banned. Where are the objections to this proposal coming from—why, from the same side. What, one can ask, is humane in this?

Socialism proposes the conclusion of an international agreement banning the development and production of new types and systems of weapons of mass destruction. Experience shows that when one type of weapon or another is added to the arsenals of states it is extremely difficult to secure its removal from these arsenals. Who, one may say, straightaway, even without discussing the problem, shies away from this proposal? Those very same politicians, those very same people. Are there signs of humanity in this? None at all.

Ever since the time of Lenin the Soviet Union and now, together with it, the entire community of socialist countries have been raising an

176

acute problem of world-wide significance—the problem of general and complete disarmament. Mankind is today, to put it metaphorically, sitting on mountains of weapons which are growing from month to month, from week to week, from day to day.

Who has recourse to all sorts of casuistry in their stubborn objections to having this burning problem even discussed properly at a forum with the participation of all the countries of the world?

This is being done by those who determine the basic guidelines of the policy of countries belonging to the other social system. In this policy there neither has been nor is a grain of humanitarianism.

This list could be lengthened, but I feel that what has been said is enough for objectively thinking people to draw the correct conclusions about what sort of foreign policy is more in harmony with humanitarianism and what sort of policy does not dovetail with it.

In its own right this aspect of our socialist foreign policy of peace has millions of visible and invisible threads linking it with the basic, vital interests of the peoples of all continents, of all countries.

There is no doubt that the principled foreign policy of our parties and countries will be reaffirmed and developed at the 25th Congress of the CPSU and the 15th Congress of the Communist Party of Czechoslovakia.

Esteemed Rector,

Esteemed Academic Council,

Permit me to thank you and all the people present here for your attention and to wish you and the scientists of your country further substantial creative successes for the weal of the Czechoslovak Socialist Republic, in the name of progress, peace, and socialism.

Faciam omnia ut sim dignus honore ac fide mihi tributis.

> *Speech at the ceremony of conferment of the title of honorary Doctor of Law of Charles University, Prague, 27 September 1975*

Ratification of the USSR–GDR Friendship Treaty. 4 December 1975

The Treaty of Friendship, Co-operation and Mutual Assistance between the Soviet Union and the German Democratic Republic, concluded during a recent visit to the Soviet Union by a Party and government delegation from the GDR, has been submitted for ratification to the Supreme Soviet of the USSR. It bears the signatures of the General Secretary of the CPSU Central Committee Leonid Brezhnev and the First Secretary of the Central Committee of the Socialist Unity Party of Germany Erich Honecker.

It may be said without exaggeration that the conclusion of this treaty is an event of historic significance not only in the relations between our countries and peoples. It is of immense importance to all the Warsaw Treaty member-countries and to the entire socialist community. Moreover, it is of signal importance to peace and security in Europe.

This treaty places the fraternal alliance between the USSR and the GDR on a higher level and is a great contribution to the promotion of treaty relations between socialist countries. Its conclusion was prepared by the entire course of the successful co-operation between the Soviet Union and the GDR in bilateral relations and on the international scene.

This new treaty bears testimony to the extensive creative work of the Central Committee of the two fraternal parties in carrying out the decisions of the 24th Congress of the CPSU and the 8th Congress of the SUPG aimed at furthering the unity of the socialist countries, ensuring closer co-operation between them, and safeguarding the peaceful labour of their peoples.

The treaty mirrors the important qualitative changes that have taken place in the situation throughout Europe as a result of the joint efforts of the socialist states. In particular, this document takes the results of the Helsinki Conference into account and will unquestionably contribute to the successful implementation of its decisions.

Its point of departure is that the results of the war are today immutable. The territorial and political realities in Europe are dependably anchored and this has opened up further possibilities for the materialization of *détente* and an improvement in the relations between nations on the basis of the principles of peaceful coexistence. Understandably, some provisions of the USSR–GDR Treaty of 12 June 1964 could not be included in the new treaty for they no longer adequately meet with the requirements of the times, the situation in Europe, and the main tendencies of international development.

The idea of military and political co-operation in the interests of peace and security is further developed and amplified in the treaty. The Soviet Union and the German Democratic Republic undertake jointly and in alliance with the other Warsaw Treaty members to ensure the inviolability of frontiers as they exist today as a result of the Second World War and post-war development, including the frontiers between the GDR and the FRG.

A provision of the treaty is that an armed attack against any of the parties to the treaty, wherever that attack may come from, will be repulsed jointly with determination by the two countries. This commitment, clearly formulated in the treaty, is of great importance not only to the GDR and the Soviet Union, not only to the socialist community, but also to the maintenance of peace in Europe.

The USSR and the GDR will continue acting together to counter any manifestation of revanchism and militarism. The new Treaty of Friendship, Co-operation and Mutual Assistance leaves no room for the illusions of those Western circles who still believe that the emergence of socialism on German soil is nothing more than an episode in history. Socialism is firmly established there for centuries to come.

Further, I should like to draw attention to the article in the treaty concerning West Berlin. Its inclusion in the treaty was motivated by concern for ensuring a normal and healthy climate over West Berlin. The USSR and the GDR declare that they are prepared to maintain and promote relations with that city on the basis of the pivotal provision of the Quadrilateral Agreement, which states that West Berlin is not a component part of the FRG and will not be administered by it in future. Respect for and the strict observance of this provision are consistent with the vital interests of the population of West Berlin, the interests of their stable relations with the external world, and the interests of European security.

The treaty is permeated with concern for strengthening world peace and security. It envisages a far-ranging action programme in international affairs by the two sides aimed at steadily improving the international situation and consolidating socialism's position on the world scene. Here a central place is held by their mutual obligation to direct their efforts to end the arms race and achieve general and complete disarmament, to exclude war from the life of nations once and for all. To complement political *détente* with military *détente* and curb the arms race is a task of immense magnitude and a most pressing question on the agenda of international life.

The new treaty is eloquent evidence that the fraternal alliance that has taken shape between the USSR and the GDR on the solid foundation of Marxism–Leninism and socialist internationalism is being consolidated still further, acquiring the firm tissue of living links between the two countries in all fields of party, state, and social life. This is consistent with the objective law of the development of co-operation between fraternal states and will still further strengthen the might and unity of the world socialist community.

The treaty has been warmly approved by the peoples of the USSR, the GDR, and other fraternal socialist countries.

From a speech at a sitting of the Presidium of the USSR Supreme Soviet on the question of the ratification of the Treaty of Friendship, Co-operation and Mutual Assistance between the USSR and the GDR of 7 October 1975

Meeting the Hungarian Foreign Minister, Moscow. 22 December 1975

We are receiving you in Moscow at the close of 1975, when the results of the past year and of the past five-year period are being summed up in our two countries. It may be noted with satisfaction that the results are impressive. The people of our countries have achieved enormous progress in the building of socialism and communism. The 11th

Congress of the Hungarian Socialist Workers' Party, which set the historic task of building a developed socialist society, was a major event in Hungary.

The Soviet Union is moving confidently towards the 25th Congress of the CPSU, which will determine new important milestones of communist construction in our country.

The Central Committees of our parties and both Leonid Brezhnev and János Kádár personally give their closest attention to the relations between our countries. In this fact alone the peoples of the USSR and the HPR see the guarantee of the further consolidation of friendship and co-operation between the Soviet Union and Hungary, which, to quote Leonid Brezhnev, have become 'a durable, permanent and important factor in the development of our countries'.

This definition is fully applicable as a characterization of our co-operation in international affairs, in questions of foreign policy. The successful completion of the Helsinki Conference was made possible largely by the co-ordinated policy and vigorous actions of the socialist countries.

This was further confirmed at the recent conference of Foreign Ministers of fraternal countries in Moscow.

In the Soviet Union we know and highly value the contribution made by the Hungarian People's Republic to the Helsinki Conference. We are confident that our co-operation will continue also in the realization of the results of that Conference and in other areas of international politics.

The Soviet Union is fully determined to promote the relaxation of tension and, to this end, to do everything in its power to facilitate, by practical actions, co-operation in Europe and in other regions of the world. At the same time, we are aware that the struggle against the adversaries of *détente* will have to be continued and that this struggle, as it has been hitherto, will not be an easy one. But our policy, as also the policy of other fraternal countries and fraternal parties adhering to the positions of Marxism–Leninism, is permeated with optimism, because this policy and our practical steps in the world meet with the vital interests of all peoples.

In the co-ordinated policy of the socialist countries an important role is played by each socialist state. But their unity and co-ordinated efforts make our common policy more productive. On this question our views coincide with those of our Hungarian friends.

In the talks with you we have exchanged views on a wide range of issues, and we feel we can state that there is complete agreement between the two countries in their assessment of the international situation and in their approach to the solution of key problems of the day. We are confident that the negotiations and talks during your visit to the Soviet Union will contribute to the further development and deepening of Soviet–Hungarian co-operation in all areas.

> *From a speech in Moscow during a*
> *visit to the USSR by Frigyes Puja,*
> *the Hungarian Minister of Foreign*
> *Affairs, 22 December 1975*

On arrival in London. 22 March 1976

We have come to London at the invitation of the British Government to exchange views with British statesmen on questions of Soviet–British relations and on urgent international problems of mutual interest. It will be appreciated that countries like the Soviet Union and Britain have much to say to each other.

Since the important summit talks in Moscow last year the relations between the USSR and Britain have changed perceptibly for the better and, it may be said, risen to a new level. In our opinion the conditions exist for the further development of this beneficial tendency. In accordance with the principles of peaceful coexistence, the Soviet Union is prepared to continue the line of promoting long-term mutually beneficial co-operation with Great Britain in different fields. This was stated unequivocally in the report of the CPSU Central Committee delivered by the Central Committee's General Secretary Leonid Brezhnev at the recent 25th Congress of the CPSU.

In the Soviet Union we feel that there is great potential for co-operation between the USSR and Great Britain in European and world affairs, if, of course, this is wanted by both sides. The Soviet Union definitely wants it. This is the position from which the Soviet Union approaches the pending meetings and talks with British leaders.

*Statement upon arrival in London
during a visit to Great Britain,
22 March 1976*

Speech in London. 23 March 1976

The purpose of our visit is to exchange views with the statesmen of Great Britain on a wide range of questions, having in mind the possibility of consolidating and furthering the positive changes that have taken place in Soviet–British relations. These changes are linked mainly with the results of the summit in Moscow in February of last year.

The Soviet Union wants a further expansion of good relations with Great Britain. This was stated distinctly by the General Secretary of the CPSU Central Committee Leonid Brezhnev at the 25th Congress, the highest forum of the Soviet Communist Party.

Our relations with Great Britain, as with other countries with a different social system, are founded on the principles of peaceful coexistence. These are dependable, tested principles. If what has been achieved is assessed from that standpoint, it may be stated that there has been progress in a number of areas of bilateral relations—political, economic, scientific, technical, and cultural.

But can it be said that what has been achieved is the limit? By no means. Two countries like the USSR and Britain could do much more to improve the situation in Europe and the world as a whole if they co-operated more closely in international affairs.

We believe that the Soviet Union's membership of the Warsaw Treaty Organization and Great Britain's membership of NATO are no barrier to finding a common language in settling urgent international problems and to joint or parallel actions in that direction.

The experience of our relations with Britain—and not only with her—shows that when there is a genuine desire for co-operation beneficial results are achieved even in the existing situation. A striking example

183

G

of this is a major undertaking such as the Helsinki Conference, in the course of which, particularly at its last stage, the Soviet Union and Great Britain co-operated quite well on some issues relating to the strengthening of stability and confidence in Europe.

We feel that the successful completion of the Helsinki Conference has created a more solid foundation for lasting peace to become a natural state for the European peoples. However, all the provisions of the Final Act must be observed strictly and in their entirety. I emphasize: precisely all, and not by arbitrary selection. This is the Soviet Union's approach to these matters. We expect the same approach from all the other countries that participated in the Conference.

As you all know, the Soviet Union recently proposed European congresses or inter-state conferences on co-operation in environmental protection, on the development of transport, and on power engineering. This proposal is entirely in keeping with the practical implementation of the Helsinki Conference's decisions and is aimed at the further materialization of *détente* in the world. Britain's voice in support of these initiatives, which meet with the interests of all European peoples, including the British people, would play a useful role in their realization. We are prepared to consider the relevant proposals of other countries, including Great Britain, aimed at achieving the same aims. In short, this is an important area of co-operation whose humanitarian aspect is clear-cut.

Of course, matters are not confined to the questions I have mentioned. You evidently know that at its 25th Congress the CPSU put forward a broad foreign policy programme, the core of which is, as before, the struggle for *détente*, for a lasting and just peace. This programme sets our Government concrete tasks on the international scene for the immediate future, namely, to secure an end to the arms race, achieve disarmament, strengthen European and world security, reduce the danger of a nuclear war, and safeguard the legitimate rights of nations.

In short, the Soviet Union will firmly continue its line of lessening the danger of war and promoting equal and mutually beneficial co-operation. On this road we count on greater understanding with Britain and all other countries urging broader international co-operation, including the expansion of trade and economic relations with countries championing world peace.

The Soviet Union advocates the further development of Soviet–British relations and giving to them a more durable foundation. We should like to hope that these views are shared by the British leaders.

Speech in London during a visit to
Great Britain, 23 March 1976

The 31st session of the UN General Assembly. 28 September 1976

Now, here in this hall, where states with different social systems are represented, we should focus our attention on what concerns us all equally: the prevention of war and the consolidation of peace.

The Soviet Union rejects the grim conclusion that putting an end to the arms race is beyond human ability. No one can prove that people must either constantly be at war or be preparing for mutual annihilation.

For almost six decades now our country has been guided in its policies by ideas of a different kind, those of peace and friendship among nations. V. I. Lenin, the founder of the Soviet State, said: 'An end to wars, peace among nations, an end to plundering and violence—that is our ideal . . ..'

The Soviet Union acts in the international arena in close unity and co-operation with its allies and friends—the fraternal socialist states. We are proud that the impact of the socialist countries on the course of world affairs is becoming ever more profound, and we are proud because that impact is used not only in the interests of those states but also for purposes of strengthening universal peace.

Any objective observer realizes that the members of the Warsaw Treaty, the countries of the socialist community, bring to international politics a feeling of respect for the independence and sovereignty of all nations and put forward concrete peace-loving initiatives and proposals and serve as a reliable bulwark for peoples fighting for national liberation and social progress.

The Leninist ideas of peace found new, vivid expression in the decisions of the highest forum of our Party, the 25th Congress of the

CPSU, held last spring. Its Programme of Further Struggle for Peace and International Co-operation and for the Freedom and Independence of the Peoples, set out in the report delivered by Leonid Brezhnev, General Secretary of the Party's Central Committee, is imbued with a sense of profound optimism and an unshakeable belief in the possibility of making peace on earth enduring.

As one of the major objectives of the Soviet Union's foreign policy, the Congress set the task of seeking to contain the arms race, and then to reverse the trend and begin disarmament. We have put forward numerous specific proposals. Some of them are long-term proposals; others, with goodwill on the part of our partners too, could be implemented in the near future.

Now, what specifically do we have in mind?

In the first place, the curbing of a further build-up of weapons of mass destruction, to be followed by their complete prohibition and elimination. The conscience of mankind demands that ultimately nuclear weapons be eliminated altogether.

The Soviet Union has been, and remains in favour of their removal from the arsenals of states, and of using nuclear energy solely for peaceful purposes. We believe that the nuclear Powers—and all other states could join them—should come to the negotiating table to examine comprehensively the problem of nuclear disarmament and to chart together ways leading to its solution. The Soviet Union is prepared to take part in such negotiations at any time.

Independently of these negotiations, nuclear weapons testing should be stopped everywhere and by all. This would put an end to the qualitative improvement of those weapons. That is the purpose of the proposal to conclude a treaty on the complete and general prohibition of nuclear weapons testing approved by the General Assembly at its last session. The start of negotiations on this question is being unjustifiably delayed. The problem here is not the absence of objective conditions—they have long existed—but the unwillingness of some nuclear Powers to begin negotiations.

The question of underground nuclear explosions for peaceful purposes cannot be allowed to become a stumbling block: the USSR and the United States have, after all, succeeded in agreeing on this matter, and have recently signed a relevant Treaty. We hope that it will soon be ratified by the United States. On our part, there will be no delay.

The problem of verification has been artificially inflated for quite some time now. Advanced techniques for identifying seismic phenomena have eliminated this point of disagreement as well. If, nevertheless, there are some who still harbour doubts on this score, we are confident that a mutually acceptable approach can be found that would remove such doubts.

In short, no room has been left for any plausible excuses which would prevent the completion of the task of prohibiting all nuclear weapons tests.

It is well known that at present international commercial exchanges of nuclear materials are increasing. In some cases, however, it is not sufficiently certain that the possession of fissionable materials could not be used for dangerous purposes or that the means of developing nuclear weapons would not fall into the hands of irresponsible persons, adventurists, or simply madmen. This is a question not of trade, but of politics and security.

Surely it follows that the world must be safely protected from all such risks. The way to achieve this is to strengthen the rules on the non-proliferation of nuclear weapons. We should redouble our efforts to make the Non-proliferation Treaty truly universal and to secure the accession to it of all states, without exception.

The Soviet Union proposes that all chemical means of warfare be completely prohibited and destroyed, as has been done in respect of bacteriological weapons. If all states are not prepared to take such a step, then, to begin with, agreement should be reached on banning and eliminating the most dangerous and lethal types of chemical weapons.

At the last session of the General Assembly, the Soviet Union proposed the conclusion of an international agreement which would preclude the development and production of new types and new systems of weapons of mass destruction.

Conventional types of weapons are not normally included among weapons of mass annihilation. But modern tanks, aircraft, cannon and even small arms have been perfected to such a degree that they have actually become instruments capable of wiping out great masses of people. Since the Second World War, the Soviet Union has repeatedly proposed that conventional types of arms and the strength of armed forces also be reduced. We believe it imperative to discuss these questions as well.

As it always has, the Soviet Union favours the dismantling of all foreign military bases on alien territories.

We consider it reasonable that a number of Asian and African states desire to turn the Indian Ocean into a zone of peace. In this connection, the essential point is that there should be no foreign military bases, which constitute the main element of a permanent military presence in the area. As for the Soviet Union, it has never had and does not have any intention of building military bases in the Indian Ocean.

In solving the problem of foreign military bases along these lines, the Soviet Union is prepared, together with other Powers, to seek ways of reducing on a reciprocal basis the military activities of non-coastal states in the Indian Ocean and the regions directly adjacent. Our country has shown its readiness to contribute to the realization of the idea of turning it into a zone of peace, but of course this should not create any obstacles to freedom of navigation or scientific research in the Indian Ocean. If due account is taken of our approach by the states concerned, the Soviet Union will be able to participate in consultations on matters relating to preparations for convening an international conference on the Indian Ocean.

Among the various methods of securing the curtailment of the arms race there is another one which, as it were, combines the various possibilities, and that is the reduction of military budgets.

Three years ago, the General Assembly approved our proposal that the military budgets of permanent members of the Security Council be reduced by ten per cent while a part of the money thus saved could be used to provide assistance to developing countries. Because of the position taken by some states, the practical solution of this problem has been blocked. Wishing to break the deadlock in this matter, we are prepared to look for mutually acceptable specific figures with which the reduction could be started. As a first step, a figure either greater or smaller than ten per cent could be agreed upon as soon as for 1977, next year. But it is necessary to begin negotiations on this question.

No one today will deny that the arms race has assumed unprecedented dimensions. This makes it imperative for all states, nuclear and non-nuclear, great and small, developed and developing, to combine their efforts to arrest it.

That is why the Soviet Union has proposed, and continues to propose, that the problem of disarmament be considered in its entirety at the broadest and most authoritative forum—a world disarmament conference. An overwhelming majority of the states of the world have declared themselves in favour of convening such a conference. But the implementation of this proposal continues to meet with the objections of some big Powers.

In this regard it has been suggested that it would be appropriate to hold a special session of the General Assembly to discuss disarmament questions. Well, this too is a suitable forum if it is viewed as an intermediate stage in the preparations for a world conference. But it must really be a special kind of session, not a routine one. We see its task as one of paving the way for a world conference and finally ensuring a real breakthrough in solving disarmament problems. Its work must reflect the grave responsibility of all states of the world, especially the great Powers.

Such, fundamentally, is our approach to the problem of stopping the arms race and of disarmament. Such is the essence of the Soviet Union's memorandum on these questions which we are submitting for consideration at this session and circulating as an official document of the United Nations.

It will be recalled that it has recently proved possible to achieve international understandings which impose certain limits on the arms race in some areas. As far as one can judge, an important agreement on the prohibition of military or any other hostile use of environmental modification techniques seems to be within reach. A number of questions relating to disarmament are now being discussed among states.

Pride of place belongs, for obvious reasons, to the continuing talks between the Soviet Union and the United States of America on strategic arms limitation. The importance of these talks far transcends the interests of just our two countries. We are ready to actively continue our efforts to translate the well-known Vladivostok understanding into the text of an agreement.

There can hardly be anyone who would doubt that the fullest

guarantees of peace will be provided by general and complete disarmament. Ever since Lenin's days, Soviet foreign policy has been aimed at achieving that ultimate goal.

But along with efforts to solve that historic task, it is possible and necessary to seek by other means, too, a reduction of the risk of the outbreak of war. Now, what is of decisive importance today? Above all, a firm agreement between states not to use force in international relations.

It could be argued that the principle of the renunciation of the use or threat of force is already embodied in the United Nations Charter. This is true.

The knots of differences among states should be untied and out-standing problems should be resolved at the conference table, by peaceful means. The principle of renunciation of the use of force must become an immutable law of international affairs. That is precisely the purpose of the proposal made from the rostrum of the 25th Congress of the CPSU concerning the concluding of a world treaty on the non-use of force in international relations.

We note with satisfaction that that proposal has met with a broad response and has aroused the interest of many states. At the same time, we are asked what the Soviet Union has in mind in terms of the specific contents of such a treaty. The answer to this question is to be found in the draft world treaty on the non-use of force in international relations which the Soviet Union is submitting to the General Assembly.

The essence of the proposed treaty lies in the idea that in their relations with each other, as well as in their international relations in general, all parties to it will strictly abide by the undertaking to refrain from the use or threat of force either against the territorial integrity or political independence of any state or in any other manner inconsistent with the purposes of the United Nations. They will accordingly refrain from the use of armed forces involving the employment of any types of weapon, including nuclear weapons, on land, at sea, in the air and in outer space and will not threaten to use such forces. They will have to reaffirm the undertaking to settle disputes among themselves solely by peaceful means in such a way as not to endanger international peace and security.

There is, of course, a fundamental difference between the launching of hostilities for the purposes of aggression and the legitimate right to repel aggression or eliminate its consequences. Can the Arabs, for instance, resign themselves to the loss of their lands? And do the colonial peoples have no right to fight for their independence till final victory? They do indeed have an inalienable right to that.

The substance of the matter is the prevention of aggression. In this case there will be no further need to use force to repel it. The source of the evil is aggression and not the desire to restore justice; that is the cause and not its effect. Underlying our draft treaty—and I want to lay special emphasis on this—is the definition of aggression worked out by the United Nations, and everyone voted in favour of that document.

The treaty takes fully into account the system of bilateral and multilateral relations of states that has developed in the world. One of its articles provides that nothing in the treaty affects the rights and obligations of states under the United Nations Charter and treaties and agreements concluded by them earlier.

It is envisaged that the treaty would be open for signature by any state at any time. This means that, firstly, it would be of a general, universal nature. Secondly, for the signatory states the treaty would enter into force upon ratification. Consequently, there would be no need to wait for the accession to the treaty of a specific number of countries. According to our draft, the Secretary-General of the United Nations would be the depositary of the treaty. The United Nations as a whole would be called upon to lend all its moral and political prestige in support of the treaty.

These are the new and concrete initiatives designed to stop the arms race and exclude the use of force in relations among states which have been proposed by the Soviet Union in this important forum. We are convinced that the fundamental strengthening of the bulwark of universal peace depends to a decisive degree on progress precisely in those two directions. The political climate in the world and the processes of relaxation of international tension prevailing in it are conducive to an undertaking of the implementation of these initiatives in a practical and serious manner.

The relaxation of tension and the attitude of states towards it are now in the spotlight of world politics. This alone shows that *détente* is not a myth or a catchword. Underlying it is a real change-over from confrontation and 'brinkmanship' to peaceful and mutually beneficial co-operation among states and the investing of such co-operation with ever greater material content.

Not a single state, not a single government—if, of course, it really wishes to remain in touch with reality—should hesitate in choosing its policy: either to promote the further reduction of tension and the elimination of the remnants of the cold war or to kindle conflict and friction. Every government, every statesman should consider it an honour to be in the mainstream of the forces working for the further reduction of tension in the world.

As for the Soviet Union, its position has been determined with utmost clarity by the decisions of the 25th Congress of the CPSU. Expressing the will of the Soviet Communist Party, of the entire Soviet people, Leonid Brezhnev has stated that our country would

'. . . do everything possible to deepen international *détente* and to embody it in concrete forms of mutually beneficial co-operation between states.'

That is our firm foreign policy line, one which the Soviet Union will steadfastly follow.

All the treaties and agreements concluded in recent years in the interests of a peaceful future for Europe should be scrupulously observed by all parties. I should like to emphasize particularly that attempts to undercut the Quadripartite Agreement on West Berlin, which has been serving the cause of improving the situation in the centre of the European continent for five years now, run counter to these interests.

In the light of the results of the Helsinki Conference new possibilities have opened up for expanding relations between states in Europe in the political, economic, scientific and technological fields, as well as in the sphere of culture, contacts, information and education. The Soviet Union has put forward concrete proposals for organizing multilateral co-operation in such important fields as energy production, transport and protection of the environment.

The task of supplementing political *détente* with military *détente* is now coming to the fore in European affairs. What does that mean primarily? It means a successful conclusion of the Vienna talks on mutual reduction of armed forces and armaments in Central Europe, where the concentration of armed forces and armaments is higher than in any other part of the world.

The Soviet Union and other socialist countries taking part in the negotiations are seeking to make the discussions constructive. We have given figures with regard to the total strength of the armed forces of the Warsaw Treaty countries stationed in the zone of reductions, including land forces. It is now our partners' turn to respond. If no attempts are made to obtain unilateral military advantages, the negotiations in Vienna will also succeed.

It is well known how important for the international situation is the state of Soviet–American relations. As a result of the agreements and understandings reached between the USSR and the United States in previous years, the necessary conditions have been created for continuing to build those relations on a constructive foundation.

As far as the Soviet Union is concerned, it is not guided in its policy by temporary considerations of the moment. The true interests of both countries, the interests of peace, are served by only one course of action—that of acting in conformity with the course jointly formulated in recent years, with the spirit and letter of the agreements that have been concluded. The Soviet Union expects that the United States will proceed precisely in that way. That will primarily determine further developments.

Relations between the Soviet Union and France are developing in a favourable direction. This is something which has been reflected in the signing of many agreements, including the Declaration on the Further Development of Friendship and Co-operation, signed in October 1975. The recent Soviet–French agreement to prevent the accidental or unauthorized use of nuclear weapons is along the same lines. As far as the Soviet Union is concerned, we will consistently follow the line we have taken in our relations with France.

A great deal of what has been achieved in relations between the Soviet Union and the Federal Republic of Germany and, above all, the conclusion of the Moscow Treaty, have marked the end of a whole phase in the post-war history of Europe. A fundamentally important page was turned in the right direction. The Soviet Union believes that further development and deepening of co-operation with the FRG—

in the expectation naturally that the policy of that country will be determined by the interests of peace, including the interests of peaceful development and neighbourliness in Europe—is desirable.

The relations between the Soviet Union and practically all states which are known as 'Western'—Great Britain or Denmark, Italy or Belgium, Canada or Sweden—are increasingly assuming the character of normal, mutually advantageous co-operation.

The successes of the policy of *détente* by no means signify that it no longer has any opponents. Ill-assorted forces often presenting a common front against it are easily found in Europe and elsewhere—in fact, they reveal themselves every day.

The fruits of the policy of *détente* must be accessible to all peoples. It is well known, however, that the independence and territorial integrity of Cyprus are still threatened. Tensions in the Middle East have not abated.

There can be no doubt that so long as the occupation by Israel of Arab lands continues, so long as the legitimate rights of the Arab people of Palestine are trampled upon, the Middle East will continue time and again to be in a state of fever.

It is now common knowledge that thousands of people have been killed or crippled in Lebanon in recent months. The tragic events which have occurred in that country are the direct result of imperialist aggression against the Arabs. The events in Lebanon are a direct consequence of the lack of an over-all settlement in the Middle East. The blow is being aimed primarily against the patriots of Lebanon and the valiant Arab people of Palestine whose just struggle cannot but evoke our admiration.

The Soviet Union believes that the crisis in Lebanon must be settled in a peaceful, democratic way by the Lebanese themselves, without any outside interference, on the basis of the preservation of the territorial integrity, independence and sovereignty of Lebanon.

The protracted nature of the tension in the Middle East gives us no grounds for concluding that the situation there is hopeless. A good basis for establishing peace in that area has been worked out through the efforts of many states, including the Soviet Union. What it boils down to is the withdrawal of Israeli troops from all Arab territories occupied in 1967; the satisfaction of the legitimate national demands of the Arab people of Palestine, including their inalienable right to create their own state; and the furnishing of international security guarantees for all states in the Middle East, including Israel.

Unfortunately, the international machinery for producing the necessary agreements on the Middle East—the Geneva Peace Conference—is still inactive. The Soviet Union is in favour of a resumption of its work, and the sooner the better, for consideration by it of all the major issues involved in a Middle East settlement.

It is becoming ever more urgent to spread *détente* to Asia. Conditions are ripening there for the consolidation of peace through the joint efforts of the Asian states. This is demonstrated by a fact of vast historical significance—the end of the war in Indo-China and the formation of a new major peace-loving state, the Socialist Republic of Vietnam. The Soviet Union is confident that the voice of an independent, united Vietnam will soon be heard from this rostrum too. We insist that the Socialist Republic of Vietnam be admitted to the United Nations without delay.

It is worth recalling, particularly in this hall, that on 14 December 1960 thunderous applause greeted the adoption of the historic Declaration on the Granting of Independence to Colonial Countries and Peoples. Its adoption signified that historically the hour had struck for the complete elimination of colonial domination in the world.

We have all witnessed the failure of the attempt to stifle with the help of arms the young independent state of the People's Republic of Angola. If there are still governments which would impede the exercise of its legitimate right to participate in the work of the United Nations, they stand to gain nothing by that action; they only stand to lose. Angola will without any doubt take its lawful and proper place in this hall.

We should like to take this opportunity to congratulate the Republic of Seychelles on its admission to the United Nations and to wish the people of that country success in the building of a new life.

Thousands of miles separate the Soviet Union from Latin America, but our people have feelings of friendship towards its peoples and wish to have good relations with Latin American countries. So much greater then are our bitterness and indignation at the unabated violations of human rights and liberties in several parts of that continent, primarily in Chile, where these rights and freedoms are being flagrantly and criminally trampled under foot. Together with all progressive mankind we demand freedom for Luis Corvalan, arrested three years ago, and for other Chilean democrats.

The present international situation is far from being monochrome. Along with the positive changes which have occurred in the world, which have been characteristic of recent times, certain phenomena of a different kind have been noted, namely, opposition to *détente*. This requires the vigilance and active efforts of all those who cherish the cause of peace. And yet the over-all political background of the world today gives grounds for looking to the future with optimism.

> *From a statement at the 31st UN*
> *General Assembly, 28 September*
> *1976*

Article in *Kommunist*. September 1976

Present Soviet aims in foreign policy, as defined by the 23rd and re-affirmed by the two subsequent Party congresses, are to secure jointly with the fraternal countries favourable international conditions for building socialism and communism; to further the unity, friendship and fraternity of the socialist countries; to assist the national liberation movement and expand all-round co-operation with the developing countries; to promote the principle of peaceful coexistence of states with different social systems, repulse imperialism's aggressive forces, and save mankind from another world war.

Our Party and its Central Committee have worked industriously and fruitfully to further the Peace Programme of the 24th Congress. Practice—and practical results are the only trustworthy criterion of the viability of a political programme—has shown that its objectives are justified and far-sighted. It has proved right the line of securing a radical improvement in international relations and—relying on the power, unity and dynamism of the socialist world and on its increasingly close alliance with all progressive and peace-loving forces—of achieving a change of course from cold war and explosive tension to *détente*, peaceful coexistence and mutually beneficial co-operation.

We are pleased to note that a substantial part of the Peace Programme has by now been put into effect. The positive change in world affairs is truly impressive. There is hardly any precedent in the history of international relations for such far-reaching improvements, vitally important not only to the fraternal socialist countries but also to the world, being achieved in so short a time.

Referring to the principal result of the Party's foreign policy in the early half of the seventies, L. I. Brezhnev observed that 'the international position of the Soviet Union has never been more stable. We have entered the fourth decade of peace. Socialism's position has grown stronger. *Détente* has become the leading trend.' We can be proud that Soviet foreign policy has contributed enormously to the favourable changes in the world, with the Peace Programme acting as a kind of catalyst in this progressive, often precipitous, process that is still not over.

Certainly, it is too early to say that positive trends have become an irreversible feature of international affairs. World peace is far from guaranteed. Serious obstacles have yet to be put out of the way. But jointly with our Warsaw Treaty allies and our friends we have done everything we can to safeguard peaceful construction in our own country and the fraternal socialist states, and to safeguard peace and international security.

Small wonder that Soviet foreign policy has won respect and support among the mass of people all over the world. 'And we shall continue this policy, with redoubled energy,' says the Central Committee report, 'working to bridle the forces of war and aggression, to consolidate world peace and assure the peoples' right to freedom, independence and social progress.'

The 25th Congress of the CPSU advanced a new foreign policy programme based on the results of the Peace Programme, of which it is a natural continuation and projection. It sets out the most urgent international priorities, advances a set of important constructive proposals, and charts concrete objectives for the further peace offensive of Soviet diplomacy.

The Programme of Further Struggle for Peace and International

Co-operation and for the Freedom and Independence of the Peoples gives pride of place to the task of the fraternal socialist countries, 'while steadily strengthening their unity and expanding their all-round co-operation in building a new society . . . [to] augment their joint active contribution to the consolidation of peace'.

And this is understandable, because the affairs and cares of the part of the world where communist ideals are being put into practice are naturally closest to our hearts. We make no secret of seeking an ever more favourable international setting for the peaceful building of socialism and communism.

But that is not all. Lenin's prediction that socialism would become an international force exerting decisive influence on all world politics is coming true before our eyes. Naturally, this imposes a special responsibility for world peace on the USSR and the fraternal countries. And this they understand very clearly. Socialism and peace are indivisible.

No other alliance or coalition past or present can compare in endurance with the socialist community. This new community of nations and states has become a powerful factor in world affairs, and has set the main trend in humanity's social and political progress. Through the very nature of socialism and thanks to their foreign policy, which exercises an ever greater influence on international relations, the socialist states are now the most dependable stronghold of peace and freedom and independence of nations.

The successful building of a new society in each of the socialist countries and their effective conduct of world affairs depend to an enormous extent on unity, class solidarity and mutual aid. The CPSU and the Soviet Government are doing their utmost to strengthen the fraternal friendship of the countries of the socialist community and to further their co-operation on the principles of socialist internationalism, true sovereignty, complete equality, interest in each other's success, and comradely mutual assistance.

Their co-operation reposes on the indestructible unity of their Communist Parties, identity of their world outlook, aims and will. This is its basis, its heart and soul, and its organizing force. One tested form of co-operation are the meetings held regularly by leaders of the Communist Parties, at which they discuss matters concerning the building of socialism and communism and foreign policy, and jointly map out a common advance.

There is effective co-operation in the framework of the Warsaw Treaty's Political Consultative Committee on questions of relations between its member-countries. Here they also discuss European and world problems of common interest, and work out an agreed political course. It is not surprising, therefore, that sessions of the PCC always turn into a major international event.

The Warsaw Treaty Organization set up twenty years ago is a time-tested instrument of political and military collaboration. It perseveres in its mission and is a dependable shield for the interests of socialism and peace. As the Central Committee Report declares, 'as long as the NATO bloc continues to exist and as long as militarist elements continue their arms drive, our country and the other signatories of the Warsaw Treaty will continue to strengthen this political–military alliance'.

Countries of the socialist community are entering the qualitatively new stage of developed socialism with its high growth rates of productive forces, higher efficiency of social production, and steadily rising standards of living. 'The ties between socialist states are becoming ever closer with the flowering of each socialist nation and the strengthening of their sovereignty, and elements of community are increasing in their policy, economy, and social life. There is a gradual levelling of their development', L. I. Brezhnev noted at the 25th Congress of the CPSU, adding that 'this process of gradual drawing together of socialist countries is now operating quite definitely as an objective law'.

This law expresses itself strikingly through the economic co-operation of the countries of the socialist community. It is mainly due to their effective use of the advantages of socialist international division of labour that they have grown into so powerful an economic force.

The fraternal countries in the Council of Mutual Economic Assistance form the world's biggest economic community. CMEA also surpasses all other international economic alignments in the rate of growth of the aggregate national economic potential. The Soviet Union alone accounts for twenty per cent of world industrial output, and in physical terms this exceeds total world output in 1950. The CMEA share of world industrial output is now approaching one-third.

The co-operation of CMEA countries is based on the Comprehensive

Socialist Integration Programme adopted in 1971. This programme gave their economic interaction a new quality. A considerable reserve has been tapped in the current five-year period and for the subsequent period by co-ordinating national economic plans and adopting a plan of multilateral integration measures for 1976–80.

The 30th session of CMEA, held in Berlin this July, was an important milestone in socialist economic integration, which increasingly directs the economic development of member-countries. The participants in the session reviewed the results of the Comprehensive Programme and reaffirmed their common resolve to continue integration and joint use of their natural wealth, material resources and manpower through co-operation and specialization in the national and common interest. This is reflected, among other things, in their decision to work out specific ten- to fifteen-year co-operation programmes for key fields of production. Cumulatively, they will give added momentum to the objective historical process of bringing closer and balancing the levels of economic development of CMEA countries.

They will make the community more close-knit, fortify the spirit of socialist internationalism among the people of the fraternal countries, and show socialism's superiority as a socio-economic system. Consistent growth of socialist economic integration will in many ways promote equal economic co-operation between all countries of the world and help recast the unequal relations imposed by imperialism, thus benefiting the international situation.

As noted by the 25th Congress, ideological co-operation among parties of the fraternal countries is expanding steadily. This is important because the ideological contention between the two systems is as relevant and sharp as ever. And in this contention, propagation of our progressive and humanitarian ideas, of the truth about socialism and its successes, and about its historical superiority over capitalism, is a powerful weapon.

In sum, Congress has again demonstrated the stability of Soviet party and government policy as concerns cementing the unity of the fraternal parties and countries, and their ever closer relations in all fields for the good of the peoples of the socialist community and in the interests of world peace and international co-operation. And it is with enthusiasm that our entire nation follows this course.

'Work for the termination of the expanding arms race, which is endangering peace, and for transition to reducing the accumulated stockpiles of arms, to disarmament' is another cardinal task set in the foreign policy programme of the 25th Congress. And, truly, nothing is more urgent today than to bridle the arms race and begin disarmament. There is no other task more crucial not only for safety today, but also for coming generations.

In this nuclear age the arms race is an incomparably greater threat to people's lives than it has been at any other time. Apart from the obvious danger of possible military consequences, it leads inevitably to disruption of political *détente*. On the social and economic plane, with the world spending about a million dollars on armaments every two minutes or nearly 300 billion a year, it robs nations of a substantial and continuously increasing portion of the wealth created by strenuous labour, and is holding up solution of vital global problems, such as extensive development of the seas of the world and outer space, development of fundamentally new sources of energy, and eradication of disease, hunger, illiteracy, and poverty.

Despite the seemingly ungovernable arms avalanche engulfing more and more countries, and despite the fact that disarmament is being variously resisted by groups that make billion-dollar profits on arms, by those who still nurse reckless schemes of settling the historical contention between the two systems by force—and exponents of the cynical 'philosophy' of building a 'radiant' future on radioactive ruins and ashes are making common cause with them—the present world situation is on the whole encouraging. Good conditions for progress to disarmament are being created by the easing of tension and by the ever more determined efforts of the peace-loving nations to curb the arms race.

There is convincing evidence that work in this direction can be successful. In recent years, for example, largely on the initiative of the Soviet Union and other countries of the socialist community, a wholly realistic—albeit initial and limited—advance has been made in the matter of disarmament.

It is the duty of all countries to make the most of all available opportunities in the interest of safeguarding their own security, as well as international peace. As concerns the Soviet Union, it is as willing as before to come to terms on the most radical disarmament measures, not short of general and complete disarmament. But since not all by far are inclined to join in solving this problem at once and in earnest, the USSR is prepared to approach disarmament gradually, stage by stage. The main thing is to secure tangible results.

The new peace programme gives the specific directions in which efforts should be made to further this aim. In particular, it would be very useful to complete the Soviet–American talks on the further limitation of strategic offensive arms, in which the Soviet Union is seeking to give effect to the Vladivostok accord of 1974 and prevent the opening of yet another channel of the arms race.

We will continue to do what we can to complete the drafting of a new Soviet–American agreement on limiting and reducing strategic arms. Its conclusion would visibly contribute to international security. A desire to facilitate this is also being voiced by the American side. We can only hope that its deeds will match its words.

The crying necessity for ending the race in mass destruction weapons, notably nuclear weapons, needs no proving. In line with its principles, the Soviet Union has always advocated and still advocates banning these weapons. And now, too, it favours solving this problem in conjunction with a total ban on the use of force in international relations. Though aware that in the prevailing conditions this can only be a strategic, long-term aim, the Central Committee of the CPSU always keeps it in sight.

A fruitful approach would be to conclude accords on stopping the manufacture of nuclear arms, stopping their supply to armies, and ending the development and manufacture of new models and types of nuclear arms with a simultaneous or early reduction of stockpiles and of nuclear arms carriers. The problem of nuclear disarmament merits close and exhaustive study with the participation of all nuclear powers. And since, for wholly understandable reasons, all nations have a stake in the matter, it could also be joined by non-nuclear countries.

If we want to prevent the qualitative improvement or development of new types of nuclear weapons, the first thing we must do is stop testing everywhere and by all countries. The Soviet Union, which proposed a treaty on the complete and general prohibition of nuclear weapons tests at the last session of the UN General Assembly, holds that negotiations sanctioned by that session should begin without delay. During these negotiations we are ready to take part in a search for an understanding on the control problem.

Like the question of peaceful underground nuclear explosions, this problem should not be an insurmountable obstacle to negotiations, as borne out by the recently concluded Soviet–American treaty on underground nuclear explosions for peaceful purposes.

It is highly important to protect the world against the spread of nuclear weapons. A sure way would be to make the now operating Non-proliferation Treaty truly universal, for so far not even all nuclear powers have acceded to it. What we also need are guarantees to prevent international co-operation in the peaceful use of nuclear energy serving as a loophole for the spread of nuclear arms.

Banning and eliminating chemical weapons, which are another means of mass annihilation, is also highly urgent. Since for reasons beyond the control of the socialist countries it has not been possible to solve this problem radically and at one go, as was the case with bacteriological weapons, everything should evidently be done to ban the deadliest chemical means of warfare. It would be a big step forward to carry out the Soviet–American understanding on a joint initiative concerning a relevant convention.

Prohibiting the development of new weapons of mass annihilation that could in deadliness prove commensurate or even superior to existing types and systems is a substantial aspect of the whole disarmament problem. This danger is growing from day to day, and especially so because, in effect, there are no serious curbs on using scientific and technical achievements for military purposes.

Wishing to prevent this turn of events and being anxious that scientific and technical achievements should be used exclusively for man's good, the Soviet Union has suggested an international agreement blocking the development and manufacture of new types and systems of mass annihilation weapons. The Disarmament Committee in Geneva, to which this issue was referred by the last UN General Assembly, is at present discussing a pertinent Soviet project.

As we see it, negotiations on a ban on developing new types and systems of mass destruction weapons should receive cardinal attention. On no account can we let a new Pandora's box be opened, threatening mankind with incalculable perils. Those politicians who take this issue lightly and fail to give it due attention will assume a grave responsibility for the tragic consequences.

In the conditions of the scientific and technical revolution practical opportunities are coming to hand for modifying nature and the climate, and, among other things, causing artificial cyclones and storms, changing the weather in large areas, altering ocean currents and the state of the ionosphere and the ozone layer, and the like. This can be used—and initial attempts have already been made—as a means of warfare. Two years ago the Soviet Union placed a proposal before the United Nations to eliminate this danger and conclude an international convention banning modifications of the natural environment for military or other hostile purposes. The Disarmament Committee in Geneva has worked out and endorsed the text of such a convention on the basis of a draft agreed by the USSR and USA, and has by now submitted it for approval to the UN General Assembly. Once it is signed and enters into force a serious barrier will have been erected against military or any other hostile use of means of modifying the natural environment.

An effective way of winding up the arms race would be to end the present continuous growth of the military expenditures of many states and to replace it with systematic reductions. The Soviet Union has repeatedly declared its readiness to take practical steps in this direction. Now, too, it is making constructive proposals.

In 1973 the UN General Assembly, acting on the initiative of the USSR, decided in favour of reducing by ten per cent the military budgets of countries which are permanent members of the Security Council and allocating part of the released funds for aid to developing countries. Implementation of this decision, in which other countries could also take part, would benefit the developed, as well as developing countries, for the economized funds could be channelled into peaceful development.

However, nothing has been done on this score so far, because some of the NATO countries that are unwilling to curb the arms race are sidestepping this natural and useful measure. Additional efforts are evidently needed to get the matter off the ground. After all, if the suggested extent of the reduction does not suit someone, we could come to terms on a figure higher than ten per cent or a lower one as a first step in 1977. In any case, the matter of reducing military budgets is exceedingly important and must be steadily pushed to a successful solution.

Like other socialist countries, the Soviet Union attaches great importance to the Vienna negotiations on reducing armed forces and armaments in Central Europe, where there is a high concentration of troops of the two most powerful military groups of states. A solution of this issue would substantially help to ease tension not only in the region concerned but also in the rest of Europe and would benefit international *détente* as a whole.

Striving for progress in Vienna, the socialist countries have suggested working out an agreement on a reduction of Soviet and American armed forces and armaments in the first stage, with the other countries directly involved undertaking not to increase their strength during the time of the negotiations and also taking on a general but clear commitment to reduce their armed forces and armaments in the second stage. This would ensure an equal contribution by each country to lessening the military confrontation in Central Europe.

The proposals of the socialist countries are based on the approximate equality of the armed forces of Warsaw Treaty and NATO countries, as this is evident from data they supplied in Vienna on the total strength of the armed forces of the Warsaw Treaty in the centre of Europe. Naturally, commitments assumed by signatories of the envisaged agreement must reflect this fact.

In the Vienna negotiations the socialist countries seek strict adherence to the principle of not impairing the security of any country, which naturally includes consideration for the true interests of their Western partners. In contrast, the Western countries keep insisting on an asymmetrical reduction that would tilt the long-time balance of strength in Central Europe in their favour.

The Soviet Union holds, however, that there are opportunities for progress. All we need is sincere desire on the part of all participants to reach an understanding. As noted at the 25th Congress of the CPSU, the Vienna negotiations will be successful if the NATO countries give up attempts to use them to win unilateral military advantages.

The Soviet Union intends to work on for accords on concrete

disarmament steps in Central Europe, and to promote military *détente* in this region in years to come.

The problem of curbing the arms race, which affects the interests of all nations without exception, cannot, of course, be settled automatically. Energetic efforts are needed by peace-loving states and joint action by all peace-loving forces. Effective use should be made of any multilateral as well as bilateral negotiating mechanism that has proved its worth.

To secure cardinal progress in disarmament (conditions for this have matured and the matter brooks no delay), all pertinent questions must be competently and comprehensively examined with due account of all circumstances by the broadest possible and most prestigious forum. For many years the Soviet Union has called for a World Disarmament Conference, and, as put down in the new Peace Programme, we will do our utmost to have it convened.

We hold that a special session of the UN General Assembly could be an intermediate stage in laying the groundwork for a broad and radical examination of the disarmament problem at a world conference. This special session, which must not be restricted either in time or by any procedural routine, would facilitate discussion of the entire range of disarmament problems, help to determine ways and means for solving them, and work out a long-term programme of practical steps, thus securing a radical change in the matter of disarmament.

Taking guidance from the foreign policy programme of the 25th Congress of the CPSU and with consideration for the trends and outlook of the political situation in the world, the Soviet Union has appealed to all UN member-states at the 31st General Assembly, and to all countries of the world, to multiply their efforts in curbing the arms race and beginning disarmament. It has submitted a special document to the Assembly, setting out its ideas about the main objectives of agreed action that would yield practical results in this large and exceedingly important area of present-day international relations.

The Soviet Union is making a tremendous contribution to ending the arms race and beginning disarmament. Our efforts directed to supplementing political *détente* with military *détente* are winning broad international backing. 'Soviet Communists are proud', L. I. Brezhnev said at the 25th Congress of the CPSU, 'of having undertaken the difficult but noble mission of standing in the front ranks of the fighters striving to deliver the peoples from the dangers ensuing from the continuing arms race.' Indeed, the Soviet Union will consider no effort too great in order to further disarmament.

Along with greater efforts to put the brake on the arms race and ultimately liquidate the whole mechanism of material preparation for war, the interests of peace and international security require additional measures to assert the principle of renouncing use or threat of force in settling controversial issues as an unbreakable rule of international relations.

Though this principle is enshrined in the UN Charter and in a large number of bilateral, regional, and broad multilateral treaties and agreements, use of force and aggression is still too frequent an occurrence. The chapters of post-war history abound in armed conflicts. Today, too, despite a considerable improvement in the international climate, seats of war danger persist, and new ones keep appearing from time to time.

The Soviet Union is consistent in its efforts to eliminate the danger of armed clashes erupting between states, to banish the use of force in mutual relations, to give greater effect to the commitment to the non-use of force and to rule out any possibility for settling international issues by force of arms. It was on a Soviet initiative, for example, that the UN countries in a 1972 resolution renounced the use or threat of force in international relations with a simultaneous perpetual ban on the use of nuclear weapons.

In furtherance of an active course in this direction, the 25th Congress of the CPSU put forward a proposal for a world treaty on the non-use of force in international relations. Promotion of this proposal is described in the foreign policy programme of the Congress as a vital international objective. Working for this objective, the USSR has put the draft of a pertinent treaty before the present UN General Assembly session. Under this treaty its signatories would undertake not to use force or to threaten force with any kind of arms, including mass destruction weapons, and to settle disputes by peaceful means without endangering world peace.

Such a treaty would pave the way for progress in disarmament and lead to a further easing of world tensions. All states, big or small, nuclear or non-nuclear, would benefit.

Certainly, conclusion of such a treaty must in no way impair the legitimate right of nations to safeguard their freedom and independence or to eliminate the consequences of aggression. There should be no illusions on this score.

Along with other peace-loving countries, the Soviet Union will do its utmost to make non-use of force a principle of international law rigorously observed by all countries.

Among the urgent international tasks the 25th Congress also listed a concentration of effort by peace-loving countries on eliminating existing military hot-beds. This applies first of all to the Middle East, which has for decades been one of the worst flashpoints on earth. The explosive situation there stems from Israel's unrelenting aggressive manoeuvres and the policy of its imperialist backers who are seeking to recover their grip on this region. As a result, Israeli troops are still occupying 60,000 sq. km of Arab territory and still ignoring the lawful national demands of the three million Arab people of Palestine, with the whole business of a Middle East settlement at an impasse.

The fratricidal conflict in Lebanon is a direct result of the subversive activity of imperialism, Zionism, and the Arab reactionary groups acting in league with them. This activity is aimed against the whole national liberation movement in the Middle East. Its principal purpose is to wipe out one of the movement's most active sections, the Palestine resistance movement, to divide the Arab countries, distract their attention from the original cause of Middle East tension, Israeli aggression, and obstruct the struggle of the Arab peoples for their national interests.

As before, the Soviet Union holds that the bloodshed in Lebanon must be stopped as soon as possible and so must outside interference in the country's internal affairs. The people of Lebanon must be given a chance to settle their difficult problems on a peaceful democratic basis ensuring Lebanon's independence, sovereignty, and territorial integrity. The interests of Middle East peace and security require that all anti-imperialist forces involved in the Lebanese crisis should come out of it not weakened and divided, but stronger and more closely united in the common interests of the struggle against Israeli aggression, against imperialist designs and manoeuvres, and for the freedom and social progress of the Arab peoples.

A radical and all-embracing political settlement of the Arab–Israeli conflict is the sole alternative to the highly critical situation in the Middle East. This must include three basic and organically linked elements: withdrawal of Israeli troops from all Arab territories occupied in 1967; recognition of the lawful rights of the Arab people of Palestine, including that of creating their own state; and provisions ensuring the right to independent existence and security for all Middle East states with pertinent international guarantees. This is a realistic and trust-worthy platform for normalizing the Middle East political situation.

The Soviet Union is for renewing the work of the international mechanism to achieve the requisite accords—the Geneva Peace Conference on the Middle East, in which all the directly interested sides, including the Palestine Liberation Organization, must participate. As reaffirmed by the 25th Congress of the CPSU, the Soviet Union is prepared to participate in international guarantees of the security and inviolability of the borders of all Middle East states within a UN framework or on any other basis. As we see it, it is also important to seek ways of ending the arms race in the Middle East, naturally in con-junction with a basic settlement there. The situation in the Middle East is a grave threat to peace and the security of nations, and requires effective steps all along the line leading to a just settlement. The USSR will actively continue contributing to this. Among other things, we have suggested an agenda for the above-mentioned conference.

A complicated and tense situation prevails in Cyprus, an area neighbouring on the Middle East. Foreign troops are still there and the military confrontation continues. Round after round of talks between the Greek and Turkish communities to find a mutually acceptable solution for the country's internal problems have brought no results. The successive UN resolutions are not being carried out. The situation is aggravated by attempts at saddling the Cypriots with a settlement suiting the interests of imperialist circles that are nursing plans of abolishing the integrity of the Republic of Cyprus, even liquidating the republic, and turning the island into a strategic NATO base. In sub-stance, these designs are the prime cause of the trials and upheavals that have fallen to Cyprus's lot.

The Soviet Union has always held and now holds that the Cyprus question can and must be settled with unqualified respect for the independence, sovereignty and territorial integrity of the Republic of Cyprus, and with sensible consideration for the interests of both communities, letting the people decide their own future independently, without any outside interference. Demilitarization of the island, providing for the withdrawal of foreign troops and abolition of all foreign military bases, is an important condition for a dependable settlement.

The Soviet proposal to put the Cyprus question before a representative international conference within a UN framework is especially timely in the prevailing conditions. It is meeting ever broader understanding and support among Cypriots and all those who sincerely wish to facilitate a just solution of the Cyprus problem in the interests of its people, security in the Eastern Mediterranean, and *détente*.

The clear and resolute Soviet position on the Middle East and Cyprus is a practical expression of its determination to support the national liberation movement and the anti-imperialist struggle of the peoples, and to help extinguish the flashpoints of war which impede normal international relations and further consolidation of world peace.

As put down in the new foreign policy programme, our country will 'do everything to deepen international *détente*, to embody it in concrete forms of mutually beneficial co-operation between states'. In our nuclear age there is no sensible alternative to *détente*. *Détente* is the means to secure more favourable external conditions for the building of socialism and communism and to radically improve the political climate in the world as a whole.

The purpose of *détente*—and now it is the leading trend in world affairs—is, first of all, to rule out outside interference in the internal affairs of states and the use or threat of force in disputes and conflicts, thus reducing the danger of another world war and letting people look to the future without fear. Yet, *détente* does not mean freezing the objective processes of history. It does not cancel out the antagonism between classes in capitalist countries, between the interests of the peoples and the interests of world imperialism, or between the two social systems. Neither does it scale down the ideological confrontation.

The policy of *détente*, which has already yielded tangible positive changes in world affairs thanks mainly to the Leninist course of the CPSU, is spreading to more and more states and has become an organic element in their conduct of foreign affairs. Many nations now enjoy its fruits. But much still remains to be done for *détente* to gain still greater depth and scope. Political *détente* must be steadily supplemented with military *détente*, and this is exactly what our country is working for.

One of the most topical problems is to expand peaceful co-operation in Europe and, in particular, to carry into effect the provisions of the Final Act of the Helsinki Conference—and this in full and in strict conformity with the way these provisions have been written into it, neither exaggerating the secondary nor belittling the primary. It is in this spirit that the Soviet Union will continue working for the implementation of the Helsinki accords by all states.

When they meet in Belgrade next year, the representatives of countries which participated in the Helsinki Conference must concentrate their attention on working out concrete measures facilitating implementation of the Final Act. It is in the common interest that the meeting should not turn into a registry of complaints and grievances.

The fight for peace, security and co-operation in Europe, the fight for its new image, is closely linked with the fight to root out recurrences of fascism and safeguard true democracy and national independence. This is precisely how the Communists of Europe put the issue.

Guided by principles of peaceful coexistence and striving for lasting peace, the Soviet Union intends to continue its policy of diverse long-term mutually beneficial co-operation with capitalist countries. Special significance attaches to the consistent improvement in Soviet–American relations—and this not only for the Soviet and American peoples but also for the further normalization of international affairs as a whole. The Soviet Union will continue doing its utmost so that these relations might become really stable and free of any transient effects. As noted in the Report to the 25th Congress, our relations with the United States have a good future, provided they continue to develop on a jointly elaborated realistic foundation allowing for the obvious difference in the class nature of the two states and in their ideology but showing firm resolve to settle differences and disputes by peaceful political means, not force or sabre-rattling.

Favourable conditions are at hand to extend the sphere of concord and co-operation with France. This is facilitated, among other things, by the Soviet–French declaration signed last year and the recent agreement on preventing accidental or unsanctioned use of nuclear weapons.

The Soviet Union also wants closer relations with the FRG, though, of course, it cannot overlook the designs of those reactionary forces in West Germany who are trying to direct its policy along a course contrary to the vital interests of peace and neighbourly relations in Europe. Our country stands for closer co-operation with Britain, Italy, Canada, Belgium, Denmark and other European states.

The USSR is prepared to extend its diverse co-operation with Japan. L. I. Brezhnev's recent meeting with a delegation of Japanese business representatives gave a strong new impulse to a mutual consolidation of economic ties. The positive results of this meeting strengthen our belief that Soviet–Japanese relations can and must follow an upward path if both sides want it so. Given a mutual interest in doing so, the Soviet Union and Japan are quite capable of determining the course of this development on their own. And we would like to hope that people in Japan understand this.

Congress has reaffirmed the long-term objective of working for 'Asian security based on joint efforts by the states of that continent'. As before, the Soviet Union will persevere in this, taking into account the positive elements that have recently appeared in the political life of the Asian continent.

New opportunities for a further improvement of the situation in Asia, for the spread of *détente* to this part of the world, and for the erection there of dependable pillars of peace have arisen with the ending of the war in Indo-China, the establishment of the united Socialist Republic of Vietnam—the outpost of socialism in Southeast Asia—as a result of the great victory of the Vietnamese people over aggression, and with the winning of independence by the peoples of the Lao People's Democratic Republic and Democratic Kampuchea.

Friendly co-operation between the USSR and India is an effective and important stabilizing factor in Asia. It is our constant concern to strengthen and expand relations with that great Asian country.

Everybody knows the principled Soviet position towards Maoist policy. But as pointed out at the 25th Congress, we are prepared to normalize relations with China on the principles of peaceful coexistence. The CPSU will go even further if Peking abandons its hostile political course against the socialist world and the interests of all nations. The next step is up to the Chinese side. Normalization of relations between the USSR and PRC would doubtless have a salubrious effect in Asia and in a broader international context.

Our country is in favour of making the Indian Ocean a zone of peace. This must above all provide for a radical solution to the problem of closing down foreign military bases, among which there have never been any Soviet ones. We are prepared to join other powers in a search for accords that would, on a reciprocal basis, reduce the military presence there and in the directly adjacent areas of states not bordering on the Indian Ocean.

The system of colonial domination has essentially been rooted out. The last of the colonial empires—the Portuguese—has fallen. Recently the people of Angola, supported by its allies and friends and by all freedom-loving countries and nations, won its independence in a courageous struggle. This is an outstanding victory.

It is still too early to say, however, that colonialism in all its shapes and forms has receded into the past. It continues to poison the world climate and is a cause of many international conflicts. It is, therefore, only right that the foreign policy programme of the 25th Congress contains the provision 'to consider as crucial the international task of completely eliminating all vestiges of the system of colonial oppression, infringement of the equality and independence of peoples, and all seats of colonialism and racialism'.

Due to the policy of the racist regimes in the Republic of South Africa and in Rhodesia, a major seat of tension has arisen of late in southern Africa. These regimes encroach most grossly on the lawful rights of the peoples of Namibia and Zimbabwe, and on those of the African majority in the RSA. They are trying to drown the freedom struggle in blood, and are committing acts of aggression against neighbouring states. The responsibility for this falls, among others, on those imperialist circles outside Africa that co-operate with, support and arm the racist regimes.

The inhuman apartheid policy is a threat to the independence and free development of African countries and peoples. It endangers peace in Africa and the rest of the world. The Soviet Union severely condemns this policy and is consistently working for the effective isolation and

213

boycott of the racist regimes in South Africa and Rhodesia. It urges strict fulfilment of the resolutions of the UN, OAU, and other international bodies and forums demanding an end to apartheid and to all other racial discrimination. The African majority in South Africa and the peoples of Namibia and Zimbabwe must be given an opportunity to determine their own future without outside interference and to live in peace and freedom.

The visibly greater positive influence of the young independent states on world affairs, their visibly greater international activity, is described in the Central Committee Report as an important phenomenon of modern international life. This incontestable fact was illustrated by the 5th Conference of Non-aligned Countries, held in Colombo in August, whose participants declared their resolve to combat imperialism, war and aggression, colonialism and neo-colonialism, and to further unity among forces working for peace, national independence and social progress.

The Soviet Union thinks highly of the anti-imperialist, anti-colonial and anti-racist orientation of the non-aligned movement. We presume that the contribution of the non-aligned countries, of all developing states, to the common cause of peace and security could be still more palpable.

We are bound with the vast majority of developing countries, with their peoples, by our common allegiance to profound peace and freedom, and by our common basic aspirations. Solidarity with them runs through the entire foreign policy programme of the 25th Congress. Backing peoples fighting for national and social liberation, furthering the independence of developing countries, protecting their national sovereignty against expansionist encroachment, and aiding their economic and social progress—all this has ranked and continues to rank among the priorities of the Soviet foreign policy willed us by the great Lenin.

The problem of restructuring international economic relations created in the capitalist epoch and serving the needs of capitalism is becoming ever more urgent. They have long since come into sharp collision with the vital interests of the vast majority of countries and the chief trend in world affairs. It was only right, therefore, for Congress to set the objective of working for 'eliminating discrimination and all artificial barriers in international trade, and all manifestations of inequality, *diktat* and exploitation in international economic relations'.

In order to secure further growth in fruitful international economic co-operation on the basis of equality and mutual advantage, the Soviet Union and the other CMEA countries have proposed that an agreement should be concluded on the principles of mutual relations between the CMEA and the European Economic Community. The USSR has also come forward with a proposal for holding European congresses or inter-state conferences on co-operation in environmental protection and the development of transport and energetics. They could discuss joint measures to safeguard the natural environment, the problems of combating pollution of the land, air and the seas of Europe, creating trans-European waterways and ground routes, concluding transport conventions, setting up all-European power grids, and finding new sources of energy. These proposals elicited considerable interest inside and outside Europe, and the Soviet Union will, of course, continue to labour to have them put into practice.

The legitimate desire of the developing countries to win and consolidate not only political, but also economic independence is a highly important aspect of the battle for a new world economic order. They must be helped to break the trammels of colonialism and neo-colonialism, and to overcome backwardness, poverty, hunger and disease in the shortest possible time. While rendering them considerable and effective material aid, neither the Soviet Union nor the socialist community as a whole can, of course, bear responsibility for the continuing and still extremely grave economic difficulties of the new states that stem from their recent colonial past and are aggravated by the economic crises gripping the capitalist system.

It is common knowledge that the aid of the USSR and other socialist countries to the developing states amounts to disinterested support by friends and allies fighting a common enemy—imperialism, colonialism and neo-colonialism. Given this aid, the developing countries are wholly capable, step by step, of putting up roadblocks to imperialist dictation and discrimination in economic relations with developed capitalist states.

Special account should be taken of the important fact that progress

H

in normalizing the world's economic situation depends on the progress of political and military *détente* and on the stability of peace.

To improve the entire range of international economic relations, the Soviet Union advocates their reconstruction on a democratic and just foundation, furthering every country's sovereignty over its natural wealth and the right of every people to choose its own way of development without outside interference, ending exploitation of developing nations by foreign capital, and creating the best possible conditions for international division of labour to benefit all mankind.

Those are the international priorities of our time to which Soviet foreign policy applies itself under the Programme of Further Struggle for Peace and International Co-operation and for the Freedom and Independence of Peoples adopted by the 25th Congress. This Programme sets scientifically reasoned and at the same time concrete and feasible objectives at the centre of world affairs. And this is its strength. It gives expression to the fruitful unity of theory and practice in Lenin's strategy of peace, the changeless basis of Soviet foreign policy. Much effort is needed to fulfil the large-scale tasks set in this new Peace Programme. But there is good reason to count on success.

The Soviet Union places its tremendous influence in world affairs, its high international prestige and powerful economic and defensive potential at the service of world peace and progress. And it is also an important point that the foreign policy programme of the 25th Congress is seen by the fraternal socialist countries as their own programme, as a platform of agreed action on the international scene by the whole socialist community. Its noble aims have won understanding and support among all peace-loving and progressive forces and all honest people on earth.

'The Leninist Strategy of Peace:
the Unity of Theory and Practice',
from the September 1976 issue of
Kommunist, *the theoretical journal*
of the CPSU Central Committee

Ratification of the USSR–Angola Friendship Treaty. 14 March 1977

A Treaty of Friendship and Co-operation between the Union of Soviet Socialist Republics and the People's Republic of Angola has been submitted for your study and approval. It was concluded on 8 October 1976, during the stay in Moscow of an Angolan party-and-government delegation. It is sealed with the signatures of the General Secretary of the Central Committee of the CPSU, L. I. Brezhnev, and the Chairman of the MPLA and President of the PRA, Agostinho Neto.

The conclusion of the treaty is a highly significant event in the relations of our peoples and states. True friendship and co-operation between the peoples of the Soviet Union and Angola began at the time of the heroic struggle of Angolan patriots for their country's liberation from colonial oppression. During those years of grave trials for the people of Angola, and now as well, the Soviet Union is their reliable supporter. And the people of Angola appreciate this. Cuba and other fraternal socialist countries and all freedom-loving nations are on Angola's side.

The crushing defeat of the armed mercenary gangs sent into the country by the colonialists, the defeat of the venal reactionary groups at home, and the successes scored by People's Angola in building a new life are acclaimed by all those who stand for peace, democracy and national freedom. Angola's successes are deeply influencing the peoples fighting against the last remaining racist regimes in southern Africa.

We are not blind to the fact that the situation in Angola and around it is still fairly complicated, because the imperialists and neo-colonialists have not given up attempts at interfering in Angola's internal affairs in the hope of regaining their former grip and continuing to plunder and exploit the Angolan people. And small wonder they are trying to turn the tables by means of intrigue and plot, if not armed intervention. Angola has considerable natural resources and wealth. The enemies of People's Angola cannot reconcile themselves to the irreversible fact that an end has come to the unmitigated plunder of the country's wealth by foreigners. They are also displeased that the plans for making Angola part of a kind of *cordon sanitaire* between Free Africa and the racist South have completely failed. This is why the people of Angola and their government still have to repulse the incendiary sallies of the imperialist forces, which are directing and financing subversive activities, acts of diversion, and sabotage by counter-revolutionary groups.

The Soviet Union will continue to side with the Angolan patriots. It has rendered the government of the People's Republic of Angola diverse aid in strengthening its independence and sovereignty, and will continue to do so.

The Western mass media continue to spread lies about Soviet policy in Africa. It would not be amiss, therefore, to recall today the words spoken by L. I. Brezhnev on 7 October 1976 at a reception for the Angolan party-and-government delegation: 'We have no "special interests" in either the south or the north or any other part of Africa, nor can we have any. We seek no advantages there for ourselves. All we want is that the sacred right of every people to decide its own future, to choose its own way of development, should be recognized. This is our steadfast principle, one that neither our Party nor the Soviet people will ever depart from.' And this principle is wholly reflected in the treaty.

In sum, the Soviet–Angolan Treaty of Friendship and Co-operation is laying a reliable political and legal foundation for further fruitful and many-sided relations between the USSR and the PRA.

The treaty submitted for ratification by the Soviet Government to the Presidium of the Supreme Soviet strikingly exemplifies the consistency of the peaceful foreign policy of the Communist Party and Soviet Government, and of their internationalist solidarity with friends in the common struggle. It serves the aims of peace, *détente* and mutual understanding among nations; it is in no way directed against any third country, does not infringe upon anybody's legitimate interests, and does not conflict with the commitments of the two countries under any other effective agreements. Both contracting sides have reaffirmed their fidelity to the purposes and principles of the UN Charter.

Furthermore, the treaty is an important contribution to the strengthening of the unity of anti-imperialist forces, the peace forces, the forces of national liberation and progress.

Precisely this is why the treaty was met with satisfaction not only by the Soviet and Angolan peoples, but also by the peoples of the fraternal socialist countries, the African states, and the people of the world.

Speech at a session of the Presidium of the USSR Supreme Soviet on the ratification of the Treaty of Friendship and Co-operation between the USSR and the People's Republic of Angola concluded on 8 October 1976

After US Secretary of State Vance's visit to Moscow. 31 March 1977

In connection with the Moscow visit of US Secretary of State C. Vance rumours, in all sorts of versions, have appeared abroad, chiefly in the United States of America, about the outcome of the talks.

It will be recalled that US President Carter also made a statement without even waiting for the Secretary of State's arrival in Washington. I must say that the rumours do not accord with the actual state of affairs. What is more, some of them distort the actual situation and that is why there is need for appropriate explanations and clarifications from our side.

I believe that every one of those present here has guessed that one of the main questions discussed during the talks held by Leonid Brezhnev with Mr Vance, and also during my own meetings with the Secretary of State, was the question of concluding a new agreement on the limitation of strategic arms, since the agreement now in force expires in October of this year.

What is the essence of the Vladivostok accord? I mean to say, what is the essence of the main issue which was examined? It would not be out of place to recall this.

Agreement was eventually reached in Vladivostok that the Soviet Union and the United States would each have 2,400 strategic arms carriers, including 1,320 MIRVs. This is the main content of the Vladivostok accord.

You know that there were many reports—both official and semi-official—saying that there was progress after Vladivostok. There were also more moderate reports. But, in general, it is true that quite a few steps forward have been taken. There were opportunities to bring things to completion. However, this did not happen.

Then all of a sudden the question arose of the so-called Cruise missile. What does this mean? There is hardly any need to dwell on the technical aspect of the matter. They tried to prove to us that the Vladivostok Agreements did not refer to the Cruise missile, that this missile, don't you see, is in general not subject to any limitations and that the Vladivostok accord concerns ballistic missiles only. We strongly objected to this attempt. At Vladivostok the question was posed differently, no green light was given there to the Cruise missile. The question was posed in this way—to work for such an agreement that would shut off all channels of the strategic arms race and reduce the threat of nuclear war.

The United States and the Soviet Union exchanged relevant official documents which sealed the Vladivostok accords. Everything, it seemed, was clear and it remained to carry the matter forward to the signing of an agreement. The delegations of the USSR and the USA at Geneva were working on some of the questions, including the legal wording of the agreement. At first things were moving. But all of a sudden a wall rose and everything was frozen. Apparently somebody, some influential forces in the USA, found all this not to their liking. And you know that great difficulties arose and these difficulties have not been removed. If one is to speak frankly, of late these difficulties have increased. What should we call this situation and this kind of position, which certain people in the United States began taking after Vladivostok? This is a line of revision, a line of revising the commitments made in Vladivostok.

We are categorically opposed to this. We are in favour of the edifice that was built through such hard work in Vladivostok, an edifice on which so many intellectual and other resources were spent, being not only preserved, but that things should be brought to a conclusion and a new agreement on limiting strategic arms should be concluded between the USSR and the USA.

We were told, and it was said to us in the last few days when the talks were on in Moscow, that one of the obstacles is the Soviet Union's possession of a certain type of bomber (it is called Backfire bomber in the USA), which it was said can be used as a strategic weapon and that this plane absolutely must be mentioned in the agreement. We categorically rejected and continue to reject such attempts. Time and again Mr Brezhnev personally explained to President Ford, specifically during the meeting in Helsinki, and later to President Carter, that it was a medium-range bomber and not a strategic bomber. Nevertheless, this question was tossed at us again. Somebody evidently needs to artificially create an additional obstacle. The Americans know best the level at which these obstacles are put up, whereas we simply acknowledge the fact that this question is raised artificially to complicate progress toward the conclusion of an agreement.

During the first talk with Mr Vance Mr Brezhnev set forth our position on all the basic questions of limiting strategic arms and concluding a new agreement. Furthermore, in several public statements Mr Brezhnev set forth the Soviet Union's policy on that question, underlining its readiness to work for an agreement. It was emphasized that an agreement accords with the interests of the United States and the Soviet Union as well as the interests of the whole world. Throughout the talks here in Moscow our side emphasized the main idea that the foundation for a new agreement that has been built up should not be destroyed, but that it should be preserved at all costs.

And truly, what would happen if upon the arrival of a new leadership in some country, all the constructive things that had been achieved in relations with other countries were scrapped? What stability in relations with other countries could we talk about in such a case? What stability can we talk about in relations between the USA and the USSR in this case? We, our side, would like to see just such stability in our relations so that these relations should be as good as possible and based on the principles of peaceful coexistence and, even better, that they should be friendly. That is our stand and we would like to see similar actions in reply from the other side, that is the United States of America.

A version is now being circulated in the USA alleging that the US representatives at the Moscow talks proposed a broad programme for disarmament, but that the Soviet leadership did not accept this programme. I must say that this version does not accord with reality. This version is essentially false. Nobody proposed such a programme to us.

I shall dwell on some facts from which you may draw certain conclusions.

For example, it is proposed to us now to reduce the number of strategic arms carriers to 2,000 or even 1,800 units and MIRVs to 1,200 or 1,100. What is more, it is simultaneously proposed to liquidate half of the rockets in our possession because they are simply disliked by somebody in the United States. They are called either 'too heavy', or 'too effective', or something else. They don't like these rockets, and that is why the Soviet Union should jettison half of these weapons. So, we would like to ask whether such a unilateral way of putting the question is a way to agreement? No, it only damages the Vladivostok accord and breaks the balance of limitations on which agreement was reached in Vladivostok.

What has changed after the Vladivostok accord? There are no changes at all. You may call it as you like, but this is no way to solve problems. It is the way of piling up one unresolved problem on another. Regrettably there are quite a few of these problems still, especially if we take the broad area of the arms race. We are all for the accord reached earlier between the USA and the Soviet Union being meticulously observed as was intended when the accord was achieved.

In advancing proposals of this kind, they seek to present them virtually as 'general and complete disarmament'. But if we want to really speak about general and complete disarmament, an extensive plan of general and complete disarmament under strict and effective control lies on the desk of the American President, the governments of other NATO countries, and the governments of all states of the world. There has been much talk about control, and especially in the post-war period, about extensive control, with the dispatching of foreign inspectors to other states, etc. Our reply to all these statements has been: yes, we are ready to agree to general and complete control during general and complete disarmament. Well, has the matter advanced after this? No, there has been no advance on this matter. The number of resolutions adopted in various bodies of the United Nations and at different kinds of international conferences on disarmament has increased. But the scale of the arms race has not been reduced by this.

During the talks with Mr Vance it was also suggested that we revise the right of the two sides to modernize existing missiles as laid down in the present agreement, just as in the Vladivostok accords. This was taken for granted. No problems arose. But no, it is now proposed to break up the agreement also in this respect, and to do so in a way that would give advantage to the United States, with the Soviet Union finding itself in a worse position. Clearly, we shall not depart from the principle of equality in this regard either. And to put forward such demands is a dubious, if not a cheap move.

Just another fact. It was proposed to us to include a clause in the agreement prohibiting the creation of new kinds of weapons. At first sight it seemed there was nothing bad in it. But I would like to remind you that the Soviet Union itself had long ago made a proposal on banning the manufacture of new kinds and new systems of weapons of mass extermination. Moreover, we have submitted a draft of the relevant international treaty to the United Nations. And what was the response? Perhaps the US Government supported this proposal? No. They did not breathe a word in support of that treaty. Even at the negotiations in Moscow they said only the most general words about the need to include into an agreement such a proposition, moreover together or, as they say, in a 'package' with other obviously unacceptable proposals. All that left a very dubious impression. If there is a serious intention in this matter, then, as I have already said, there is a concrete proposal. At first when we raised the question of banning new kinds of weapons, we were asked: what do you mean? Could anything more novel than nuclear weapons be thought up? But when we cited relevant facts, and these are known not only to us, but also to scientists in other countries, the attitude to this proposal of ours somewhat changed. I cannot therefore say that our proposal met with a negative attitude on the part of all the other states. No, it didn't. But on the part of major states, on the part of the USA, it unfortunately got no support.

Let us speak frankly. If both our countries stand for banning new kinds of weapons of mass extermination, then let us discuss the draft treaty we have. If you have amendments to the Soviet draft, put them forth. Let us discuss these amendments. If you have no amendments, then let us conclude this treaty.

I say it again—our draft treaty is already in the hands of the US Government. And wouldn't it be better to state definitely whether or not the US Government is prepared to sign such a treaty? To mix this idea with other questions and propose examining all of them in a 'package' means to bury the 'package' and, together with it, the idea itself. This is not a new method, of course. It has long been used by some persons.

It seems to us that in international affairs in general, including relations between the USA and the Soviet Union, it would be better to examine relevant problems on a more realistic, on an honest basis.

The more trickery in these affairs, attempts to tread on one's partner's foot, so to speak, the more difficulties this will bring about. This does not promote an improvement in Soviet–US relations, the cause of *détente* or the strengthening of peace. It is necessary to stress this in connection with the latest statements which have appeared in US newspapers and, regrettably, not only in the newspapers.

I should like to add a few words more.

If the US is prepared to ban new kinds of weapons, why, then, is the need to produce the B-1 strategic bomber, so beloved by some people in the US, defended all that much? The same is true of the manufacture of the Trident atomic submarine. L. I. Brezhnev spoke of these new American weapons systems in his speeches and in his remarks during the official negotiations with the American side, and did so repeatedly. So what we have now is that certain declarations by the American side do not tally with the actual readiness to ban new kinds of weapons of mass extermination.

One would rather not speak on this theme, but one has to. In his latest statement the President of the USA used the word 'sincerity' when referring to the Soviet leadership's attitude to questions of strategic arms limitation. I would like to say: we do not lack sincerity. We have plenty of it. It is on this basis that we are building all our policy and we would want all to build their policies on the same basis, so that deeds do not differ from words.

US representative Mr Vance described his proposals mentioned above as the basis for a broad and all-encompassing agreement. But it is easy, after an objective study of these proposals, to draw the conclusion that they pursue the aim of getting unilateral advantages for the USA to the detriment of the Soviet Union, its security and the security of its allies and friends. The Soviet Union will never agree to this. This was openly said by Leonid Brezhnev to the US Secretary of

State during the first talk. He said the same during the last talk held yesterday.

Reading some of the statements made in the USA you probably noticed that not only some what they call 'all-encompassing proposals' have been made to us, but also an alternative 'narrow proposal'. What is this 'narrow proposal'? We are simply told—let us conclude an agreement that will concern ballistic missiles and strategic bombers. At the same time it is proposed to ignore the Cruise missile and the Soviet bomber called Backfire, which I have already reminded you is not a strategic weapon at all.

It looks as if a concession is being made to us, but it is a very strange concession. We are given what does not belong to the United States. Having called a non-strategic aircraft strategic, some persons then say: we are prepared not to include this bomber in the agreement at this stage, if the Soviet Union gives the green light to the manufacture and deployment of US Cruise missiles.

So, according to this narrower agreement, the Cruise missile would be totally excluded from the agreement. Such a decision would signify that sealing one channel, ballistic missiles, would simultaneously be opening a new channel which could be wider and deeper—production of Cruise missiles, which are nuclear arms carriers. I emphasize— nuclear arms carriers. But it is our task to prevent nuclear war and deliver mankind from nuclear war. Is it not the same thing to be killed by weapons delivered by a Cruise missile or by weapons delivered by a ballistic missile? The result is the same. Besides, the production of Cruise missiles will devour no less money—dollars, pounds sterling, roubles, francs, lire, etc. Do the peoples stand to gain by this? What, one may ask, will be the use of such an agreement for security? And will this be security at all?

No, it will not be the security which peoples sincerely want. It will not be even a semblance of security. Frankly speaking, that is why we also rejected the so-called narrow agreement. We declared that it does not present a solution for the problem and does not even come close to solving the problem. That is what the US Secretary of State took back when he left Moscow.

We do not know how all this will be presented to public opinion in the USA. Judging by the first signs the actual state of affairs has been distorted. The results of the exchange of opinions and the statements made to the US Secretary of State were also distorted. Leonid Brezhnev's statements were also distorted.

None of this helps to provide a productive solution of problems, though we sincerely wish them to be solved. But we are ready to continue talks on all these problems. The Soviet leaders have the necessary patience. I would like discussions, regardless of where they are held—here in Moscow, in Washington or in other places—to finally come to a favourable conclusion.

Leonid Brezhnev emphasized: 'We stand firmly for good relations with the United States, just as with other countries of the world. We stand for relations based on the principles of peaceful coexistence, for friendly relations. And possibilities for that are far from exhausted. They are not exhausted, insofar as they concern the United States and the Soviet Union.'

We do not intend to belittle the substantial differences that now exist between the positions of the USA and the Soviet Union. The Secretary of State was told this frankly. But does this mean that there are insurmountable obstacles? No, it does not. We would like to hope that the leadership of the United States will adopt a more realistic stand, that it will give greater consideration to the security interests of the Soviet Union and its allies and will not strive for unilateral advantages.

I would like to touch upon yet another problem. This is the question of military budgets. How many times have our Central Committee, the Supreme Soviet, the Soviet Government and Leonid Brezhnev personally in his speeches and in confidential talks with the leaders of respective countries belonging to a different social system raised the question of reducing military budgets! We also submitted this proposal for discussion by all states. And this proposal, like the proposal on banning the production of new types of mass destruction weapons, has met with extensive support. Regrettably, we see how the budgets of some states, the USA included, grow and follow an ascending line. This is a very wide-ranging topic and right now I do not want to go into detail on it. I want to give every emphasis to the fact that war budgets must be reduced and the funds in question should be rechannelled into peaceful purposes.

I am not going to read you the complete list of the proposals submitted by the Soviet Union over the past few years for consideration by the appropriate international organizations and other governments, the proposals that are intended to ensure *détente*, peace, disarmament, and better relations between states. That list includes more than seventy proposals. I will only mention some of them in order to put things in their proper place, to restore the truth and to expose the lies that some foreign newspapers and politicians have of late been persistently propagating. They allege that the Soviet Union is guilty of spurring on the arms race. Way back in 1946, immediately after the war, the Soviet Union made a proposal on concluding a convention prohibiting the use of nuclear energy for military purposes. And who was the sponsor of the proposal on the non-proliferation of nuclear weapons? The Soviet Union, the Soviet state, and not the country that today claims to be virtually the champion of general and complete disarmament.

Such a treaty has been concluded. Unfortunately, not all the states have joined it and this is bad.

On the initiative of the Soviet Union the Moscow Treaty Banning Nuclear Weapon Tests in Three Media has been concluded. Moreover, we have made a proposal on the universal and complete prohibition of nuclear weapon tests. This proposal has received broad-based support in the United Nations. Do you think the United States has supported our proposal? No, it has not. Even today that proposal is on the agenda of certain governments. If the US Government and its allies want to do something good they should adhere to the will of the overwhelming majority of the world's states and conclude a comprehensive agreement on the complete prohibition of nuclear weapon tests. We will continue to work vigorously for the positive solution of that problem.

Our country has made a proposal on banning the modification of the environment for military purposes. I must point out that, by and large, the United States has supported this proposal, although a number of the provisions of our draft treaty have been weakened by it to the displeasure of a number of states. Nevertheless, the overall result, the final result, is positive and, apparently, an appropriate international convention will soon be signed.

Now take the proposal on banning bacteriological weapons. Who made this proposal? Perhaps those who now state that it is they who are the advocates of radical disarmament and curbing the arms race? No, that proposal was also made by the Soviet Union, and we take pleasure in stating that an appropriate agreement has been concluded.

We have made a proposal on the non-use of force in international relations. Although the overwhelming majority of states have voted for the Soviet proposal, unfortunately certain countries without which the agreement cannot be made effective still show a manifestly negative attitude to it. What arguments are raised against that proposal? They say that there is the UN Charter which already has appropriate provisions. I can only say to that that the Charter lays down general guidelines, whereas importance is attached not only to general guidelines, but also to the practical policies of states. Therefore, the conclusion of the treaty proposed by us would mean a great step forward. I would like to express the hope that the US Government and its allies will heed the opinion of the majority of the world's countries and the idea will be eventually translated into an international treaty.

Not so long ago, during a Bucharest session of the Political Consultative Committee the participating states of the Warsaw Treaty jointly proposed that all the participating countries of the Helsinki Conference commit themselves not to be the first to use nuclear weapons against one another. One may ask: what is bad about this proposal?

Indeed, if no one will be the first to use nuclear weapons, then there will be no state to be the second and, hence, the third, fourth and fifth to use them. And this means that the danger of nuclear war will be pushed back in general. That is one of the effective proposals aimed at strengthening peace and *détente*.

The NATO member-states, however, without any particular discussions, though they say there was a difference of views, declared their negative attitude to this proposal. We do not regard the discussion of this matter to be over. Perhaps technically this item is not on NATO's agenda, but in reality it remains and will continue to be discussed until the problem of the non-use of nuclear energy for military purposes is resolved.

We stand for the United States joining more effectively and more actively in the positive solution of relevant problems.

We are trying to convince the USA, and our explanations today are directed precisely towards that end.

The Soviet Union pursues a consistent policy of peace, of international *détente*, a policy of curbing the arms race, a policy of disarmament. It is a Leninist policy of peace. You have heard about it at our Party Congresses and at plenary meetings of the Party's Central Committee. This is our basic line, we shall follow it persistently, and no one will push us off that road. But we shall also give a rebuff to anyone who tries to improve his position to the detriment of our interests or the interests of our friends and allies.

This is the just basis on which we are conducting and would like to conduct in the future our affairs with the United States.

Do not think that the critical remarks against the USA, in particular in connection with the question of strategic weapons, lessen to any extent our desire to see good relations between the USA and the Soviet Union or, better still, friendly relations. But this depends not only on us. We will embark upon and cover our part of the road. But there is the other part of the road which must be travelled by the United States. I should like to believe that it will cover its part of the road.

I will touch on two more questions. Some people pretend that these questions have no direct relation to the problem which was discussed as the principal one during the stay in Moscow of the US Secretary of State. But this is far from being so.

The first question I would like to formulate thus: this is the question of not handing strategic weapons over to third countries, and of taking no action whatsoever to circumvent the agreement with the signing of which we are now concerned. On this question we formulated a concrete proposal. It was discussed. At any rate, we posed it at Geneva in the course of the talks between the American and Soviet delegations. But our representatives received no substantial reply.

We attach no small importance to the solution of this question.

The second question is about the advance deployment of American nuclear weapons in Europe, around Europe and in other areas from where these weapons can reach Soviet territory.

Even during the concluding of the first agreement on the limitation of strategic weapons we made official statements to the effect that we should return to that question. In the interests of reaching an understanding in Vladivostok, we did not suggest that the agreement should include as a binding condition the dismantling of US nuclear facilities based in forward areas. In the light of the latest US proposals, however, we take a different view of the matter. This question concerns our security and the security of our allies. We have the right to raise the question of dismantling the US forward bases. This concerns nuclear-powered submarines, bombers capable of delivering nuclear weapons, and aircraft-carriers in a certain area of Europe (you know quite well which area is meant). Call this whatever you like, a toughening of the position or a change in the position. But, I repeat, we face this question now in connection with the latest American proposals.

Concluding my statement, I would like to point out that we are invariably loyal to our peace policy and will unswervingly pursue this policy. It is the policy of our Party, its Central Committee and the policy of the entire Soviet people. It was dwelt upon on many occasions by Leonid Brezhnev, when he spoke from the rostrum of the Central Committee and in many other speeches, including those in Tula and at the recent Trade Union Congress.

But we shall never relinquish our legitimate interests and our security. We can conduct affairs, including affairs with the United States, only on the basis of equality, not to the detriment of our legitimate interests. If the other side does the same, I think both sides can look to the future with optimism.

We have a preliminary understanding about a meeting of the Ministers of Foreign Affairs of the two countries in Geneva. I think we shall have plenty to talk about.

Mr Gromyko then answered journalists' questions.

Question: What can you say about the statements coming from the White House that in case the strategic arms limitation talks fail the United States will develop and deploy new strategic weapons?

Answer: I can only say that if anyone takes this road he will have to take full responsibility for the consequences of such actions. It is our belief that every effort should be made to curb the arms race, i.e. to achieve positive results in the talks.

Question: What other aspects of arms limitations and disarmament were discussed during the talks with C. Vance and what is the Soviet Union's stand on this score?

Answer: I have given you a sufficient list of the problems discussed.

I will only add that concerning some issues that remain open at the present time—and the USA has objections to most of them—we agreed that our representatives will evidently have to meet, and maybe more than once, in order to remove the existing differences. Such meetings can be useful. This is the positive side of Mr Vance's visit.

Question: Does the US President's line on the question of 'human rights' affect the solution of the strategic arms problem?

Question: Do you consider the campaign being conducted in the United States by certain quarters in relation to the invented 'human rights' issue as a deliberate whipping up of tension?

Answer: The second question helps me to answer the first one. I cannot say that we spoke about 'rights' when discussing any aspect of the problem of preparation of a new agreement on the limitation of strategic arms. Of course not. But the fact of the matter is that all that is being said in the United States lately about 'human rights'—and all present here know what and how much talk there is over there on this subject—naturally poisons the atmosphere, worsens the political climate. Does this help to settle other questions, including those related to strategic weapons? No, it does not help. On the contrary, it interferes. Answering to the point, I would say the following: we do not force ourselves on anyone at all as teachers, since the matter concerns the internal affairs of a state, and only states themselves can decide their own internal affairs. I emphasize it, internal affairs. But we will permit nobody else to strike up the pose of teachers and to tell us how to decide our internal affairs. I stress this, our internal affairs.

I shall recall the documents which in 1933 President Roosevelt and Litvinov, Minister of Foreign Affairs of the USSR at the time, exchanged on the establishment of normal diplomatic relations between the Soviet Union and the United States. It was clearly stated there that one of the main conditions for the normalization of relations between the USA and the Soviet Union is non-interference in each other's internal affairs. Incidentally, this was recorded on the initiative of the American side. This does not mean that we, too, would not have proposed this ourselves. If this principle was correct then, then it is also correct today. The thesis about non-interference in the internal affairs of states is a component of our general Leninist foreign policy. We shall not retreat

231

from it. No noise, howling or screaming will swerve us off this road. We shall move along our own road, with no need of the kind of teachers whom I have just mentioned.

Question: What do you think about the selling of arms and military equipment by the great powers to the developing countries?

Answer: First of all, I would like to note that US President Jimmy Carter himself stated that the number one supplier of arms to other countries is the United States. A lot of both American and Soviet arms and arms of other countries are travelling around the world today. Why? Because there are many hot-beds of tension, there are many places where people are waging a legitimate struggle either for the liberation of their territories, as is the case in the Middle East, or for other inalienable rights of theirs. Where is that wise man or those wise men who, in this situation, can decide today the question of stopping the trade in arms, while leaving aside the solution of problems which build up seats of tension? If this question suggests anything, then it suggests that it is necessary to tackle these problems and solve them.

Take, for example, Rhodesia. Twenty-four out of every twenty-five people there are black Africans and one is white. Who must wield power in that country? I think the answer is clear from these figures. I would like to develop this thought. What system that country should have must be decided by the people themselves. Not by outside forces, not by some instructors and not by all those types who like to travel about and teach people how they should arrange their domestic affairs.

Question: Could you talk in more detail about the purpose of your possible meeting next May in Geneva with the US Secretary of State?

Answer: We agreed to discuss in detail and meticulously the Middle East problem. In passing I must say that Mr Vance and the US Government stressed the role of the two powers, as co-chairmen of the Geneva Conference, in settling that problem. I mentioned in my statement that we do not rule out the appearance by that time of questions on which an exchange of views may perhaps take place.

Question: In your opinion what benefits resulted from the meeting with Secretary of State Mr Vance, having in view benefits for improving mutual understanding between the USSR and the USA?

Answer: I would answer this question in the following way: the visit of the US Secretary of State was necessary and indeed useful, because we must know each other well. I mean not a superficial acquaintance, but knowledge of the position, knowledge of the policies of the countries on the problems concerned. We also diverge on some questions, and important questions they are. I have already spoken about this and do not think there is any necessity to repeat it. Some agreement was reached to continue discussions on unsolved matters on which we could not find a common language with the USA. The exchange of views may be held not necessarily at a high level, but, say, at the level of experts or counsellors. Then we could see where we stand. We hope that the American side will show a serious attitude to these accords. For our part we promise to be serious.

Question: Was any exception made in regard to the Cruise missile in the Vladivostok agreements?

Answer: No exception was made.

Declaration at a press conference held in Moscow following the visit of US Secretary of State Vance in March 1977

The 32nd session of the UN General Assembly. 27 September 1977

At every session of the General Assembly we take satisfaction at seeing the growing ranks of member states of the United Nations. Their number has now reached almost 150. This is yet another indication of the positive changes occurring in world affairs. It signifies that the peoples one after another continue to gain freedom and independence, thereby confirming the inexorable advance of the process of national liberation.

But what matters most is that the constant influx of new members adds to the political weight and capabilities of the United Nations and enhances the over-all potential of the policy of peace. Indeed, the main objective of all the activities of the United Nations as laid down in its Charter is 'to save succeeding generations from the scourge of war'.

Our country made its irrevocable choice long ago. The essence of

Soviet foreign policy is to ensure a peaceful creative life for our people and peace for all peoples on earth. For sixty years now we have been firmly and unswervingly following this line bequeathed to us by the founder of the Soviet State, Vladimir Lenin.

In this year of the sixtieth anniversary of the Great October Socialist Revolution the peaceful goals and humanitarian principles of the foreign policy of the Soviet Union will acquire the force of fundamental law and as such will be enshrined in the new Constitution of the USSR.

The same objectives are served by the concrete foreign policy actions of the Soviet Union, by the initiatives which we take in international affairs. Many of them have been enunciated from this very rostrum. In a condensed form they are set forth in the Programme of Further Struggle for Peace and International Co-operation and for the Freedom and Independence of Peoples adopted by the Twenty-fifth Congress of the CPSU, the highest political forum of our Party.

As an integral part of the world socialist system our country acts in the international arena in close unity with fraternal socialist states. We are proud that the entire world is increasingly recognizing the fact that the socialist community of states commits its growing resources and the full weight of the prestige of its foreign policy on the side of fruitful co-operation among peoples, their security, and universal peace.

But is it not true that work for a stronger peace is no less pressing today than it was yesterday? Indeed, it has proved possible in recent years to make headway in this direction. In various parts of the planet people have felt tangibly that it is easier to breathe, that the threat of war is receding. The process of *détente* is becoming pivotal to the development of international relations. But it is clear that in the current situation, with its pluses and minuses intricately intertwined, this process is not yet immune from pitfalls or even reverses.

Faced with the clear prospect of improvement in the international climate, certain groups are intensifying their attempts to launch an offensive to push the world back to the time of the cold war. These groups have a stake in an unrestrained arms race, the preservation of old centres of tensions and the creation of new ones, and the perpetuation of the remnants of colonialism and racism.

As a matter of fact we are confronted with the following alternative:

either the world will follow the road of renouncing the use of force, the road of disarmament and equal, mutually beneficial co-operation, or it may plunge even more deeply into the arms race and find itself on the brink of a nuclear catastrophe. That is why our country is laying such a stress on the need to continue and consolidate *détente*.

One hears it said at times: 'You know, *détente* is an abstract thing, nobody really knows what it is all about.' Such an argument is spurious and far-fetched. But if it is really necessary to clarify the meaning which the USSR gives to the concept of a relaxation of tensions, this has been done most authoritatively by Leonid Brezhnev.

He said in his speech in the city of Tula last January:

'*Détente* means, first of all, the overcoming of the cold war and transition to normal, stable relations among states; *détente* means willingness to resolve differences and disputes not by force, not by threats or sabre-rattling, but by peaceful means, at the conference table. *Détente* means a certain trust and ability to take into consideration each other's legitimate interests.'

We note with satisfaction that an increasing number of responsible statesmen are coming to the conclusion that in a nuclear age there is no reasonable alternative to the policy of *détente* and peaceful coexistence.

The policy of *détente* cannot be allowed to mark time, still less to take a downward turn. It must be constantly nourished with new initiatives and brought within the reach of an ever greater number of states; in short, we must ensure what one might call the materialization of *détente*.

The United Nations has a weighty role in this respect also. All member states of the United Nations, no matter how diverse their positions and views, are called upon to step up their efforts to deepen and strengthen *détente*.

The General Assembly could determine, in terms of the present-day situation, the top priority areas in which states could exert peaceful efforts and the line of conduct which they should follow in relations with each other.

What, specifically, do we have in mind?

It is necessary, above all, to scrupulously protect the assets of *détente* that have already been accumulated and to prevent them from being squandered. And the assets accumulated in recent years are quite impressive. It is necessary to assist actively in the implementation of multilateral treaties and agreements which serve the interests of strengthening international security and developing peaceful relations, as well as of United Nations decisions aimed at reaching these goals.

Another appropriate channel for directing efforts for the benefit of peace and peaceful relations among states is, of course, that of taking resolute steps to contain the arms race and to turn the course of events towards disarmament.

In the post-war period the arms race has been spiralling upwards continuously, but we were not the ones who have caused this. This race was forced on the world by others. However, at every stage the Soviet Union has proposed, backing its proposals up with concrete deeds, that an end be put to the dangerous competition and that funds be diverted to the noble endeavour of improving the conditions of life for the peoples of the world. And that is still our position.

The Soviet proposals in the field of disarmament are well known. At the last session of the General Assembly we submitted them again in a summarized form in our memorandum on questions of ending the arms race and on disarmament. It emphasized our willingness to search for new measures in the field of disarmament, as well as to advance towards general and complete disarmament.

We do not in the least underestimate the significance of some constraints placed on the arms race in a number of areas in recent years. The Soviet Union has made its contribution, together with other countries, in the preparation and implementation of a whole series of relevant international treaties and agreements. These either curtail the build-up of certain types of weapons or ban the arms race in certain environments.

The latest example of this is the signing of the Convention on the Prohibition of Military or Any Other Hostile Use of Environmental Modification Techniques. In our view, all states without exception should accede to it if they want to support by deeds their words about peace.

Nonetheless, in realistic terms very little has been done so far. In fact physical disarmament and the elimination of the material means of warfare have not even started yet. The armies of nations have not been reduced by a single aircraft or a single tank as called for in United Nations resolutions.

If one listens to the pronouncements of certain statesmen, one might get the impression that they appear to be in favour of putting an end to this. But what, I ask, is the actual state of affairs?

A closer look at what are sometimes proposed as 'comprehensive' disarmament recipes reveals that the objectives pursued are diametrically opposed to that of reaching agreements. It would seem that the intent here is roughly as follows: what about making a proposal known in advance to be unacceptable to our counterpart? He then will reject it, thereby giving us a convenient excuse, first, to blame him for that and, secondly, by invoking his rejection, to take steps to build up armaments which, in the absence of such camouflage, would appear quite unseemly.

Can one really on the one hand propose various 'drastic reductions' while on the other hand authorizing the development of new and, bluntly speaking, merciless, terrifying types of weapons such as the neutron bomb? No wonder the world literally shuddered when it learned of the secret programmes to manufacture that weapon. How can one qualify this inhuman weapon as 'humane'? After all, it is intended to be used directly against human beings and is in the same category as such cruel and barbaric means of warfare as bacteriological or chemical weapons. In our view, the United Nations must resolutely demand that the plans for the production of new types and systems of weapons of mass destruction, including the neutron bomb, should be discontinued.

A special session of the United Nations General Assembly on disarmament is to be convened next year. We shall have to conduct there not merely a wide exchange of views on fundamental approaches to the disarmament problem at the present stage. We shall have to identify jointly the main areas where states should concentrate their priority efforts in the field of disarmament. The Soviet Union would like that session to be businesslike and to help with practical preparations for a successful convening in the immediate future of a world disarmament conference.

Next, efforts in favour of *détente* presuppose such actions by states as would contribute to an early peaceful settlement of situations of conflict and to the preclusion of new situations of that kind arising.

Acting in conformity with the decisions of the 25th Congress of the

CPSU, our country continues to actively press for the elimination of the remaining hot-beds of war. Of course, the most dangerous of those is the one in the Middle East.

For its part the Soviet Union will go on doing all in its power to bring about such a settlement in the Middle East as would establish a lasting peace there without infringing the legitimate rights and interests of any people or any state of the region.

From this high rostrum our country declares once again that we have been and remain advocates of the just cause of the Arabs, whose lands have been unlawfully taken away and are still retained by force of arms. Those lands must be returned unconditionally to the Arab peoples.

But if there is any need to reiterate once again that Israel has a right to exist as an independent and sovereign state in the Middle East, then on behalf of the Soviet leadership, on behalf of the Soviet Union, I say again that we have always adhered and will continue to adhere to precisely that line.

The Soviet Union is in favour of an early reconvening of the Geneva Peace Conference with the participation on an equal footing of all parties concerned, including representatives of the Palestine Liberation Organization.

The Soviet Union, as co-chairman of the Conference, intends to do its utmost to have it convened and make it work successfully, and it expects the other co-chairman—the United States of America—also to follow that line.

For more than a year now tensions have also persisted in Cyprus. No one will convince us that it is impossible to solve this problem without impairing the independence, sovereignty or territorial integrity of Cyprus. It is clear that there a most intricate knot has been tied, but given goodwill it can be untied by peaceful means. The Soviet Union is prepared to facilitate this, and our relevant proposals remain valid.

For many years now the question of withdrawing foreign troops from Korea has been on the order of the day. Is it really essential that the United Nations should admit its impotence in this respect? We think otherwise. There are quite a few possibilities for solving this question so as to prevent a potential conflict from erupting in that part of the world.

Attempts to strengthen and expand military blocs run directly counter to the spirit of *détente*. The Soviet Union and other countries of the socialist community have recently put forward a proposal that at least no action should be taken that could result in enlarging the existing closed groupings and political–military alliances, or creating new ones. However, the attitude of the Western countries to this initiative of the socialist states was, to put it mildly, cool. It would appear that its realization would run counter to their designs.

Let us take the Vienna talks on the reduction of armed forces and armaments in Central Europe. They have now been going on for four years, and throughout all those years our Western counterparts have stubbornly sought to ensure for themselves unilateral military advantages and to encroach upon the security interests of the socialist countries. Thus, these talks have so far produced no practical results. We urge that we should proceed to a real search for an understanding rather than just talk about the desire for an agreement.

The relaxation of tensions creates still more favourable conditions for completing, within the shortest possible time, the liberation of all colonial countries and peoples, for eliminating the racist regimes, and for eradicating apartheid and the last vestiges of national oppression and discrimination of all kinds.

Today, colonialism is on the brink of total collapse. Conditions are improving for the further development of the struggle of peoples for their national liberation. A vivid example of this is the glorious victory of the peoples of Indo-China over imperialist aggression. That victory has opened up favourable prospects for the establishment of peace in South-East Asia and on the entire Asian continent.

It is with special feeling that we welcome the entry into the United Nations of the Socialist Republic of Vietnam. Justice has been restored: the united socialist State of Vietnam has taken its rightful place in this Organization. A large state, which has consistently taken a peaceful stand, has joined the United Nations. We wholeheartedly congratulate our Vietnamese friends.

We also welcome the admission of a new African State, the Republic of Djibouti.

When a conflict breaks out in a particular part of the world, more often than not there is, lurking in the background, either a desire to cling to colonial privileges or there are actions of a neo-colonialist nature.

Let us look at what is happening in southern Africa. It is now the biggest colonialist and racist enclave in the world. An enormous majority of the population in the Republic of South Africa, Rhodesia and Namibia are deprived of the most elementary human rights. This would seem to be a boundless field of activity where those who clamour for human rights could best apply their efforts. But for some reason or other, they shut their eyes to the intolerable plight of millions of people. What is more, they actually connive at the shameful acts of these racist regimes; they support them and cover up their crimes.

We do not conceal the fact that in Africa, as elsewhere, our sympathies lie with the states that have embarked on a progressive path of development, a path of social and economic transformation for the benefit of the masses. We openly declare our complete solidarity with the peoples fighting for the liquidation of the remaining strongholds of colonialism and racism. The Soviet Union will do its utmost to ensure that the desire to establish peaceful, neighbourly relations with one another prevails among African states as well as all other states that have gained independence, and that the sources of discord and conflict stoked up between them by imperialism and reaction be eliminated.

It would not be an exaggeration to say that there is another major world problem, and if it is not solved it is difficult to expect *détente* to be irreversible. What I have in mind is the development of equal mutually beneficial economic relations between all states, in short, the restructuring of international economic relations on a just and democratic basis.

We shall continue to give all possible assistance to the countries which have embarked on the road of independent development. But is it not clear to everyone that developing states will hardly be able to stand squarely on their feet if they remain hobbled by hundreds and thousands of tethers of neo-colonialist exploitation?

Now, a few more words about another aspect of the development of friendly relations between states. What we have in mind is cultivating the feelings of friendship and trust among all peoples and increasing mutual exchanges in cultural and other humanitarian fields. We have in mind also the need to encourage respect for human rights and fundamental freedoms for all, without distinction as to race, sex, language or religion, as determined, *inter alia*, by the international covenants on human rights. This has always been our approach to these questions and it has been clearly reflected in the draft of the new Constitution of the USSR.

But let no one have any doubts about something else: any attempts at preaching to us, at reading us sermons or, still worse, at interfering in our internal affairs under contrived pretexts have encountered and always will encounter a most resolute rebuff. We are ready to say it once again from this high rostrum: it is high time to realize that by acting in a spirit of psychological warfare the most that one could hope for would be to poison the international atmosphere and to sour relations between states. We should like to think that all this will be taken seriously.

An exceptionally important area where the policy of *détente* is being implemented in practice is the sphere of bilateral relations between states.

For about ten years now Soviet–French relations have been developing steadily without a hitch. The joint documents signed as a result of the recent visit of Leonid Brezhnev to France convincingly demonstrate that the joint actions of the two countries are making a major contribution to the cause of the relaxation of tensions and the development of co-operation in Europe and elsewhere.

Our relations with the Federal Republic of Germany have now been brought onto a normal path, which is a major accomplishment in itself if we recall how strained they were in the not too distant past. We intend to go on expanding and deepening our ties with the FRG in various fields. It is clear, however, that it does not all depend on us. There are circles in the FRG that are still exploiting some issues in a manner which is far from conducive to the favourable development of relations between our two countries.

We are satisfied with the way in which our relations are shaping up with Finland, Italy, Austria, Britain and other Western states, even though not all possibilities have yet been exhausted. Relations with these countries as well as with the other participants in the European Security Conference in Helsinki have now been put on a solid foundation—namely, in the principles and understandings embodied in the Final Act. The Soviet Union strictly adheres to all the provisions of that outstanding international document. We expect the same of all the other states whose highest representatives affixed their signatures to the Final Act of the Conference.

The meeting of representatives of states that participated in the Helsinki Conference is due to open in Belgrade in a few days' time. We do not overestimate the significance of that meeting, nor do we underestimate it. For its part, the Soviet Union is prepared to do everything so that the meeting may proceed constructively and become yet another milestone on the road embarked upon at Helsinki.

Relations between the Soviet Union and the USA merit special consideration. It is difficult to conceive of further progress in the policy of *détente* unless there is at least a minimum of trust and mutual understanding between them. The experience of the late 1960s and the first half of the 1970s indicates that when both countries are guided by principles of equality, mutual interest in the fate of peace, and non-interference in internal affairs, it becomes possible not only to reach a number of major agreements and arrangements but also to establish useful co-operation in many areas.

Unfortunately, it must be noted that recently Soviet–American relations have experienced a certain stagnation, if not a downright slump. To a somewhat lesser extent that has affected the practical aspects of bilateral ties. However, more complications have emerged now than before regarding issues of broad international concern. We, the Soviet Union, stand for the improvement of relations with the United States, for Soviet–American co-operation in the interests of our peoples, in the interests of peace. But we say just as clearly that the efforts of one side alone are not sufficient for this. In response to the relevant remarks by President Carter about the desire of the United States to develop relations with the Soviet Union, Leonid Brezhnev has said that if there was an intention to translate those words into the language of practical deeds we would willingly seek mutually acceptable solutions.

The Soviet Union invariably pursues a policy of neighbourly relations with Japan. Soviet–Japanese co-operation is developing successfully in a number of areas. In some other areas that is not the case. In our opinion the cause lies in the unhealthy sentiments regarding the Soviet Union that are still strong in some Japanese circles. Besides, those feelings are being whipped up by outside forces. We are convinced that the situation can and must change for the better in the interests of the peoples of our two countries and of peace in Asia.

For many years now Soviet–Indian relations have served as an important stabilizing factor on the vast continent of Asia. They provide a good example of friendly co-operation based upon the principles of peaceful coexistence and enshrined in a relevant treaty. It is our firm intention to continue promoting the development, intensification and enrichment of our ties with India.

A few words now about our relations with a large neighbouring country, China. Our position in this respect was defined by the 25th Congress of the CPSU. From the rostrum of the Congress Leonid Brezhnev stated:

'As regards China, as well as other countries, we adhere firmly to the principles of equality, respect for sovereignty and territorial integrity, non-interference in each other's internal affairs and the non-use of force. In short, we are prepared to normalize relations with China in accordance with the principles of peaceful coexistence.'

And that position of ours remains fully valid.

For the Soviet Union—and we are confident this is true of others—the struggle for the deepening of *détente* is at the same time the struggle for the complete elimination of the risk of nuclear conflict. Widening the scope of *détente* means at the same time pushing back the risk of mankind finding itself under the crushing steam-roller of a nuclear war. These are in fact two most important aspects of securing a genuinely solid and genuinely lasting peace on earth. It was precisely the atmosphere of *détente* that made it possible to undertake some major actions with a view to reducing the nuclear threat.

However, there is still a lot more to be done. We call upon the United Nations and its member states to continue and intensify their efforts to reduce step by step the likelihood of the aforementioned threat in order to subsequently remove it from the lives of human beings.

Of course the most radical and effective means of preventing nuclear war would be the complete elimination of nuclear weapons. The Soviet Union has favoured this course ever since that very moment when the world saw the first ominous silhouettes of nuclear explosions. Now, as before, we repeat our readiness to sit down at any time, together with all the other nuclear Powers, at the negotiating table to examine the problem of nuclear disarmament in its entirety and jointly to work out concrete ways for its practical solution.

But while there are no such negotiations—through no fault of our own—one cannot sit twiddling one's thumbs. Any steps would do in this respect provided they bring us closer, even by an inch or two, even gradually but steadily, to a complete removal of the threat of nuclear conflict.

The United Nations has played a certain role in creating a favourable political climate as regards the problem of averting a nuclear war. It suffices to recall the resolution adopted five years ago on the non-use of force in international relations and the permanent prohibition of the use of nuclear weapons. And yet we should like to see a more active United Nations in this matter, one which is of the greatest concern to mankind.

Using the full weight of its prestige the United Nations could, on behalf of all its member states, solemnly call upon all states to act in such a way as to prevent the emergence of situations which could cause a dangerous strain in relations between them and to avoid armed conflicts.

This applies particularly to states with nuclear weapons. What is required of them is continuous restraint in their mutual relations and a readiness to negotiate and settle their differences by peaceful means.

This is closely connected with strict observance of the principle of renunciation of the use or threat of force in international relations involving both nuclear weapons and conventional armaments. This principle has already been enshrined in a series of recent bilateral and multilateral agreements, including the Final Act of the Helsinki Conference on Security and Co-operation in Europe.

The United Nations would accomplish a great deal by calling on all states to start negotiations to conclude a world treaty on the non-use of force in international relations.

The joint initiative of the socialist countries advanced last November also had to do with the prevention of nuclear war. This is a proposal addressed to the countries that participated in the Helsinki Conference to conclude a treaty whereby each would engage not to be the first to use nuclear weapons against the other. This would be of tremendous significance not only for Europe but for the world at large.

I shall mention yet another area where in our view it is possible to arrive at an agreement that would reduce the threat of war. Nuclear countries could start negotiations with a view to working out arrangements concerning the withdrawal of ships with nuclear weapons on board from certain areas of the world's oceans.

Other steps are also possible to curb the arms race. On a broader plane this would meet with the desire of non-nuclear states to establish zones of peace completely free from nuclear weapons. They could include both individual countries or groups of states and vast geographical regions or even entire continents.

In this connection, we reaffirm our sympathetic attitude to the idea of turning the Indian Ocean into a zone of peace. The main prerequisite for this is the dismantling of the foreign military bases that exist there and the prevention of the establishment of new ones. It is precisely from this position that the Soviet Union approaches this idea. And it is from the same angle that we are holding consultations with the United States on certain problems relating to the Indian Ocean.

An extremely important question which attracts the closest attention throughout the world is the limitation of strategic arms. The need to contain the threat of nuclear war, to achieve progress in other areas of the struggle to end the arms race and for disarmament, the strengthening of international security and the further development of the process of *détente* call for the speediest solution of this pressing issue.

As far as the Soviet Union is concerned, its stand is well known. The USSR has invariably sought to achieve an agreement on the limitation of strategic arms and has done and is doing everything in its power to that end. We are prepared to go even further and to proceed to negotiations on the reduction of existing stockpiled arsenals of strategic weapons.

What is the state of affairs in this respect?

It is an open secret today that the USSR and the United States were able some time ago to agree to a considerable extent on a new Soviet–American agreement on the limitation of strategic offensive arms on the basis of the well-known Vladivostok agreements. Yet subsequently much of what was agreed upon has been called into question—not by us.

What is the reason for this? The reason is clear. What is involved here above all is the decision of the United States to begin deploying a new type of strategic weapon, the so-called Cruise missile. Thus yet another channel has been opened for the strategic arms race and of course it would be naive to think that the other side would be a passive onlooker.

So what will happen in the long run? Certainly not the strengthening of security—this is openly admitted even in the United States—and certainly not a reduction in military expenditures. The result will be greater rivalry, more billions which could be used far more sensibly thrown into the bottomless pit of the arms race, and consequently greater dangers for peace.

Even now it is not easy to reach agreement in the field of limiting strategic arms but the situation would become much more complicated if we had to deal with weapons whose limitation hardly lends itself or does not lend itself at all to verification by the other side. And this could spell extreme danger in the military and political fields. Is this really what the USSR and the United States should strive for?

No, it certainly is not. It may be said with confidence that a positive conclusion of the Soviet–American talks on the limitation of strategic arms is extremely important for the peoples of our two countries, for the peoples of the entire world. As a result of recent meetings in Washington some progress has been achieved in bringing the positions of the two sides closer together, and this is all to the good. However, there still remain issues to be agreed upon. It is important now to ensure successful completion of the talks. I repeat that we are doing everything possible to that end in the firm belief that a mutually acceptable agreement at the Strategic Arms Limitation Talks is quite feasible, of course on the basis of strict observance of the principle of the equality and equal security of both sides. We cannot backtrack from this unchallengeable position.

While speaking of nuclear missiles, we should not forget that there may emerge new and terrifying means for the annihilation of peop . Is it not true that the threat of war will increase many times if ever more new types and systems of weapons of mass destruction are developed? Two years have elapsed since the Soviet Union proposed the conclusion of an international agreement which would ban their emergence.

Negotiations are under way and this of course is a positive factor, but progress has been rather slow.

In the meantime, ever more sophisticated means of killing people go into production from laboratories and experimental facilities. It is the duty of the United Nations to call upon all states to put a dependable road-block in the way of the emergence of new types and systems of weapons of mass destruction.

Today the problem of the non-proliferation of nuclear weapons is most acute. It is a fact that many states have not yet become parties to the Treaty on the Non-proliferation of Nuclear Weapons, and some of those countries are near-nuclear states or have already attained the capability of manufacturing such weapons. Is it really necessary, for example, to speak of the grave consequences for the security of the peoples of Africa and for universal peace which might result from actions taken by the Republic of South Africa in order to get hold of nuclear weapons?

The Soviet Union is a convinced advocate of the peaceful uses of nuclear energy. Our country is already co-operating in this field with many states and we are prepared to expand that co-operation. However, we are categorically opposed to a state of affairs in which the peaceful uses of the atom would become a channel for the proliferation of nuclear weapons, and yet this is a real and growing danger. What is required here is co-ordination of the efforts of many states and an elaborate international system of safeguards and controls. We intend to co-operate constructively in this area.

The prohibition of all nuclear weapon tests would be a major step towards lessening the threat of a nuclear war and deepening *détente*. As is well known, the Soviet Union has proposed that a treaty be concluded to this effect. Moreover, to meet the wishes of some countries we have expressed our willingness to take part in the search for a generally acceptable agreement on the question of verification. Today we are taking yet one more step forward: under an arrangement with the United States and Great Britain we have consented to suspend underground nuclear weapon tests for a certain period of time even before the other nuclear Powers accede to the future treaty.

The Government of the USSR proposes including in the agenda of the 32nd session of the United Nations General Assembly, as an

247

I

important and urgent question, an item entitled 'Deepening and consolidating the relaxation of international tensions and the prevention of the risk of nuclear war'.

At the same time, the Soviet Union is submitting for consideration by the General Assembly two draft documents: 'Declaration on deepening and consolidating the relaxation of international tensions' and 'Resolution on the prevention of the risk of nuclear war'.

We should like to express the hope that the Assembly at this session will give thorough consideration to these documents and address a corresponding appeal to all states of the world.

Increasingly broad opportunities to work for the benefit of peace are opening up before the United Nations in conditions of *détente*. The key to the success of this noble mission is the strict adherence of all the members of this body to the United Nations Charter. The Charter contains all that is essential for preserving and strengthening peace on earth. It is now a matter of the practical deeds of states.

Our country will work tirelessly for the benefit of peace, hand in hand with fraternal socialist states, together with all our allies and friends, and with realistically minded forces which put the ensuring of peace and the prevention of the risks of war above transitory considerations. Our country will constantly labour for peace.

Leonid Brezhnev recently said:

'The Soviet Union will always be an active participant in any negotiations or any international action aimed at developing peaceful co-operation and strengthening the security of the peoples.

'It is our belief—it is our firm belief—that realism in politics and the will for *détente* and progress will ultimately prevail and that mankind will be able to step into the twenty-first century in conditions of peace, secure as never before. And we shall do all in our power to make this a reality.'

I trust that this appeal of the Soviet State will evoke a grateful response from those who cherish peace.

From a statement at the 32nd session of the UN General Assembly, 27 September 1977

During a visit to the United States. 1 October 1977

The general discussion in which the different governments are stating their views about the international situation has only just begun. From what has already been said from the rostrum of the General Assembly and on the basis of our many contacts here we can quite definitely draw the conclusion that the predominant tendency in the world is towards *détente* and its deepening, as has been declared time and again by Leonid Brezhnev.

From the rostrum of the 25th Congress of the CPSU and on other occasions Leonid Brezhnev has clearly and unambiguously stated our position relative to the United States. Its substance is that we are prepared not only to maintain the level that has been reached in Soviet–US relations but also to go further, to promote our relations with the USA in different areas, in the political and economic fields, in trade, in cultural contacts, and so on. Moreover, we have repeatedly declared that we are prepared to look for a common language with the United States on the major and most pressing international problems. Central among them has always been the question of ending the arms race and achieving disarmament. We have submitted concrete proposals at international forums, including the UN General Assembly, and for the consideration of states on a bilateral basis, including the discussion of questions of this kind with representatives of the United States, in this case with President Carter.

We have always stressed that our relations should be maintained and developed, noting that good relations are in the interests of both the Soviet and the American people. We have always emphasized that major outstanding international issues, and there are many of them, must be settled. The Middle East problem has been a fixture on the agenda for many years. We have always made it plain that there must be a just settlement of that problem, one providing protection of the legitimate rights of the Arabs. Such a settlement would ultimately bring lasting peace in that region, with the result that all the states— the Arab countries and Israel—could occupy a dignified place as independent, sovereign states. We abide by this line to this day and have clearly stated this in our talks here in the United States, in the White House.

At the talks in Washington both sides have given considerable attention to the possibility of signing a new, i.e. the second, agreement on a limitation of strategic arms. The Soviet stand is based on the immutable and just proposition that neither side should receive unilateral advantages as a result of an agreement. This is the only basis on which agreement can be reached. It may be said that as a result of the talks held in Washington over the past few days the positions of the two sides have drawn closer together and that today the situation is better than it was yesterday. It may be said that the two powers—the Soviet Union and the United States—have now entered onto the road leading to agreement.

However, it still cannot be stated that all questions have been settled. Some still remain outstanding, but I would nonetheless move them to the background. Some, possibly most of them even, could be brought to a settlement by the delegations of the two countries in Geneva. The main questions, as you all know, are settled at a different political level, but there has been progress in key questions.

Even on the basis of what has been accomplished in the past, everyone who regards politics realistically will readily draw the conclusion that it is easier to resolve key political issues at summit level. This concerns both the USA and the Soviet Union. But the question arises of how this meeting should best be organized. Without preparation or with preparation? How best to go to the meeting—confidently, in the knowledge that a positive result is assured, or uncertainly, with eyes closed, along the lines of what will be will be? I would say that the first is the most suitable way.

On behalf of Leonid Brezhnev personally and of the Soviet leadership as a whole I have stated this view also to President Carter. He said that this view was absolutely correct. However, the President did not conceal his desire for a meeting with Leonid Brezhnev. As a matter of fact, he had stated this before. It would thus be good if such a meeting were prepared fittingly and held. It would be an important step in the promotion of Soviet–US relations and would be of great significance to the cause of peace.

At the meetings with US representatives and at the UN General Assembly we touched upon other questions, in particular, European problems, a wide spectrum of questions relating to ending the arms race and achieving disarmament, and questions relating to the Middle East and Africa.

As regards the latter, the most acute problem that has come to the forefront of attention is that of settling the situation in the south of Africa—in Zimbabwe and Namibia—where troops of the Republic of South Africa are still stationed, although they should not be there, and in the South African Republic itself. Most of the population of the RSA are black. Two policies have come into collision there. One is aimed at preserving the existing colonialist and racist practices, leaving the existing racist regime in power and keeping the black population, who comprise the majority, in a state of colonial oppression. This is the policy pursued today by the racist regimes in these regions.

The other is the clear and lucid policy of the Soviet Union and its friends and allies, the other socialist countries. Its aim is that freedom should be granted to the local population without delay. We are often told that the local population are not used to governing themselves. How can they grow used to it when to this day they are governed by colonialists? It is said that they are incapable of governing themselves. But where are the scales on which the ability of this population to govern themselves is weighed? And if such scales exist, they have been manufactured by the colonialists.

We have no doubt that these people are capable of settling their internal affairs by themselves. We also have meetings with the leaders of these movements on the spot, and they tell us unequivocally that if only they are given the opportunity they will have no difficulty in assuming power and organizing the administration of their country. For that reason, on behalf of the entire Soviet people and the Soviet leadership, the Soviet delegation at the UN General Assembly emphatically condemns racist colonialist policy.

From an interview on Soviet television during Mr Gromyko's visit to the United States in October 1977

**During the visit of David Owen, British Foreign Secretary, to Moscow.
10 October 1977**

David Owen's visit is taking place at a time which witnesses an historic
event in the life of the Soviet people—the adoption of the new Constitution of the USSR. To use the words of Leonid Brezhnev, the new
Constitution is the concentrated result of the Soviet Union's six
decades of development. It shows the genuine democracy of the Soviet
socialist system and formalizes the peaceful principles and aims of
Soviet foreign policy.

These aims and principles are concretely expressed in the practical
actions of the CPSU and the Soviet Government on the world scene,
in Soviet foreign policy initiatives aimed at deepening and widening
détente, preventing a nuclear war, curbing the arms race, and achieving
disarmament. We can note with satisfaction that in recent years these
initiatives have led to a series of important treaties and agreements
that in large measure have helped to improve the political situation in
the world.

Unquestionably, *détente* remains the predominant tendency in the
development of international relations. At the same time, it must be
seen that the process of reducing tension is resisted by some Western
circles who are endeavouring to push the world back to the cold war.

However, the logic of the development of international relations is
obviously the following: either progress along the road of *détente* or
descend into tension and a mounting threat of nuclear war. It is therefore
vitally important to continue stepping up efforts to promote and
consolidate international *détente*.

Disarmament is the highroad of *détente*. As regards the Soviet
Union, it is, as Leonid Brezhnev said, working to end the arms race—
this is our programme objective.

We hold that in disarmament, particularly in curbing the nuclear
arms race, any steps and measures are good if they draw us closer,
even a little at first, even gradually but steadfastly, to the removal of the
threat of a nuclear conflict. In this context I should like to note in
particular the immense importance of the understanding reached by
the Soviet Union and Great Britain relative to the conclusion of an
agreement on the prevention of an accidental outbreak of nuclear war.

At the current session of the UN General Assembly the Soviet Union called upon all countries to contribute their utmost to the further assertion of *détente* and to ensure the elimination of the nuclear threat. Everybody knows the proposals submitted by us on this score. We are convinced that they meet with the interests of all peoples, of all the states of the world.

In order to consolidate world *détente* it is necessary to take practical steps to continue improving the international climate in Europe and reduce the danger of war on that continent. To this end the approaches must be opened to the settlement of the question of reducing armed forces and armaments in Central Europe, on, needless to say, the basis of the principle of non-prejudice to the security of any side.

One cannot overestimate the significance of the countries that participated in the Helsinki Conference signing a treaty under which none of them would be the first to use nuclear weapons against each other. The proposal of the socialist countries that the existing closed military groups should not be enlarged or new ones formed is likewise aimed at consolidating peace in Europe.

The progress that has been achieved in recent years in promoting *détente* and peaceful, neighbourly co-operation in Europe is in many ways due to the fact that the relations between the European participants in the Helsinki Conference have been given a solid foundation in the shape of the principles and understandings formulated and recorded in the Final Act of that conference. The Soviet Union urges the strict fulfilment of all of that document's provisions *in toto*.

We believe that the present Belgrade meeting of representatives of the countries which had participated in the Helsinki Conference should be yet another element in the build-up of peaceful, neighbourly relations in Europe.

Of course, we have given due attention to the discussion of questions concerning the bilateral relations between our countries and to the ways and means of further promoting these relations to the benefit of the two countries and in the interests of peace in Europe and the rest of the world. I think you will agree that on the whole they are developing beneficially, particularly after they had received a considerable impulse from the results of the Soviet–British summit in February 1975.

I am confident that by acting in a spirit of the concrete under-standings reached then and subsequently, our countries can and should co-operate constructively in international affairs and expand mutually beneficial relations in all the fields interesting them. We are prepared to work in that direction on the understanding that the British side makes analogous efforts.

> *Speech during the visit to the USSR of David Owen, Secretary of State for Foreign and Commonwealth Affairs of Great Britain, 10 October 1977*

The 33rd session of the UN General Assembly. 26 September 1978

It has become customary for representatives of practically all states to expound the views of their governments concerning the crucial issues of war and peace at regular sessions of the United Nations General Assembly. Indeed, the United Nations, the most representative inter-national forum, is the right place to raise to their full stature issues on whose solution largely depends the future of mankind.

The United Nations was established specifically for these purposes. It emerged immediately after the fiery steam-roller of the Second World War had driven over Europe and a considerable part of the rest of the world. Today, memories of those days are still fresh in our minds. Words fail to describe fully what that war visited upon people.

Both the generation that had to live through the war and the present generation realize that the victory won over the forces of fascism and aggression is of world historic significance. It changed the political image of the planet and brought to an unprecedented pitch the activities of forces working for peace, national liberation and social progress. The sword of justice fell on the heads of those who had instigated the aggression. Such are the lessons taught by history itself, the most authoritative teacher.

Looking back over the path traversed in international affairs over the post-war decades, including the troubled years of the cold war, peoples, governments and political figures—unless, of course, they are laymen in politics—cannot afford to ignore the major imperative of directing every effort to prevent another military catastrophe which would be even more disastrous for mankind than the two world wars taken together.

The fact that it has proved possible to avoid a major war for almost a third of a century is undoubtedly a great achievement of the people of the world. They are increasingly making it felt that they hate war, reject and curse it as a means for resolving international disputes and controversies.

Representatives of the Soviet Union, speaking at various international forums on behalf of our people and the Communist Party, which is the nucleus of the political system of Soviet society, have always emphasized the theme of peace—and they will continue to do so. The fundamental law of the Soviet State, its new Constitution, states: 'The USSR steadfastly pursues the Leninist policy of peace and stands for strengthening the security of nations and broad international co-operation.'

We are implementing that policy hand in hand with our friends and allies. The recent meeting of Leonid Brezhnev with the leaders of fraternal Parties and states in the Crimea has shown with new strength that the socialist community stands firmly on the course of peace, *détente* and international co-operation.

The fraternal socialist states are justly proud that through their consistent activities, year after year, month after month, and even day after day they are making no small contribution to preserving peaceful conditions for the life and creative work of the peoples on Earth.

Yet it would be naive to deny that peace will not become more durable or *détente* more reliable unless the efforts of socialist states are reciprocated by other countries. This in turn calls for a willingness to resolve controversial issues at the negotiating table, without seeking unilateral advantages, differences in social systems notwithstanding.

The participants in the General Assembly session will probably agree that we have not gathered here merely to express our satisfaction that so far peace has been preserved. What is much more important is to mobilize additional efforts and find new possibilities to shield people from aggression and a world conflict in the future as well.

The will of the Soviet people and the policy of our state was expressed in a penetrating and meaningful manner by Leonid Brezhnev in these words: 'The major thrust of our struggle for peace in the present conditions is to lessen the risk of another world war, of the mass annihilation of people through the use of nuclear weapons.'

It is indeed true that all peoples are inspired by one idea, one aspiration—and that is peace. Yet the situation in different parts of the world is shaping up differently, for the world is full of contradictions and the influence exercised by those forces which are working for stronger international security and the freedom of peoples and by those which, on the contrary, are attempting to encroach on them, is felt differently in various parts of the world.

The continent of Europe has made the greatest headway towards establishing durable peace. It is in Europe that major peace moves on a collective and bilateral basis have been accomplished in recent years. Several hurdles have been surmounted one after another in improving relations between countries with opposing social systems. The political climate in Europe today is clearly healthier than before.

The results of the Conference on Security and Co-operation in Europe have been a fresh and considerable impetus. It is no secret that from time to time attempts are made to put the durability of those results to the test. Nevertheless, *détente* has been, and continues to be, the dominant trend in European international life. And surely this is demonstrated by the development of relations between the Soviet Union and other socialist countries, on the one hand, and France, the FRG, Italy, Finland, the Scandinavian and many other states, on the other.

Europe now appears to have reached a stage where the opponents of *détente* are hard put to reverse the course of events. Yet, this does not mean, of course, that the fruits of improved relations between states will fall into the hands of the peoples by themselves. On the contrary, sustained efforts are required, and here states, provided they are on the side of *détente*, have great opportunities for mutually beneficial co-operation in the most diverse fields. For its part, the Soviet Union will spare no effort to this end.

Close attention is riveted today on the continent of Africa. Africa with its 400-million population is seething. Newly liberated states are in the process of self-assertion, shedding away the last shackles of colonialism. Following the adoption by the United Nations in 1960 of the historic Declaration on the Granting of Independence to Colonial Countries and Peoples almost all of them have gained their national freedom. Almost all, but not all. The colonial order still persists in Rhodesia, Namibia and South Africa with its barbaric forms of racial discrimination.

How many words and what a huge amount of paper are spent on casting aspersions on the policy of the Soviet Union and other socialist countries in connection with the situation in some parts of Africa. And who is doing all that? Those who are clinging to the remnants of colonialism and racism. Being aware that what they are doing is hardly popular, to say the least, they are attempting to cover up their neo-colonialist moves and to deceive the peoples. Apparently such devices will be resorted to in the future as well. Yet, deceit will get no one very far: the people will know how to tell the truth from a lie.

Colonialism and racism must be eliminated fully and irrevocably on the African continent as well. Those who want to preserve the racist regimes, so hateful to the African peoples, must realize that their cause has been lost—and lost irretrievably.

As in the past, we are making no secret of the fact that our sympathies are on the side of the peoples fighting for their national independence and social progress. But we are not seeking any advantages for ourselves either in Africa or in the developing countries on other continents. The Soviet Union is not coveting political domination, concessions or military bases.

When the states of Africa or other areas of the world request aid to repel aggression, we repeat, aggression, or an armed attack, they have every right to expect support from their friends. Or, perhaps, the United Nations Charter provision on the 'inalienable right to individual or collective self-defence' is no longer valid?

The objective inexorable laws of historical development will prevail: the day is not far off when the hour of independence will strike for the peoples of southern Africa too, and when the entire African continent, to the last inch, will become free.

There is an area situated at the crossroads of three continents which can be described as a 'powder keg', just as the Balkans once used to be called. This area is the Middle East. There is hardly anyone who would dare to say that the situation there is not fraught with the risk of another explosion.

What is the root cause of such a situation? It lies in the fact that ten years after the aggression its consequences have still not been eliminated, while the aggression itself goes unpunished. Israel continues to hold sway over the territories it has seized. Unfortunately, even in the Arab world there are some politicians who display no concern for Arab lands and who are inclined to neglect the legitimate rights of the Arabs, notably the Palestinian Arabs, and to cringe and surrender to the demands of the aggressor and his patrons.

The Soviet Union has repeatedly stated its willingness to take part in ensuring peace in the Middle East and to participate in the most stringent international security guarantees for all states of that area. Israeli spokesmen contend that they have no use for international guarantees. This is no more than empty polemical bravado. If Israel genuinely cared for its security, real not illusory security, it would seek a political solution. For the fact is that with the existing means of warfare the distance from the borders to which a neighbouring state has withdrawn its guns is of little consequence. What is required here is a radical breakthrough towards a situation where the guns would be silent altogether.

Only a solution that would guarantee the right to independence and the security of all states and peoples in the Middle East, including the Arab people of Palestine, who are fully entitled to a national home, a state of their own, can lay down the foundation for a durable peace in that area.

The entire accumulated experience, particularly recent experience, indicates that a radical and comprehensive settlement in the Middle East can be achieved only on the basis of joint efforts by all the sides directly concerned. Separate deals at the expense of the Arabs have only side-tracked the solution of the problem.

And such precisely is the nature of the understandings reached at the recent three-sided meeting at Camp David. If a realistic look is taken at things, no grounds can be found to believe that they, as claimed, bring closer a Middle East settlement. On the contrary, what this is all about is a new anti-Arab step making it difficult to achieve a just

258

solution of this pressing problem. That is why a campaign of artificial and affected optimism can mislead no one.

There is machinery specifically established to achieve peace in the Middle East, and it is the Geneva Peace Conference. And the sooner an end is put to attempts to keep it in a state of paralysis, the nearer will be the moment when the solution of the Middle East problem can be tackled with a chance of success.

For many years and decades the peoples of Asia, that most populous continent of the world, have been concerned with how to ensure peace, security and possibilities for development and progress in the area. The key to this in our view lies in joint action by all Asian states without exception. This is particularly urgent in the present conditions when developments in Asia are revealing certain disquieting traits. It has not happened by chance that among Asian countries there is a growing realization of the fact that conflicts, crude pressure and interference in internal affairs, which not so long ago went so far as to assume the dimensions of military intervention, and the attempts to pit Asian states one against the other should give way to a stable peace.

It is from this perspective that the creation of a unified Vietnam which has expelled the aggressors from its territory and which is today pursuing a peace-loving policy is of tremendous significance. The Socialist Republic of Vietnam, which heroically lived through all the hardships of a long and bitter war, is now courageously defending its sovereignty. From the United Nations rostrum the Soviet Union once again declares its solidarity with Vietnam and states that hegemonistic claims with which it is being confronted are inadmissible.

The Soviet Union favours good relations with those Asian states which in turn seek mutual understanding and good-neighbourliness with us. Such are our relationships with most Asian states and in several cases they go back a good many years. Along with interest in equal and mutually advantageous co-operation based on the principles of mutual respect, strict observance of sovereignty and non-interference in each other's internal affairs, we are united with those countries by our common concern for strengthening peace and security in Asia, our joint struggle against the designs of the forces of imperialism, colonialism and racism.

One shining example of multi-faceted friendly co-operation, of peaceful coexistence of states with different social systems are Soviet–Indian relations. These relations, abounding in long-standing traditions of good-neighbourliness, are steadily on the rise in their development on the firm basis of the 1971 Treaty of Peace, Friendship and Co-operation. They are consonant with the vital interests of the peoples of the two countries and constitute an important and effective factor for peace on the Asian continent and throughout the world.

And if we do not have such relationships with all Asian states, the responsibility for that is not ours. It rests squarely on those who persist in following a hostile line with respect to our country, a line which is hostile to the cause of peace in general. Those who, while themselves pursuing hegemonistic aims, try to peg the label of hegemonism on others are making a travesty of the facts.

Of course, the line followed by Japan is not immaterial for the interests of peace in the Far East and the Pacific. Unfortunately, its policy has been showing some disquieting trends. One may well wonder whether that country might not eventually step onto the path which led in the past to enormous sufferings for other peoples and plunged Japan into a catastrophe. I would not like to make any final conclusions, yet serious attention should be paid to this matter. We believe that our anxiety is shared by many.

Our policy with regard to Japan has been, and will remain in the future, a policy of principle. We stand for good relations with that country, for genuine neighbourliness. However, appropriate moves by Japan are required.

Let us now turn to yet another continent—Latin America. Its role in world affairs is on the rise and what is particularly noteworthy is that Latin American countries increasingly seek to have an independent say. Accordingly, there are growing opportunities for co-operation between those countries and states in other parts of the world. This is a positive and important factor of international life. The Soviet Union wishes nothing but good to the countries and peoples of Latin America.

During the current General Assembly session another independent state, the Solomon Islands, is becoming the 150th member of the United Nations. Oceania is very far from us but we want to maintain normal and, where possible, friendly relations with the countries of that area as well. Here too we regard with sympathy the aspiration of the peoples to gain independence and to free themselves from foreign tutelage, both in the literal and the figurative meaning of the word.

In this connection the actions of the United States in respect of Micronesia, in a bid to lay their hands on those territories which are temporarily under their trusteeship, and to make them serve their own military and strategic plans in violation of the United Nations decisions and in circumvention of the Security Council, cannot be ignored.

What follows from this review of the state of affairs in the world, brief as it is? First of all, it is a fact that despite the contradictory nature of current world developments, the international situation on the whole is better than ten or, say fifteen years ago.

At the same time, it is clear that the international situation does not depend solely on the state of affairs in this or that area of the world. There are international problems which it is difficult or even impossible to fit into a geographical framework. And the most crucial, burning and truly global problem affecting all countries and peoples is the ending of the arms race and disarmament.

The truth which is recognized today by all is that enormous resources are being spent to manufacture engines of destruction. It is indeed a fact that in this time of peace more than 25 million men wear military uniforms. And there are many more people who are directly or indirectly engaged in military production. All this represents a colossal drain on the material and intellectual resources of mankind.

There are those who may say that something is nevertheless being done to contain the arms race. Recently, for example, a special session of the United Nations General Assembly devoted to disarmament took place. It reflected the determination of peoples to do away with the arms race and to direct the course of events towards disarmament and, eventually, general and complete disarmament. The session did adopt a comprehensive document which, on the whole, is a good one.

The Soviet Union can note with satisfaction that many ideas proposed by it became an organic part of the Final Document. Like all those who are not only paying lip service to, but are also really seeking, disarmament, we believe that the decisions taken at the special session must be translated into the language of practical deeds by states, failing which they will remain an empty phrase.

Taking a sober view of things, it is to be recognized, however, that the arms race has not diminished one whit. A group of states, and it is known which, has decided to earmark additional enormous appropriations for an arms build-up over many years to come. The decision taken by the NATO Council session in Washington and the subsequent steps to intensify military preparations in a number of countries cannot be viewed otherwise than as a challenge to those who are working for disarmament.

Regardless of all the attempts of the instigators of the arms race to make things look as if the security of states will be all the more reliable the bigger their military arsenals are, the facts are quite different. As the amount of weapons grows and new and ever more destructive types of weapons emerge, the risk of war also increases. People will not accept any excuses such as references to a 'threat from the USSR'. Such references are completely spurious.

Who but the Soviet Union is making one proposal after another designed to halt the arms race, to check it from this or that angle and to prevent the development of new means of warfare? And who is rejecting these proposals out of hand? The opponents of disarmament.

By now—and Western statesmen recognize this—an approximate equality or parity in arms has come into being. The Soviet Union—and we reaffirm this—does not intend to change this correlation in its favour. What is more, we have been and are proposing now that the levels of military confrontation be reduced, i.e., that the security of each and every one be ensured with lesser quantitative and qualitative parameters of armaments and armed forces.

As Leonid Brezhnev quite definitely emphasized, 'there is no type of arms and, above all, of weapons of mass destruction that the Soviet Union would not be prepared to see limited and banned reciprocally, in agreement with other states, and then to eliminate them from the arsenals'.

Our country has a comprehensive programme for curtailing the arms race. Our proposals were put forward here in the United Nations only a few months ago. It will be recalled that they will remain the subject of further discussion in various bodies dealing with disarmament. We will never tire of taking such initiatives and they will not become tarnished because of this, since the need for specific action in all the sectors of the struggle for disarmament, for the prevention of another war is increasing rather than diminishing.

In circumstances where the arms race is being stepped up, and the world in this respect is sliding downhill, the first thing to do is to stop completely any further quantitative and qualitative build-up of arms. Clearly, this applies above all to states with a large military potential.

It will be recalled that on a practical plane the Soviet Union has urged the discussion of a set of sweeping measures which could be carried out within a specified limited period: cessation of the production of all types of nuclear weapons; cessation of the production of, and prohibition of, all other types of weapons of mass destruction; cessation of the development of new types of conventional armaments of great destructive capability; renunciation by the permanent members of the Security Council, and by countries which have military agreements with them, of the expansion of their armies and the build-up of their conventional armaments. We expect these proposals to be treated in a most serious way and to be examined in practical terms.

The greatest threat to peace—and this is something which is now recognized everywhere—stems from the nuclear arms race. Consequently, priority should be given to nuclear disarmament. On this matter we see eye to eye with most states of the world, including the developing countries.

Why is it not possible to couch in treaty language an obligation by states to discontinue the production of all types of nuclear weapons so as to move then to a gradual reduction of their stockpiles, and all the way to their complete destruction? But such obligations cannot materialize out of thin air; they are produced in the course of negotiations on whose necessity we have been insisting.

In the opinion of the Soviet Union what is required is that all the nuclear powers as well as a certain number of non-nuclear states get together at a conference table and that an exact date for the beginning of the negotiations be set. And this session of the General Assembly should have its say in this regard and make an appropriate appeal to all the nuclear Powers in the first place.

Any major task, particularly that of nuclear disarmament, calls for maximum realism once you have begun to tackle it. In the world of today it is inconceivable to expect that task to make any headway unless action is taken at the same time to strengthen political and international legal guarantees for the security of states. In this connection, the proposal to conclude a World Treaty on the Non-use of Force in International Relations is becoming ever more urgent.

While emphasizing as a great achievement of the peoples the fact that peace has been preserved for more than a third of a century now, we should not forget even for an instant how great are the dangers that lie in wait for mankind. To fully deliver the peoples from the threat of nuclear war—this is what underlies our proposals.

The same purpose is served by the concrete initiatives of the Soviet Union, and today we are stressing them again, expecting that they will elicit the understanding and support of the General Assembly.

What is involved here in the first place is the strengthening of security guarantees for non-nuclear states. And secondly, it is the non-stationing of nuclear weapons on the territory of states where there are no such weapons at present.

You will recall that recently our country has taken a step conducive to instilling among non-nuclear states greater confidence in their security. The Soviet Union has declared that it will never use nuclear weapons against countries which renounce the production and acquisition of nuclear weapons and do not have them on their territory.

Following us, the United States and the United Kingdom, for their part, made declarations to the effect that they would not use nuclear weapons against non-nuclear states. On the whole, this could be regarded as a positive fact were not such declarations replete with all kinds of reservations rendering them valueless.

The Soviet Union has not confined itself to a solemn declaration regarding the non-use of nuclear weapons against non-nuclear states which renounce the production and acquisition of nuclear weapons and which do not have them on their territory. We have expressed our readiness—and it still stands—to enter into special agreements to that effect with any of these countries. The USSR calls upon all the other nuclear Powers to act in a similar manner and to assume corresponding obligations.

It is clear at the same time that if the problem of safeguarding non-nuclear states from the use of nuclear weapons against them is to be tackled in the most effective manner, agreed guarantees on the part of the nuclear Powers and a multilateral arrangement are required. In other words, it is necessary to have an international agreement which would be based on a pledge by those Powers not to use or threaten to use nuclear weapons against non-nuclear states which are party to such an agreement, provided the latter do not produce, acquire or have such weapons on their territory. A similar obligation could be extended to the armed forces and installations under the jurisdiction and control of non-nuclear states, that is, to make it even more sweeping in scope.

Do non-nuclear states stand to benefit from their participation in this kind of an international agreement? Of course they do. They would be provided with security guarantees universally formalized in international law, whereas they themselves would not be required to do anything but to strictly observe their non-nuclear status. At the same time, this would be to everyone's advantage, for the threat of a nuclear conflict would diminish and the climate throughout the world would improve.

Taking all this into consideration and in response to a relevant appeal of the special session of the United Nations General Assembly on disarmament, the Soviet Union has proposed the inclusion in the agenda for this session as an important and urgent matter an item entitled 'Conclusion of an International Convention on the Strengthening of Guarantees of the Security of Non-nuclear States'. Seeking to put things onto a practical footing from the outset, we have also submitted the draft text of such a Convention.

We feel that one of the merits of our initiative is that, given the goodwill of states, and, of course, of nuclear states in the first place, it may yield practical results fairly soon. Following discussion on this question at the current session of the General Assembly, the Committee on Disarmament could immediately proceed to negotiate the text of the Convention so that as soon as possible it would be open for signing by all states of the world.

I should like to turn now to our second proposal concerning the non-stationing of nuclear weapons on the territories of states where there are no such weapons at present. It can hardly be disputed that this is a reliable way to prevent nuclear weapons from spreading all over the globe.

Here, too, we take into account the point of view expressed by a large group of states. Many countries are becoming increasingly aware of the risks stemming from nuclear weapons and they are not at all eager to have them on their territories.

In our view, this could be achieved through an international agreement to be based on a clear and simple pledge by the nuclear Powers not to station nuclear weapons on territories where there are no such weapons at present. Such an obligation would cover all types of nuclear weapons: warheads, bombs, shells, mines, etc., whether deployed as combat systems or kept in depots and storage facilities. At the same time, non-nuclear countries would formalize their intention to refrain from any steps which, directly or indirectly, could lead to the presence of nuclear weapons on their territory.

If all the nuclear Powers agree not to station nuclear weapons where there are no such weapons at present—and our country has already declared its willingness to do so—it would not be too difficult to reach international agreement. The Soviet Union would like to hope that the United Nations General Assembly will respond favourably to its proposal.

Implementation of the initiatives which we are advancing at this session would also result in a much stronger regime of the non-proliferation of nuclear weapons without affecting in any way the possibilities of using nuclear energy for peaceful purposes. By the same token, our proposals, which are consonant with the idea of creating nuclear-free zones, provide even greater leeway for putting these ideas into practice through the collective or individual efforts of states.

The need to prevent the development of new types and new systems of weapons of mass destruction is being increasingly felt. On our initiative, the Committee on Disarmament has started negotiations to that effect. But their progress is slow. The Soviet Union is in favour of reaching agreement on this extremely important matter and of stepping up the preparation of special agreements on individual types of weapons wherever necessary.

This applies, first and foremost, to such inhuman weapons as neutron weapons. The situation would become much more dangerous if the plans for their production, stockpiling and deployment materialized. It is in the interests of peace that those plans be irrevocably abandoned.

Rapid progress in military science and technology, this frenzy of armaments, so to speak, is increasing the risk that a point could be reached beyond which it would be absolutely impossible to verify compliance with the existing arms limitation agreements and those which are in the process of being drafted.

Wherever disarmament negotiations are taking place and whoever are their participants, our line is a line towards achieving concrete results. An early conclusion of the Soviet–American talks on limiting strategic offensive arms is of particular importance. The essence of the problem lies in setting limits for the deployment of the most dangerous and destructive types of armaments to be followed by negotiations on a substantial decrease in their levels.

It is to be hoped that a sober-minded and well-considered line in the United States policy with regard to this extremely important matter will prevail, for a new agreement is equally needed by the Soviet Union, the United States and the world at large.

Many countries on various continents welcomed the beginning of negotiations between the Soviet Union and the United States on certain questions related to the problem of disarmament and the cessation of the arms race, including the talks on the limitation and subsequent reduction of military activities in the Indian Ocean and on the limitation of the sales of conventional arms.

Positive results could have been achieved long ago at the talks concerning the Indian Ocean. However, since last February they have been 'frozen' through no fault of ours. This is giving concern to many states which cherished hopes that the talks would help turn the Indian Ocean into a zone of peace.

Now, what is required, in the first place, to limit the sale of conventional armaments and their transfers to other countries? The political basis for solving this question is to be found in international legal criteria which would take care both of the task of limiting arms sales and of the legitimate interests of peoples fighting against aggression, for their freedom and independence.

Certain progress has been achieved of late in the negotiations between the USSR, the USA and the United Kingdom on the complete and general prohibition of nuclear weapon tests. It has been agreed that the treaty under preparation must impose a ban on any test explosions of nuclear weapons in any environment. It is all the more important to bring these negotiations to a successful conclusion. But for some reason or other our negotiating partners are stalling.

It is in all earnest that the Soviet Union has been raising the question of limiting conventional armaments and armed forces. Even today the role of conventional armaments is quite important while the efforts by states to limit them are insufficient.

No real headway has yet been made at the Vienna talks on the reduction of armed forces and armaments in Central Europe. Throughout the talks we have witnessed one and the same line pursued by our Western partners: you socialist countries should reduce more and we less. Of course, there is no proof, nor can there possibly be, that such a unilateral approach is justified. This is nothing but an artificial piling-up of obstacles.

Our position is simple: without effecting any changes in the correlation of armaments and armed forces, their level, nonetheless, should be reduced by both sides. Some people who want to inflict damage on the socialist countries by changing the correlation of forces in favour of NATO ought to curb their appetite.

The socialist countries have recently put forward in Vienna new proposals whose constructive nature is recognized in the West, too. We are expecting a practical and positive response to them.

It is appropriate to stress in connection with the disarmament problem how acute are the problems of economic development of many countries which are asking for assistance. They are compelled to overcome great difficulties. Suffice it to say that according to United Nations data, one and a half billion people, that is over one-third of mankind, are deprived of elementary medical aid while some 700 million people suffer from systematic malnutrition. At the same time, enormous amounts of money, unprecedented in history, are being wasted on war preparations. And what is more, military appropriations keep getting bloated.

The Soviet Union has been proposing for a long time that military budgets, primarily those of the permanent members of the United Nations Security Council, be reduced by a certain percentage and that part of the funds thus saved be used to provide assistance to developing countries. This would be a major step of tremendous importance. Yet, what we hear in reply is: before cutting down military budgets they should become a subject for study. However, such study could take decades and decades and go on and on. To reduce is to reduce military budgets without engaging in any red-tape, even under a pseudo-scientific cover. This calls for a political decision.

In order to overcome the stalemate, we propose reaching agreement on the reduction by states having a large economic and military potential of their military budgets not in terms of percentage points, but in absolute figures of analogous magnitude. Such reductions could begin in the coming fiscal year and cover a period of three years, with ten per cent of the funds released as a result of reductions being channelled towards increasing aid to developing countries.

It must be emphatically stressed that the reduction of military budgets is being given priority not only as an urgent task but also as one which can fairly easily lend itself to solution, provided, of course, there is a desire to solve it.

The peoples of the whole world would heave a sigh of relief if the burden of taxation were reduced. Today, many are reflecting upon the reason why some states—and, not least, the economically developed ones—are experiencing economic upheavals. Our answer is as follows: instead of throwing away immense material resources on the conveyors which are continuously producing missiles, tanks, planes, guns and other means of killing people, these resources should be diverted to peaceful purposes. The resources thus released could be used to improve the living standards of the peoples, to satisfy their primary needs, such as housing, better medical care, education and science, and finally, simply to combat famine.

All this emphasizes the great responsibility for solving the problems that face mankind in the field of disarmament. This rests primarily with those who determine the foreign policies of states.

So, from whatever angle you view the problem of ending the arms race and of disarmament, the Soviet Union is ready to seek appropriate international arrangements. We have submitted concrete proposals to that effect. Naturally, we will be willing to consider proposals of other states, too, aimed at accomplishing this historic task.

The Soviet Union appreciates the efforts by non-aligned states to help get the disarmament problem off the ground. The activity of the non-aligned countries in this direction, just as in other areas of the struggle for peace, is growing and this constitutes a positive phenomenon in international life.

The General Assembly can do a great service to peace if it facilitates the convocation of a World Disarmament Conference. It is at such a forum that decisions binding on states could be adopted.

It is good that the United Nations is now more actively involved with questions of disarmament. This helps the relevant talks to be more in the limelight of public opinion: let those who, contrary to the will of the peoples, are spurring the arms race feel ill at ease. Everywhere in the world a moral atmosphere should be generated which would make the opponents of disarmament feel pilloried.

There is no people that does not crave peace. As to the Soviet people, we can say with full responsibility: it does not seek war, nor will it start one. This applies fully to our friends and allies as well. But outside the socialist community, too, there is no people that does not want peace. In the states that pursue a militarist course the watershed lies not between the peoples themselves, but between the peoples, on the one hand, and the leaders at the helm of policy of those states who have sold their heart and soul to the interests of small groupings which are making profits from military production, on the other.

States are faced with a great many international problems. And their number and complexity are unlikely to diminish in time. But what are the conditions and what is the atmosphere in which it is easier to solve those problems? Clearly, it is easier in the atmosphere of *détente* in the world, not in conditions of an aggravated situation, in a heated atmosphere. This is attested to by the experience of many years.

The principle of non-interference in the internal affairs of states, no matter what contrived pretext is used to violate it, has been and remains a cornerstone of international life, of the further progress of *détente*. Every people with self-esteem and every state with self-esteem have given and will continue to give a decisive rebuff to such attempts. The Soviet Union has not tolerated and will not tolerate interference in its internal affairs.

The course of the Soviet Union's foreign policy of peace, *détente* and disarmament is a firm course. It stems from the fundamental requirements of the social system of our state, expresses the will of the entire

Soviet people, and translates into life the directives of principle adopted by congresses of the Communist Party of the Soviet Union.

Despite the complexity of the international situation, Soviet people are looking into the future with optimism. Our confidence rests on the fact that the will of the people for peace is indomitable, that the forces favouring the maintenance and consolidation of peace prevail over those who want to turn the course of world development in the opposite direction.

Assessing world developments in this way, we ourselves are ready and call upon all other states to work without respite, notably in the United Nations, to bring all peoples closer to a reliable peace and to make the dam built against war impenetrable and insurmountable.

From a statement at the 33rd session of the UN General Assembly, 26 September 1978

INDEX